TWENTIETH CENTURY VIEWS

The aim of this series is to present the best
in contemporary critical opinion on major
authors, providing a twentieth century perspective on their changing status in an era
of profound revaluation.

Maynard Mack, *Series Editor*
Yale University

SAUL BELLOW

A COLLECTION OF CRITICAL ESSAYS

Edited by

Earl Rovit

Prentice-Hall, Inc. Englewood Cliffs, N.J.

A SPECTRUM BOOK

Library of Congress Cataloging in Publication Data

Rovit, Earl H
    Saul Bellow:
    (Twentieth c
book)
    Bibliography
    1. Bellow, Sa
PS3503.E4488Z84
ISBN 0–13–07487
ISBN 0–13–07486

Quotations from the following works of Saul Bellow are used by kind permission of The Viking Press, Weidenfeld and Nicolson, and Saul Bellow:

The Adventures of Augie March. Copyright © 1949, 1951, 1952, 1953 by Saul Bellow.
Seize the Day. Copyright © 1956 by Saul Bellow.
Henderson the Rain King. Copyright © 1958, 1959 by Saul Bellow.
Herzog. Copyright © 1961, 1963, 1964 by Saul Bellow.
The Last Analysis. Copyright © 1962, 1965, 1972 by Saul Bellow.
Mr. Sammler's Planet. Copyright © 1969, 1970 by Saul Bellow.

Grateful acknowledgment is made to the Vanguard Press for permission to quote from these works of Saul Bellow:

Dangling Man. Copyright © 1944 by the Vanguard Press, Inc. Copyright renewed 1971 by Saul Bellow.
The Victim. Copyright © 1947 by Saul Bellow.

10 9 8 7 6 5 4 3 2 1

PRENTICE-HALL INTERNATIONAL, INC. (*London*)
PRENTICE-HALL OF AUSTRALIA PTY. LTD. (*Sydney*)
PRENTICE-HALL OF CANADA LTD. (*Toronto*)
PRENTICE-HALL OF INDIA PRIVATE LIMITED (*New Delhi*)
PRENTICE-HALL OF JAPAN, INC. (*Tokyo*)

Contents

SAUL BELLOW

Introduction

by Earl Rovit

When literary criticism concerns itself with the work of a contemporary—particularly a novelist with the craft and vitality of Saul Bellow—something very like a game of hide-and-seek often takes place. The writer gains a small reputation with his first publications; the critics (who, of course, are partly responsible for that reputation) seek to define or delimit the literary categories under which they think the writer can be subsumed. As the writer produces more work, the critics have a vested interest in defending their earlier judgments. They are likely to maintain that the writer hasn't really changed his position at all; that he's merely shifted his posture slightly. Or if the later work is quite radically different from the earlier, criticism is under some compulsion to insist that the change in direction was inevitable; that this apparent break in continuity was actually inherent in the writer's earlier work. And the game of hide-and-seek continues. The writer adds titles to his *oeuvre,* convinced that each fresh contribution is unique, and the critics pursue with their nets of accumulated definition. In this slippery conflict, the critic has several advantages. He speaks with the authority of an outsider, and he reads each new work through a filter of all that the writer has written previously. It is the rarest of critics who can maintain his focus on a single novel without blurring that focus with his experience of the writer's total work. Because the critic operates in terms of hindsight, he is likely to feel that he knows where the writer is and where he has to go. The writer, alas, hasn't been able to read his next book yet, and he is not only not sure exactly where he is, but he frequently hasn't the faintest idea of where he ought to, or even, *can* go. It is thus completely natural that there be an element of friction between the critics and the writer, between the professional hunters and the quarry who is equally loath to be caught or to be left entirely alone. The writer wants his work to be read, the critic wants to interpret and evaluate. Each needs the other, but their respective desires can never be wholly compatible.

Now approaching his sixtieth birthday, with over thirty years of active publication behind him, Saul Bellow has been more successful than most writers in standing up to the rigors of the chase and in resisting the processes of marmoreal exegesis. On the basis of his first two novels, *Dangling Man* (1944) and *The Victim* (1947), he was categorized rather stringently as an academic, *Partisan-Review*-oriented, New Critical, Jewish novelist. However, the appearance of the free-swinging picaresque *The Adventures of Augie March* (1954) startlingly shattered this restrictive definition. The Jamesian "paleface" seemed to have broken out of his bookish tower in order to roam the literary prairies as a full-fledged "redskin." Undaunted, the critical cavalry laid chase, only to be ambushed by *Seize the Day* (1956). The wide open spaces of Augie's catch-as-catch-can world had been inverted into the claustral, introspective labyrinths of Tommy Wilhelm's upper Broadway. The critics were naturally wary. Was this move regressive or progressive? Had Bellow, like a fighting bull, returned to his *querencia* for a respite, or had he again eluded his pursuers with a brilliantly deceptive feint? *Henderson the Rain King* (1959) compounded the confusion: Bellow's high-spirited African romance was part spoof, part high jinks, part fantasy, and wholly serious in a comically open way. With the publication of *Herzog* (1964) and *Mr. Sammler's Planet* (1970), Bellow returned with a vengeance to the enclosed urban mindscapes of Joseph, Leventhal, and Tommy Wilhelm. In general, criticism has come to accept these latter as the most characteristic boundaries of Bellow's fiction. Perhaps the critics had become fatigued by the long pursuit and were now content to remain on the peripheries of Bellow's world; and perhaps the sheer quantity of his work had grown sufficiently large that it was impossible for him to do anything completely new and unprepared for in his earlier work. Whatever the reasons, the topographical contours of Bellow's fictional world have come to be considered more or less settled. Critics may dispute vigorously the comparative meanings and values of this world, but there seems to be a relatively satisfied consensus as to what it consists of.

It is dominantly urban in setting, Jewish middle-class intellectual in texture, gently or savagely ironic in tone. Its time span moves from a remembrance of immigrant communities shortly after World War I, through the years of the Depression and World War II, and up to the present. (Although the Holocaust is only infrequently referred to directly, its shadow hovers over the whole time period in foreboding or reminder.) This city-centered world shifts between Chicago and New York, and although there are sporadic interludes in the countryside and trips to Mexico, Europe, Africa, and Israel, Bellow's narrative seems most at home with subways rumbling underfoot and skyscrapers looming in the polluted air. Yet, for all the people who throng its streets, Bellow's world is a lonely one. His typical protagonists live their daily routines of work, play, and crisis so exclusively and introspectively that when they do meet a friend or stranger, the encounter tends to be charged with a passion that the meeting hardly merits. Preeminently, it is an explosively comic world—frequently grotesque, sometimes poignant, occasionally maudlin or bitter. Bellow consistently aims his ridicule at both the absurdly deficient culture within which his protagonist strives to live a meaningful life, and the pathetic illusions and self-deceptions that his protagonist brings to this desperate struggle. In a statement that might serve as a thematic emblem of much of his work, Bellow once wrote: "It is obvious that modern comedy has to do with the disintegrating outline of the worthy and humane Self, the bourgeois hero of an earlier age." Bellow has tried to guard against the varied temptations that this statement implies. He has tried to resist a sentimental nostalgia for the unrecoverable values of that earlier age; he has insisted intently that the new is not necessarily good just because it is new, nor is it even inevitably better than what may be left of the old. His is fundamentally an uncomfortable middle-of-the-road position, the tense stance of the rationalist who despairs of rational solutions to human frustration but who is constrained to accept no guide superior to rationality—crippled, incomplete, and irresolute as it may be.

I think that it is the inherent ambivalence of this posture—indelibly manifest in his style and in the structures and thematic concerns of his fiction—that has made Bellow vulnerable to attack from the two extremes on either side of him. To the traditionalists, he appears to be surrendering too much to the assaults of history and change; through their eyes, he may seem fashionably cynical, pessimistic, or irresponsible. From the opposite camp, he has been subject to harsher charges: naïveté, sentimentality, and, ultimately, compromising his ideals: being willing to accept the tepid principle of "making do" rather than daring to leap beyond rationality. In the increasing furor of the late 1960s, when—as with so much else in American culture—literary criticism became severely polarized, Bellow's work was particularly susceptible to attacks from both the New Left and the Old Right. The characterizations of Moses Herzog and Artur Sammler were often fused and confused with the person of Bellow himself, and the understandable but unjust demand that the artist find solutions that his society could not was laid upon him and his works as a measure of their fatal deficiency. This particular furor appears to have abated, at least temporarily, and Bellow is now on the verge of being regarded as an elder statesman of American letters—a position of eminence subject to even greater dangers, I believe, than the political exacerbations of the late '60s.

At any rate, the general stature of Bellow's work must assuredly be beyond serious cavil today. Along with the poet, Robert Lowell, he is one of the three or four writers of his generation whose name and accomplishments come first to mind as the legitimate heirs of the giants of the '20s who dramatically launched American letters into international significance. Thrice a recipient of the National Book Award for Fiction, he has been generously honored as one of our foremost contemporary novelists. A resounding commercial success since his publication of *Augie March*, he has been far from neglected by the academic critics. Doctoral dissertations, theses, monographs, book-length studies, and a host of learned essays attest to the widespread concern that his novels have generated in the scholarly community. Almost every critic occasionally concerned with modern literature has found the time to focus his attention on Bellow, and there is an abundance of interesting and relevant material readily available to the Bellow student.

In this volume of critical essays on Bellow's work, my intentions have been modest and, I hope, honorable. In the space afforded to me, I have tried to achieve certain limited ends. I have attempted to include essays or parts of longer works that, collectively, treat as full a sampling of Bellow's ample production as possible. Although there are no detailed studies directed exclusively at *Dangling Man* or *The Adventures of Augie March* here, I offer in compensation Irving Malin's examination of Bellow's only full-length play, *The Last Analysis*—a work that is frequently ignored by Bellow's critics. Cognizant of the rich variety of manners and modes in contemporary literary criticism, I have also tried to select essays that represent widely different critical perspectives, methodologies, and thematic interests. Further, I have aimed, in general, not to reduplicate valuable material that is easily accessible to the serious student of Bellow's work. Toward these ends, I have been especially fortunate in securing the generous cooperation of many hands. Professors Denis Donoghue and Marcus Klein, whose earlier published essays on Bellow are well established in the canon of Bellow criticism, were gracious enough to extend their thoughts in appenda to their original pieces for inclusion in this volume. Professor Poirier has revised his original review of *Herzog*. And my editorial chores were considerably lightened by my being the recipient of new essays by Professors Malin, Pearce, Porter, Siegel, and Sullivan, which appear for the first time in this anthology.

In the end, of course, the critics and their criticism fall away as they must, and all that is left are the works themselves—to thrive or to slumber or to disappear. Ultimately, in the continuing dialectic between novelist and critic the novelist does manage to secure the last word, but only after the critics have collectively established the intellectual context within which that word will be heard. It is my hope that this collection of essays will give a just representation of what that context now is for the work of Saul Bellow.

Saul Bellow

by Gordon Lloyd Harper

The interview "took place" over a period of several weeks. Beginning with some exploratory discussions during May of 1965, it was shelved during the summer, and actually accomplished during September and October. Two recording sessions were held, totaling about an hour and a half, but this was only a small part of the effort Mr. Bellow gave to this interview. A series of meetings, for over five weeks, was devoted to the most careful revision of the original material. Recognizing at the outset the effort he would make for such an interview, he had real reluctance about beginning it at all. Once his decision had been reached, however, he gave a remarkable amount of his time freely to the task—up to two hours a day, at least twice and often three times a week throughout the entire five-week period. It had become an opportunity, as he put it, to say some things which were important but which weren't being said.

Certain types of questions were ruled out in early discussions. Mr. Bellow was not interested in responding to criticisms of his work which he found trivial or stupid. He quoted the Jewish proverb that a fool can throw a stone into the water which ten wise men cannot recover. Nor did he wish to discuss what he considered his personal writing habits, whether he used a pen or typewriter, how hard he pressed on the page. For the artist to give such loving attention to his own shoelaces was dangerous, even immoral. Finally, there were certain questions that led into too "wide spaces" for this interview, subjects for fuller treatment on other occasions.

The two tapes were made in Bellow's University of Chicago office on the fifth floor of the Social Sciences Building. The office, though large, is fairly typical of those on the main quadrangles: much of it rather dark with one brightly lighted area, occupied by his desk, immediately before a set of three dormer windows; dark-green metal bookcases line the walls, casually used as storage for a miscellany of books, magazines, and correspondence. A set of *The Complete Works of Rudyard Kipling* ("it was given to me") shares space with examination copies of new novels and with a few of Bellow's own books, including recent French and Italian translations of *Herzog*. A table, a couple of typing stands, and various decrepit and mismatched chairs are scattered in apparently haphazard fashion throughout the room. A wall rack just inside the door holds his jaunty black felt hat and his walking cane. There is a general sense of disarray, with stacks of papers, books, and letters lying everywhere. When one comes to the door, Bellow is frequently at his typing stand, rapidly pounding out on a portable machine responses to some of the many letters he gets daily. Occasionally a secretary enters and proceeds to type away on some project at the far end of the room.

During the two sessions with the tape recorder, Bellow sat at his desk, between the eaves which project prominently into the room, backlighted by the dormer windows which let in the bright afternoon sun from the south. Four stories below lie Fifty-ninth Street and Chicago's Midway, their automobile and human noises continually penetrating the office. As the questions were asked, Bellow listened carefully and often developed an answer slowly, pausing frequently to think out the exact phrasing he sought. His answers were serious, but full of his special quality of humor. He took obvious pleasure in the amusing turns of thought with which he often concluded an answer. Throughout, he was at great pains to make his ideas transparent to the interviewer, asking repeatedly if this was clear or if he should say more on the subject. His concentration during these sessions was intense enough to be tiring, and both tapes were brought to a close with his confessing to some exhaustion.

Following each taping session, a typescript of his remarks was prepared. Bellow worked over these typed sheets extensively with pen and ink, taking as many as three separate meetings to do a complete revision. Then another typescript was made, and the process started over. This work was done when the interviewer could be present, and again the changes were frequently tested on him. Generally these sessions occurred at Bellow's office or at his apartment, overlooking the Outer Drive and Lake Michigan. Once, however, revisions were made while he and the interviewer sat on a Jackson Park bench on a fine October afternoon, and one typescript was worked on along with beer and hamburgers at a local bar.

Revisions were of various sorts. Frequently there were slight changes in meaning: "That's what I really meant to say." Other alterations tightened up his language or were in the nature of stylistic improvements. Any sections which he judged to be excursions from the main topic were deleted. Most regretted by the interviewer were prunings that eliminated certain samples of the characteristic Bellow wit: in a few places he came to feel he was simply "exhibiting" himself, and these were scratched out. On the other hand, whenever he could substitute for conventional literary diction an unexpected colloquial turn of phrase—which often proved humorous in context—he did so.

Interviewer. Some critics have felt that your work falls within the tradition of American naturalism, possibly because of some things you've said about Dreiser. I was wondering if you saw yourself in a particular literary tradition?

Bellow. Well, I think that the development of realism in the nineteenth century is still the major event of modern literature. Dreiser, a realist of course, had elements of genius. He was clumsy, cumbersome, and in some respects a poor thinker. But he was rich in a kind of feeling which has been ruled off the grounds by many contemporary writers— the kind of feeling that every human being intuitively recognizes as primary. Dreiser has more open access to primary feelings than any American writer of the twentieth century. It makes a good many people uncomfortable that his emotion has not found a more developed literary form. It's true his art may be too "natural." He sometimes conveys his understanding by masses of words, verbal approximations. He blunders, but generally in the direction of truth. The result is that we are moved in an unmediated way by his characters, as by life, and then we say that his novels are simply torn from the side of life, and therefore not novels. But we can't escape reading them. He somehow conveys, without much refinement, depths of feeling that we usually associate with Balzac or Shakespeare.

Interviewer. This realism, then, is a particular kind of sensibility, rather than a technique?

Bellow. Realism specializes in *apparently* unmediated experiences. What stirred Dreiser was simply the idea that you could bring unmediated feeling to the novel. He took it up naïvely without going to the trouble of mastering an art. We don't see this because he makes so many familiar "art" gestures, borrowed from the art-fashions of his day, and even from the slick magazines, but he is really a natural, a primitive. I have great respect for his simplicities and I think they are worth more than much that has been praised as high art in the American novel.

Interviewer. Could you give me an example of what you mean?

Bellow. In a book like *Jennie Gerhardt* the delicacy with which Jennie allows Lester Kane to pursue his conventional life while she herself lives unrecognized with her illegitimate daughter, the depth of her understanding, and the depth of her sympathy and of her truthfulness impress me. She is not a sentimental figure. She has a natural sort of honor.

Interviewer. Has recent American fiction pretty much followed this direction?

Bellow. Well, among his heirs there are those who believe that clumsi-

ness and truthfulness go together. But cumbersomeness does not necessarily imply a sincere heart. Most of the "Dreiserians" lack talent.
On the other hand, people who put Dreiser down, adhering to a "high
art" standard for the novel, miss the point.

Interviewer. Aside from Dreiser, what other American writers do you
find particularly of interest?

Bellow. I like Hemingway, Faulkner, and Fitzgerald. I think of Hemingway as a man who developed a significant manner as an artist, a life-
style which is important. For his generation, his language created a
life-style, one which pathetic old gentlemen are still found clinging to.
I don't think of Hemingway as a great novelist. I like Fitzgerald's novels
better, but I often feel about Fitzgerald that he couldn't distinguish
between innocence and social climbing. I am thinking of *The Great
Gatsby.*

Interviewer. If we go outside American literature, you've mentioned that
you read the nineteenth-century Russian writers with a good deal of
interest. Is there anything particular about them that attracts you?

Bellow. Well, the Russians have an immediate charismatic appeal—
excuse the Max Weberism. Their conventions allow them to express
freely their feelings about nature and human beings. We have inherited
a more restricted and imprisoning attitude toward the emotions. We
have to work around puritanical and stoical restraints. We lack the
Russian openness. Our path is narrower.

Interviewer. In what other writers do you take special interest?

Bellow. I have a special interest in Joyce; I have a special interest in
Lawrence. I read certain poets over and over again. I can't say where
they belong in my theoretical scheme; I only know that I have an at-
tachment to them. Yeats is one such poet. Hart Crane is another. Hardy
and Walter de la Mare. I don't know what these have in common—
probably nothing. I know that I am drawn repeatedly to these men.

Interviewer. It's been said that one can't like *both* Lawrence and Joyce,
that one has to choose between them. You don't feel this way?

Bellow. No. Because I really don't take Lawrence's sexual theories very
seriously. I take his art seriously, not his doctrine. But he himself
warned us repeatedly not to trust the artist. He said trust the work
itself. So I have little use for the Lawrence who wrote *The Plumed
Serpent* and great admiration for the Lawrence who wrote *The Lost
Girl.*

Interviewer. Does Lawrence at all share the special feeling you find attractive in Dreiser?

Bellow. A certain openness to experience, yes. And a willingness to trust
one's instinct, to follow it freely—that Lawrence has.

Interviewer. You mentioned before the interview that you would prefer
not to talk about your early novels, that you feel you are a different
person now from what you were then. I wonder if this is all you want
to say, or if you can say something about how you have changed.

Bellow. I think that when I wrote those early books I was timid. I still
felt the incredible effrontery of announcing myself to the world (in

part I mean the WASP world) as a writer and an artist. I had to touch a great many bases, demonstrate my abilities, pay my respects to formal requirements. In short, I was afraid to let myself go.

Interviewer. When do you find a significant change occurring?

Bellow. When I began to write *Augie March.* I took off many of these restraints. I think I took off too many, and went too far, but I was feeling the excitement of discovery. I had just increased my freedom, and like any emancipated plebeian I abused it at once.

Interviewer. What were these restraints that you took off in *Augie March?*

Bellow. My first two books are well made. I wrote the first quickly but took great pains with it. I labored with the second and tried to make it letter-perfect. In writing *The Victim* I accepted a Flaubertian standard. Not a bad standard, to be sure, but one which, in the end, I found repressive—repressive because of the circumstances of my life and because of my upbringing in Chicago as the son of immigrants. I could not, with such an instrument as I developed in the first two books, express a variety of things I knew intimately. Those books, though useful, did not give me a form in which I felt comfortable. A writer should be able to express himself easily, naturally, copiously in a form which frees his mind, his energies. Why should he hobble himself with formalities? With a borrowed sensibility? With the desire to be "correct"? Why should I force myself to write like an Englishman or a contributor to *The New Yorker?* I soon saw that it was simply not in me to be a mandarin. I should add that for a young man in my position there were social inhibitions, too. I had good reason to fear that I would be put down as a foreigner, an interloper. It was made clear to me when I studied literature in the university that as a Jew and the son of Russian Jews I would probably never have the right *feeling* for Anglo-Saxon traditions, for English words. I realized even in college that the people who told me this were not necessarily disinterested friends. But they had an effect on me, nevertheless. This was something from which I had to free myself. I fought free because I had to.

Interviewer. Are these social inhibitors as powerful today as they were when you wrote *Dangling Man?*

Bellow. I think I was lucky to have grown up in the Middle West, where such influences are less strong. If I'd grown up in the East and attended an Ivy League university, I might have been damaged more badly. Puritan and Protestant America carries less weight in Illinois than in Massachusetts. But I don't bother much with such things now.

Interviewer. Did another change in your writing occur between *Augie March* and *Herzog?* You've mentioned writing *Augie March* with a great sense of freedom, but I take it that *Herzog* was a very difficult book to write.

Bellow. It was. I had to tame and restrain the style I developed in *Augie March* in order to write *Henderson* and *Herzog.* I think both those books reflect that change in style. I wouldn't really know how to describe it. I don't care to trouble my mind to find an exact description for it, but it has something to do with a kind of readiness to record impressions arising from a source of which we know little. I suppose that all of us have a primitive prompter or commentator within, who from earliest years has been advising us, telling us what the real world is. There is such a commentator in me. I have to prepare the ground for him. From this source come words, phrases, syllables; sometimes only sounds, which I try to interpret, sometimes whole paragraphs, fully punctuated. When E. M. Forster said, "How do I know what I think until I see what I say?" he was perhaps referring to his own prompter. There is that observing instrument in us—in childhood at any rate. At the sight of a man's face, his shoes, the color of light, a woman's mouth or perhaps her ear, one receives a word, a phrase, at times nothing but a nonsense syllable from the primitive commentator.

Interviewer. So this change in your writing—

Bellow. —was an attempt to get nearer to that primitive commentator.

Interviewer. How do you go about getting nearer to him, preparing the way for him?

Bellow. When I say the commentator is primitive, I don't mean that he's crude; God knows, he's often fastidious. But he won't talk until the situation's right. And if you prepare the ground for him with too many difficulties underfoot, he won't say anything. I must be terribly given to fraud and deceit because I sometimes have great difficulty preparing a suitable ground. This is why I've had so much trouble with my last two novels. I appealed directly to my prompter. The prompter, however, has to find the occasion perfect—that is to say, truthful, and necessary. If there is any superfluity or inner falsehood in the preparations, he is aware of it. I have to stop. Often I have to begin again, with the first word. I can't remember how many times I wrote *Herzog*. But at last I did find the acceptable ground for it.

Interviewer. Do these preparations include your coming to some general conception of the work?

Bellow. Well, I don't know exactly how it's done. I let it alone a good deal. I try to avoid common forms of strain and distortion. For a long time, perhaps from the middle of the nineteenth century, writers have not been satisfied to regard themselves simply as writers. They have required also a theoretical framework. Most often they have been their own theoreticians, have created their own ground as artists, and have provided an exegesis for their own works. They have found it necessary to take a position, not merely to write novels. In bed last night I was reading a collection of articles by Stendhal. One of them amused me very much, touched me. Stendhal was saying how lucky writers were in the age of Louis XIV not to have anyone take them very seriously. Their obscurity was very valuable. Corneille had been dead for several days before anyone at court considered the fact important enough to mention. In the nineteenth century, says Stendhal, there would have been several public orations, Corneille's funeral covered by all the papers. There are great advantages in not being taken *too* seriously. Some writers are excessively serious about themselves. They accept the ideas of the "cultivated public." There is such a thing as overcapitalizing the

A in artist. Certain writers and musicians understand this. Stravinsky says the composer should practice his trade exactly as a shoemaker does. Mozart and Haydn accepted commissions—wrote to order. In the nineteenth century, the artist loftily waited for Inspiration. Once you elevate yourself to the rank of a cultural institution, you're in for a lot of trouble.

Then there is a minor modern disorder—the disease of people who live by an image of themselves created by papers, television, Broadway, Sardi's, gossip, or the public need for celebrities. Even buffoons, prize fighters, and movie stars have caught the bug. I avoid these "images." I have a longing, not for downright obscurity—I'm too egotistical for that—but for peace, and freedom from meddling.

Interviewer. In line with this, the enthusiastic response to *Herzog* must have affected your life considerably. Do you have any thoughts as to why this book became and remained the bestseller it did?

Bellow. I don't like to agree with the going view that if you write a bestseller it's because you betrayed an important principle or sold your soul. I know that sophisticated opinion believes this. And although I don't take much stock in sophisticated opinion, I have examined my conscience. I've tried to find out whether I had unwittingly done wrong. But I haven't yet discovered the sin. I do think that a book like *Herzog,* which ought to have been an obscure book with a total sale of eight thousand, has such a reception because it appeals to the unconscious sympathies of many people. I know from the mail I've received that the book described a common predicament. *Herzog* appealed to Jewish readers, to those who have been divorced, to those who talk to themselves, to college graduates, readers of paperbacks, autodidacts, to those who yet hope to live awhile, etc.

Interviewer. Do you feel there were deliberate attempts at lionizing by the literary tastemakers? I was thinking that the recent deaths of Faulkner and Hemingway have been seen as creating a vacuum in American letters, which we all know is abhorrent.

Bellow. Well, I don't know whether I would say a vacuum. Perhaps a pigeonhole. I agree that there is a need to keep the pigeonholes filled and that people are uneasy when there are vacancies. Also the mass media demand material—grist—and literary journalists have to create a major-league atmosphere in literature. The writers don't offer to fill the pigeonholes. It's the critics who want figures in the Pantheon. But there are many people who assume that every writer must be bucking for the niche. Why should writers wish to be rated—seeded—like tennis players? Handicapped like racehorses? What an epitaph for a novelist: "He won all the polls"!

Interviewer. How much are you conscious of the reader when you write? Is there an ideal audience that you write for?

Bellow. I have in mind another human being who will understand me. I count on this. Not on perfect understanding, which is Cartesian, but on approximate understanding, which is Jewish. And on a meeting of sympathies, which is human. But I have no ideal reader in my head, no.

Let me just say this, too. I seem to have the blind self-acceptance of the eccentric who can't conceive that his eccentricities are not clearly understood.

Interviewer. So there isn't a great deal of calculation about rhetoric?

Bellow. These are things that can't really be contrived. People who talk about contrivance must think that a novelist is a man capable of building a skyscraper to conceal a dead mouse. Skyscrapers are not raised simply to conceal mice.

Interviewer. It's been said that contemporary fiction sees man as a victim. You gave this title to one of your early novels, yet there seems to be very strong opposition in your fiction to seeing man as simply determined or futile. Do you see any truth to this claim about contemporary fiction?

Bellow. Oh, I think that realistic literature from the first has been a victim literature. Pit any ordinary individual—and realistic literature concerns itself with ordinary individuals—against the external world, and the external world will conquer him, of course. Everything that people believed in the nineteenth century about determinism, about man's place in nature, about the power of productive forces in society, made it inevitable that the hero of the realistic novel should not be a hero but a sufferer who is eventually overcome. So I was doing nothing very original by writing another realistic novel about a common man and calling it *The Victim.* I suppose I was discovering independently the essence of much of modern realism. In my innocence, I put my finger on it. Serious realism also contrasts the common man with aristocratic greatness. He is overborne by fate, just as the great are in Shakespeare or Sophocles. But this contrast, inherent in literary tradition, always damages him. In the end the force of tradition carries realism into parody, satire, mock-epic—Leopold Bloom.

Interviewer. Haven't you yourself moved away from the suggestion of plebeian tragedy toward a treatment of the sufferer that has greater comic elements? Although the concerns and difficulties are still fundamentally serious, the comic elements in *Henderson,* in *Herzog,* even in *Seize the Day* seem much more prominent than in *Dangling Man* or *The Victim.*

Bellow. Yes, because I got very tired of the solemnity of complaint, altogether impatient with complaint. Obliged to choose between complaint and comedy, I choose comedy, as more energetic, wiser, and manlier. This is really one reason why I dislike my own early novels. I find them plaintive, sometimes querulous. *Herzog* makes comic use of complaint.

Interviewer. When you say that you are obliged to choose between complaint and comedy, does it mean this is the only choice—that you are limited to choosing between just these two alternatives?

Bellow. I'm not inclined to predict what will happen. I may feel drawn to comedy again, I may not. But modern literature was dominated by a tone of elegy from the twenties to the fifties, the atmosphere of Eliot in "The Waste Land" and that of Joyce in *A Portrait of the Artist as a Young Man.* Sensibility absorbed this sadness, this view of the artist as the only contemporary link with an age of gold, forced to watch the sewage flowing in the Thames, every aspect of modern civilization doing violence to his (artist-patrician) feelings. This went much farther than it should have been allowed to go. It descended to absurdities, of which I think we have had enough.

Interviewer. I wonder if you could say something about how important the environments are in your works. I take it that for the realist tradition the context in which the action occurs is of vital importance. You set your novels in Chicago, New York, as far away as Africa. How important are these settings for the fiction?

Bellow. Well, you present me with a problem to which I think no one has the answer. People write realistically but at the same time they want to create environments which are somehow desirable, which are surrounded by atmospheres in which behavior becomes significant, which display the charm of life. What is literature without these things? Dickens's London is gloomy, but also cozy. And yet realism has always offered to annihilate precisely such qualities. That is to say, if you want to be ultimately realistic you bring artistic space itself in danger. In Dickens, there is no void beyond the fog. The environment is human, at all times. Do you follow me?

Interviewer. I'm not sure I do.

Bellow. The realistic tendency is to challenge the human significance of things. The more realistic you are the more you threaten the grounds of your own art. Realism has always both accepted and rejected the circumstances of ordinary life. It accepted the task of writing about ordinary life and tried to meet it in some extraordinary fashion. As Flaubert did. The subject might be common, low, degrading; all this was to be redeemed by art. I really do see those Chicago environments as I represent them. They suggest their own style of presentation. I elaborate it.

Interviewer. Then you aren't especially disturbed by readers of *Henderson*, for example, who say that Africa really isn't like that? One sort of realist would require a writer to spend several years on location before daring to place his characters there. You're not troubled by him, I take it?

Bellow. Perhaps you should say "factualist" rather than "realist." Years ago, I studied African ethnography with the late Professor Herskovits. Later he scolded me for writing a book like *Henderson*. He said the subject was much too serious for such fooling. I felt that my fooling was fairly serious. Literalism, factualism, will smother the imagination altogether.

Interviewer. You have on occasion divided recent American fiction into what you call the "cleans" and the "dirties." The former, I gather, tend to be conservative and easily optimistic, the latter the eternal naysayers, rebels, iconoclasts. Do you feel this is still pretty much the picture of American fiction today?

Bellow. I feel that both choices are rudimentary and pitiful, and though I know the uselessness of advocating any given path to other novelists,

I am still inclined to say, Leave both these extremes. They are useless, childish. No wonder the really powerful men in our society, whether politicians or scientists, hold writers and poets in contempt. They do it because they get no evidence from modern literature that anybody is thinking about any significant question. What does the radicalism of radical writers nowadays amount to? Most of it is hand-me-down bohemianism, sentimental populism, D. H. Lawrence-and-water, or imitation Sartre. For American writers radicalism is a question of honor. They must be radicals for the sake of their dignity. They see it as their function, and a noble function, to say Nay, and to bite not only the hand that feeds them (and feeds them with comic abundance, I might add) but almost any other hand held out to them. Their radicalism, however, is contentless. A genuine radicalism, which truly challenges authority, we need desperately. But a radicalism of posture is easy and banal. Radical criticism requires knowledge, not posture, not slogans, not rant. People who maintain their dignity as artists, in a small way, by being mischievous on television, simply delight the networks and the public. True radicalism requires homework—thought. Of the cleans, on the other hand, there isn't much to say. They seem faded.

Interviewer. Your context is essentially that of the modern city, isn't it? Is there a reason for this beyond the fact that you come out of an urban experience?

Bellow. Well, I don't know how I could possibly separate my knowledge of life, such as it is, from the city. I could no more tell you how deeply it's gotten into my bones than the lady who paints radium dials in the clock factory can tell you.

Interviewer. You've mentioned the distractive character of modern life. Would this be most intense in the city?

Bellow. The volume of judgments one is called upon to make depends upon the receptivity of the observer, and if one is very receptive, one has a terrifying number of opinions to render—"What do you think about this, about that, about Viet Nam, about city planning, about expressways, or garbage disposal, or democracy, or Plato, or pop art, or welfare states, or literacy in a 'mass society'?" I wonder whether there will ever be enough tranquillity under modern circumstances to allow our contemporary Wordsworth to recollect anything. I feel that art has something to do with the achievement of stillness in the midst of chaos. A stillness which characterizes prayer, too, and the eye of the storm. I think that art has something to do with an arrest of attention in the midst of distraction.

Interviewer. I believe you once said that it is the novel which must deal particularly with this kind of chaos, and that as a consequence certain forms appropriate to poetry or to music are not available to the novelist.

Bellow. I'm no longer so sure of that. I think the novelist can avail himself of similar privileges. It's just that he can't act with the same purity or economy of means as the poet. He has to traverse a very muddy and noisy territory before he can arrive at a pure conclusion. He's more exposed to the details of life.

Interviewer. Is there anything peculiar about the *kind* of distractions you see the novelist having to confront today? Is it just that there are more details, or is their quality different today from what it used to be?

Bellow. The modern masterpiece of confusion is Joyce's *Ulysses.* There the mind is unable to resist experience. Experience in all its diversity, its pleasure and horror, passes through Bloom's head like an ocean through a sponge. The sponge can't resist; it has to accept whatever the waters bring. It also notes every microorganism that passes through it. This is what I mean. How much of this must the spirit suffer, in what detail is it obliged to receive this ocean with its human plankton? Sometimes it looks as if the power of the mind has been nullified by the volume of experiences. But of course this is assuming the degree of passivity that Joyce assumes in *Ulysses.* Stronger, more purposeful minds can demand order, impose order, select, disregard, but there is still the threat of disintegration under the particulars. A Faustian artist is unwilling to surrender to the mass of particulars.

Interviewer. Some people have felt your protagonists are seeking the answer to a question that might be phrased, How is it possible today for a good man to live? I wonder if you feel there is any single recurring question like this in the novels?

Bellow. I don't think that I've represented any really good men; no one is thoroughly admirable in any of my novels. Realism has restrained me too much for that. I should *like* to represent good men. I long to know who and what they are and what their condition might be. I often represent men who desire such qualities but seem unable to achieve them on any significant scale. I criticize this in myself. I find it a limitation.

Interviewer. I'm sorry; what exactly is this limitation?

Bellow. The fact that I have not discerned those qualities or that I have not shown them in action. Herzog wants very much to have effective virtues. But that's a source of comedy in the book. I think I am far more concerned with another matter, and I don't approach this as a problem with a ready answer. I see it rather as a piece of research, having to do with human characteristics or qualities which have no need of justification. It's an odd thing to do, it shouldn't be necessary to "justify" certain things. But there are many skeptical, rebellious, or simply nervous writers all around us, who, having existed a full twenty or thirty years in this universe, denounce or reject life because it fails to meet their standards as philosophical intellectuals. It seems to me that they can't know enough about it for confident denial. The mystery is too great. So when they knock at the door of mystery with the knuckles of cognition it is quite right that the door should open and some mysterious power should squirt them in the eye. I think a good deal of *Herzog* can be explained simply by the implicit assumption that existence, quite apart from any of our judgments, has value, that existence is worth-ful. Here it is possible, however, that the desire to go on with his creaturely career vulgarly betrays Herzog. He wants to live? What of it! The clay that frames him contains this common want. Simple *aviditas vitae.* Does a man deserve any credit for this?

Interviewer. Would this help to explain, then, why many of the difficulties which Herzog's mind throws up for him throughout the novel don't ever seem to be *intellectually* resolved?

Bellow. The book is not anti-intellectual, as some have said. It simply points to the comic impossibility of arriving at a synthesis that can satisfy modern demands. That is to say, full awareness of all major problems, together with the necessary knowledge of history, of science and philosophy. That's why Herzog paraphrases Thomas Marshall, Woodrow Wilson's Vice-President, who said what this country needs is a good five-cent cigar. (I think it was Bugs Baer who said it first.) Herzog's version: what this country needs is a good five-cent synthesis.

Interviewer. Do you find many contemporary writers attempting to develop such syntheses or insisting that significant fiction provide them?

Bellow. Well, I don't know that too many American novelists, young or old, are tormenting their minds with these problems. Europeans do. I don't know that they can ever reach satisfactory results on the grounds they have chosen. At any rate, they write few good novels. But that leads us into some very wide spaces.

Interviewer. Do the ideas in *Herzog* have any other major roles to play? The "anti-intellectual" charge seems to come from people who don't feel the ideas are essential either in motivating the action, the decisions Herzog makes, or in helping him to come through at the end.

Bellow. To begin with, I suppose I should say something about the difference in the role ideas play in American literature. European literature—I speak now of the Continent—is intellectual in a different sense from ours. The intellectual hero of a French or a German novel is likely to be a philosophical intellectual, an ideological intellectual. We here, intellectuals—or the educated public—know that in our liberal democracy ideas become effective within an entirely different tradition. The lines are less clearly drawn. We do not expect thought to have results, say, in the moral sphere, or in the political, in quite the way a Frenchman would. To be an intellectual in the United States sometimes means to be immured in a private life in which one thinks, but thinks with some humiliating sense of how little thought can accomplish. To call therefore for a dramatic resolution in terms of ideas in an American novel is to demand something for which there is scarcely any precedent. My novel deals with the humiliating sense that results from the American mixture of private concerns and intellectual interests. This is something which most readers of the book seem utterly to have missed. Some, fortunately, have caught it. But in part *Herzog* is intended to bring to an end, under blinding light, a certain course of development. Many people feel a "private life" to be an affliction. In some sense it is a genuine affliction; it cuts one off from a common life. To me, a significant theme of *Herzog* is the imprisonment of the individual in a shameful and impotent privacy. He feels humiliated by it; he struggles comically with it; and he comes to realize at last that what he considered his intellectual "privilege" has proved to be another form of bondage. Anyone who misses this misses the point of the book.

So that to say that Herzog is not motivated in his acts by ideas is entirely false. Any *Bildungsroman*—and *Herzog* is, to use that heavy German term, a *Bildungsroman*—concludes with the first step. The first *real* step. Any man who has rid himself of superfluous ideas in order to take that first step has done something significant. When people complain of a lack of ideas in novels, they may mean that they do not find familiar ideas, fashionable ideas. Ideas outside the "canon" they don't recognize. So, if what they mean is ideas à la Sartre or ideas à la Camus, they are quite right: there are few such in *Herzog*. Perhaps they mean that the thoughts of a man fighting for sanity and life are not suitable for framing.

Interviewer. Herzog rejects certain of these fashionable ideas, doesn't he —the ideas à la Sartre or à la Camus?

Bellow. I think he tests them first upon his own sense of life and against his own desperate need for clarity. With him these thoughts are not a game. Though he may laugh as he thinks them, his survival depends upon them. I didn't have him engage in full combat with figures like Sartre. If he had chosen to debate with Sartre in typical Herzogian fashion he would perhaps have begun with Sartre's proposition that Jews exist only because of anti-Semitism, that the Jew has to choose between authentic and inauthentic existence, that authentic existence can never be detached from this anti-Semitism which determines it. Herzog might have remembered that for Sartre, the Jew exists because he is hated, not because he has a history, not because he has origins of his own—but simply because he is designated, created, in his Jewishness by an outrageous evil. Sartre offers a remedy for those Jews who are prepared to make the authentic choice: he extends to them the invitation to become Frenchmen. If this great prince of contemporary European philosophy offers Herzog ideas such as this to embrace (or dispute), who can blame him for his skepticism toward what is called, so respectfully, Thought, toward contemporary intellectual fare? Often Herzog deals with ideas in negative fashion. He needs to dismiss a great mass of irrelevancy and nonsense in order to survive. Perhaps this was what I meant earlier when I said that we were called upon to make innumerable judgments. We can be consumed simply by the necessity to discriminate between multitudes of propositions. We have to dismiss a great number of thoughts if we are to have any creaturely or human life at all. It seems at times that we are on trial seven days a week answering the questions, giving a clear account of ourselves. But when does one live? How does one live if it is necessary to render ceaseless judgments?

Interviewer. Herzog's rejection of certain ideas has been widely recognized, but—

Bellow. —why he rejects them is not at all clear. Herzog's skepticism toward ideas is very deep. Though Jews are often accused of being "rootless" rationalists, a man like Herzog knows very well that habit, custom, tendency, temperament, inheritance, and the power to recognize real and human facts have equal weight with ideas.

Interviewer. You've spoken also of the disabling effects of basing a novel on ideas. Does this mean structuring a novel according to a philosophical conception?

Bellow. No, I have no objection to that, nor do I have any objection to basing novels on philosophical conceptions or anything else that works. But let us look at one of the dominant ideas of the century, accepted by many modern artists—the idea that humankind has reached a terminal point. We find this terminal assumption in writers like Joyce, Céline, Thomas Mann. In *Doktor Faustus* politics and art are joined in the destruction of civilization. Now here is an idea, found in some of the greatest novelists of the twentieth century. How good is this idea? Frightful things have happened, but is the apocalyptic interpretation true? The terminations did not fully terminate. Civilization is still here. The prophecies have not been borne out. Novelists are wrong to put an interpretation of history at the base of artistic creation—to speak "the last word." It is better that the novelist should trust his own sense of life. Less ambitious. More likely to tell the truth.

Interviewer. Frequently in your fiction the hero strives to avoid being swallowed up by other people's ideas or versions of reality. On occasion you seem to present him with something like the whole range of contemporary alternatives—say, in *Augie March* or *Herzog*. Was this one of your intentions?

Bellow. All these matters are really so complicated. Of course these books are somewhat concerned with free choice. I don't think that they pose the question successfully—the terms are not broad enough. I think I have let myself off easily. I seem to have asked in my books, How can one resist the controls of this vast society *without* turning into a nihilist, avoiding the absurdity of empty rebellion? I have asked, Are there other, more good-natured forms of resistance and free choice? And I suppose that, like most Americans, I have involuntarily favored the more comforting or melioristic side of the question. I don't mean that I ought to have been more "pessimistic," because I have found "pessimism" to be in most of its forms nearly as empty as "optimism." But I am obliged to admit that I have not followed these questions to the necessary depth. I can't blame myself for not having been a stern moralist; I can always use the excuse that I'm after all nothing but a writer of fiction. But I don't feel satisfied with what I have done to date, except in the comic form. There is, however, this to be added—that our French friends invariably see the answers to such questions, and all questions of truth, to be overwhelmingly formidable, uncongenial, hostile to us. It may be, however, that truth is not always so punitive. I've tried to suggest this in my books. There may be truths on the side of life. I am quite prepared to admit that being habitual liars and self-deluders, we have good cause to fear the truth, but I'm not at all ready to stop hoping. There may be some truths which are, after all, our friends in the universe.

Dangling Man

by Denis Donoghue

Saul Bellow's novel, *Dangling Man*, appeared in 1944 when few readers had fiction on their minds and even dangling had to be postponed.[1] But the hero, Joseph, was neither the first nor the last victim of modern perception. The marks of his anguish are visible in much of twentieth-century literature.

The dangling man is conscious of being in an interim situation, waiting either for nothing or for a Godot answerable to his dignity and his imagination. He is in prison. His deepest feeling is a sense of displacement. He may live in a hotel, like the hero of *Seize the Day*, but, wherever he is, he feels "out of place." He has no contact, no roots: "Someone had said, and Wilhelm agreed with the saying, that in Los Angeles all the loose objects in the country were collected, as if America had been tilted and everything that wasn't tightly screwed down had slid into Southern California. He himself had been one of these loose objects." [2]

In *Dangling Man* Joseph feels himself imprisoned in one room. "I, in this room, separate, alienated, distrustful, find in my purpose not an open world, but a closed, hopeless jail. My perspectives end in the walls." In this situation action seeps away. The hero devotes himself to the niceties of routine in the hope of mistaking them for deep rituals. To keep up his morale he rises early, buys his cigars, drinks a Coca-Cola, and—like the victim in *Seize the Day*—is down in the lobby by eight o'clock.

These characters are more acutely aware of the symptoms of their malaise than of its cause. Henderson in *Henderson the Rain-King* hears a voice within which repeats, "I want, I want, I want," but he is not sure what he wants. He is afflicted, like Eliot's image of Hamlet, with a radical disease at once vague and exorbitant. If he is articulate

1 Saul Bellow, *Dangling Man* (London: Weidenfeld and Nicolson, second edition, 1960), p. 30.

2 Saul Bellow, *Seize the Day* (London: Weidenfeld and Nicolson, 1957), p. 22.

as well as suffering, like Bellow's Augie March, he tries to find some cause of his tumult. Augie laments that his life has no inherited images of value to set against the rush of events. Instead of the silken images of Sicilian lovers Augie has only "deep city vexation." [3] But prophetically charged moments are rare in Bellow's fiction: the nearest we come to them is in *Henderson the Rain-King,* where Henderson tries to talk to his faithful Romilayu who is digging his way out of the prison. "I told that man next door I had a voice that said, *I want.*" [4] So the dangling man feels that he has lapsed from an older, finer self. And he invents an Eden of warmth and resonance from which he has been displaced. What he retains is a scruple, an uncomfortable possession. Einhorn names it for Augie: "But wait. All of a sudden I catch on to something about you. You've got *opposition* in you." Augie thinks of this: "I did have opposition in me, and great desire to offer resistance and to say 'No.' " Bellow's heroes share this scruple. It is easy to think of it as, simply, imagination. The exemplary imagination is always wayward, insisting upon its right to criticize, because it is like the conscience of its bearer and it will not allow him the pleasure of facility. Meanwhile, and necessarily, the heroes are painfully introspective. Wilhelm's eyes peer into the dark of himself, disliking what they see. This partly explains Henderson's sense of his own body, the huge thing, the face like Grand Central Station. A moral Tarzan with the additional burdens of imagination and conscience, Henderson is long past the stage of swinging from branch to branch. He flounders. He has no direction. All he knows now is that, somehow, he must maintain "a sense of his own being." Some of the obstacles come, then, from within; others from outside, often embodied in an older, more successful brother—Amos in *Dangling Man,* Simon in *Augie March.* These brothers want to help, but the only help they can imagine makes the victims mere ciphers, functions. And the hero's "opposition" balks at this indignity.

It is time to ask what exactly these characters want. The short answer is: equilibrium. Or, in another version, they want to know how to live, what to do. Joseph gives a more elaborate answer: "to know what we are and what we are for, to know our purpose, to seek grace." When Augie sees the exiled Trotsky in Acatla he becomes enthusiastic, especially about the exile, and he thinks of the impression the man gave "of navigation by the great stars, of the highest considerations, of being fit to speak the most important human words and universal terms." So the search for value is not so much a search for the truth,

[3] Saul Bellow, *The Adventures of Augie March* (London: Weidenfeld and Nicolson, 1954), p. 117.
[4] Saul Bellow, *Henderson the Rain-King* (London: Weidenfeld and Nicolson, 1959), p. 318.

a message, or a revelation; it is an attempt to respond to the experience of life by producing a man adequate to its challenge. Augie says
at one point: "You invent a man who can stand before the terrible
appearances. This way he can't get justice and he can't give justice,
but he can live." As far as it goes, this is fine, but later, in the in-
flammable conversation with Mintouchian, Augie has a darker insight:

> "You will understand, Mr. Mintouchian, if I tell you that I have al-
> ways tried to become what I am. But it's a frightening thing. Because
> what if what I am by nature isn't good enough?" I was close to tears as
> I said it to him. "I suppose I better, anyway, give in and be it. I will
> never force the hand of fate to create a better Augie March, nor change
> the time to an age of gold."

The novel ends with a little self-indulgence; Augie, alone, travelling
hopefully, a Columbus from Chicago reminding us that Columbus
found his America. It is softer than the tone of great Comedy.

In the earlier novels the search for value was invariably the great
preoccupation. In *Dangling Man* the hero surrenders, gives up the
struggle on the last page, like Hans Castorp going down to the war:

> I am no longer to be held accountable for myself; I am grateful for
> that. I am in other hands, relieved of self-determination, freedom can-
> celled.
> Hurray for regular hours!
> And for the supervision of the spirit!
> Long live regimentation!

In *The Victim* the search is oblique and evasive. The book is concerned with guilt, borne by Asa and embodied in his relation to Kirby
Allbee. The guilt is given as a condition of Asa's being, and the best
pages deal with his moral analysis and Allbee's appalling speculative
earnestness. Asa is the conscience and the imagination of his race; a
good man. But the novel allows external circumstance to lift his burden. It lets this Job off, makes Cordelia live to marry Edgar. The
facts of the case are given as an inner condition, a mode of sensibility,
but the solution is circumstantial. Allbee brings in a whore and dese-
crates the holy bed of Asa and Mary; so Asa can drive him away, and
the guilt evaporates. It is a contrivance. In *Henderson the Rain-King*
again the hero is too easily redeemed, set free with a symbolic lion
cub and a child's friendship.

We can summarize this by saying that Bellow's heroes seek value,
equilibrium, salvation—Henderson's word—an earthly condition in
which body and soul may live. The condition, if it were possible,
would allow the self a genial relation to its world. Henderson gave
up hunting because it seemed "a strange way to relate to nature."

Augie looks with anguish at the eagle which Thea is training to kill lizards. Aggression, aggression, aggression. The self will not take the offensive, it will not profit from the sufferings of others, it will return a verdict for reason "in its partial inadequacy and against the advantages of its surrender," as Joseph says. Bellow's characters reach a dark moment in which they feel that reason has nothing to do with action. Augie's conjunction with Stella on a mountain of wet grass in Mexico is followed by the reflection that, "After much making with sense, it's senselessness that you submit to." Tommy Wilhelm sees himself as a man "who reflected long and then made the decision he had rejected twenty times."

Basically, these characters want to be assured of their own existence. Augie meditates that, "Personality is unsafe in the first place. It's the types that are safe. So almost all make deformations on themselves so that the great terror will let them be." The great terror takes many desolately prosaic forms, including the boredom of one day following another, the Indian file of tedium. Joseph says, "It may be that I am tired of having to identify a day as 'the day I asked for a second cup of coffee' or 'the day the waitress refused to take back the burned toast,' and so want to blaze it more sharply, regardless of the consequences."

There is another demand; that a man be his own master, agent in his own action. The philosopher Clarence Irving Lewis has argued that "a being which could not act would live out its life within the bounds of immediacy. It could find no difference between its own content of feeling and reality. There could be no self, because there could be no other-than-self: the distinction could not arise." [5] Bellow's heroes want to choose, because their humanity depends upon the hazard of choice, but they fear that the irrational may be a categorical condition, like the air we breathe. Hence the image of dissociation. These men seek salvation within their own being and from their own resources. They find no sustenance in other people, in society. Society is what went wrong: the body politic and the world's body are bankrupt. The only mode of society which Bellow's men take seriously is the family. Augie is devoted to his family and to the idea of the Person. But he has no vision of society as a great family, in which a man might live with due autonomy while being a member of something larger than himself. And often, outraged by a society which has failed and deceived them, these characters seek moral simplicity as an entirely private possession. Henderson goes through the heart of darkness into the desert, impelled to "simplify."

[5] Clarence Irving Lewis, *An Analysis of Knowledge and Valuation* (La Salle, Illinois: Open Court, 1946), p. 21.

In theory, there is no conflict between this desire and the urge to "love." Bellow often quotes Simone Weil: "To believe in the existence of human beings as such is love." This is the ground of his entire fiction. But in practice it rarely obtains. Joseph spends a lot of time pondering the difference between persons and things. In *The Victim* Schlossberg defines, for Asa's benefit, what it means to be human.[6] Henderson tells Romilayu: "The only decent thing about me is that I have loved certain people in my life." But there is an incorrigible vacuum between theory and practice, between profession and realization. Bellow's characters live on the assumption that belief in the existence of human beings as such must come later; after they have managed to secure a belief in their own existence. They do not take much stock in the idea that precisely by committing ourselves to the existence of other people our own existence is certified. They think that they can say "I" before saying "Thou."

But all these matters are exactingly complicated by *Herzog*, the residence of another of Bellow's dangling men.

In the original *Dangling Man*, as we have seen, Joseph suffers from "a feeling of strangeness, of not quite belonging to the world, of lying under a cloud and looking up at it." He feels himself cut adrift from the past, living in a spectral present tense in which Tuesday is the same as Saturday because both are featureless. So we register the first difference in *Herzog*, that a verifiable past is Moses's ball and chain. But at least he has a past. Like Wilhelm in *Seize the Day*, he is "a visionary sort of animal," but he commits himself to his own experience. Wilhelm "had cast off his father's name," but Moses keeps the name and the image. His father and mother are dead, but they range through his story, carrying the brute weight of their existence. Moses never repudiates them. Like *The Adventures of Augie March*, this is a Jewish story, a family story. Indeed, it is closer in spirit to *Augie March* than to any of the other books, before or after. Bellow has given up the allegorical neatness of *The Victim* in preference for the richer idiom of fact and event. Equally, he has evaded the symbolic itch of *Henderson the Rain-King*: we are not required to take a course in "the Africa within." Herzog's experience is given to us in the same terms in which it is given to him; specific acts, casualties, and sufferings. We are not allowed to substitute a formula for the things given. Nor is he. The plot is a commitment to live through the terms of its reference: Herzog keeps going, he strikes through every proffered mask, and because God is finally Good he is eventually allowed to reach a quiet place, the rediscovered Berkshires of his spirit. Bellow has often found trouble in making an appropriate Act Five, but the

---

[6] Saul Bellow, *The Victim* (New York: Viking Press, 1956), p. 146.

end of *Herzog* is entirely convincing, Moses lying down, containing himself, feeling the strength of his quietness for the first time. Tommy Wilhelm believed that the "easy, tranquil things of life" might still be recovered, that even yet life might be "reduced to simplicity again." The simplicity is realized in *Herzog*, but it is not a reduction; life is enhanced in those quiet Berkshires.

So the book is animated by Bellow's constant concern; Fact and Value, the relation between the terms; the redemption of the event, the thing done, because it is done in a certain spirit. Herzog knows that he must do a great deal of mind-work if he is to preserve his vigilance and be ready to deal with his experience as it comes to him and he goes to meet it. "Awareness was his work; extended consciousness was his line, his business." But he knows that this can't be the answer: we have been conscious for centuries, and, look, we have not come through. The quality of our consciousness is wrong, to begin with. We need the consciousness of appreciation, not the consciousness of possession; the open hand, not the grip of claw. There is a long passage, late in the book, where Herzog ponders these matters. "Not thinking is not necessarily fatal," he reflects. "Did I really believe that I would die when thinking stopped?" This is the first sign of health, the old body standing up to defend itself against the destructive consciousness. "Go through what is comprehensible and you conclude that only the incomprehensible gives any light." Further: "And consciousness when it doesn't clearly understand what to live for, what to die for, can only abuse and ridicule itself." The knowledge of these fundamental things is not obtained in the head. It is a sixth sense, closely in touch with the other five; or perhaps it is an ur-sense prior to any other. And if it has a special intimacy with one of the five, it is with the sense of touch: we come to know what to live for by touch, in the silence of wonder. Herzog has spent much of his life abusing and ridiculing himself, writing manic letters to men good and bad, living and dead, for fear his mind will stop and, stopping, bring him crashing to the ground. The turning-point comes when he gives up the abuse and the struggle to convert experience into mind; and simply waits. The human imagination, he says at one point, "starts by accusing God of murder." It cultivates a grievance. No more of that: let the dead grievances bury their dead. Herzog has lived most of his life converting experience into words, as if words alone were certain good: "I go after reality with language." But he comes to discover that words are destructive, subversive, if sought in the wrong spirit. "Perhaps I'd like to change it all into language, to force Madeleine and Gersbach to have a *conscience*. There's a word for you."

So this is a book of genial words reaching into silence. At the end, Herzog finds that he has said everything he needs to say, at least for the present; there will be no more talk, no messages, no unmailed letters to Nietzsche. Now, for a saving while, he will live modestly among tangible things, trusting to the emergence of light without force or pressure. So his last fictive moments are spent among wine bottles, hats, roses, a Recamier couch, Mrs. Tuttle's broom. Forty pages earlier he wrote: "The dream of man's heart, however much we may distrust and resent it, is that life may complete itself in significant pattern. Some incomprehensible way. Before death. Not irrationally but incomprehensibly fulfilled." [7] This is his "rage for order," but he discovers that he stands a better chance of finding order when the rage is stilled, and he tries to trust the world. This does not mean that he calls off the hunt or sacks his imagination; it means that he prescribes new conditions, sets a new quiet key.

There is a beautiful incident which, more than another, gives the spirit of the discovery. Herzog makes a mad dash to Chicago with a dim plan to kill his wife and her lover. He takes his father's gun and the required bullets. As he travels he works himself up to the necessary steam of venom. When he comes to the house, he looks in the back window and sees the lover, Gersbach, giving the child—Junie—her bath. It is all ordinary, almost handsome. Herzog knows that there can be no question of killing. This does not solve his predicament; his story does not become a fairy-tale, but it shows him that some crucial things in life have nothing to do with the higher mind-work, they simply are what they are.

So the book makes a strange and beautiful figure. The first half is all steam, mania, *angst;* energy lurching, an expense of spirit in a waste of hate and shame. Some of this is brilliantly done; especially when Herzog is brought home by the Himmelsteins and a browbeating session leaves the victim distracted. (Himmelstein is first cousin to old Einhorn in *Augie March.*) Bellow's feeling for this scene is impeccable; where the browbeater is thick, ignorant, and right, while the victim is all sensibility and wrong. He is not quite as good when the scene is academic and clever; the visit of Shapiro to the Herzogs is a bright parade of highbrow lore, Moses the odd-man out, but it is unconvincing, a set piece too set in its ways.

Bellow is a man's novelist. His female characters tend to be done with far smaller resource, as in *Herzog* Ramona, given in great detail, is a piece of cardboard while Father Herzog, a brief sketch, is authentically "there." Bellow's prose can deal with women only when they are magisterial figures in the landscape of the past; and then they are nearly men. If a woman is thirty-five and about to become the hero's mistress, the chances are that she will reveal herself the

7 Saul Bellow, *Herzog* (New York: Viking Press, 1964), p. 303.

product of scissors-and-paste. The reason is, perhaps, that in Bellow's fiction these women are there merely to give the hero something more to suffer; they merely add to the noise and fret of his life. And, strictly speaking, anyone could do this for him. In the novels since *Augie March* Bellow's imagination is devoted to this problem, among many; how to lure the facts into peace without denying their recalcitrance, how to reach solid ground, how to live. Women have very little to do with this part of the story: the hero's problem is now personal and representative.

I mention this limitation to suggest that Bellow's resources as a novelist, more impressive than ever, are not unlimited. But he is one of the important novelists because of the depth at which his options are made and his sense of the pressure they have to meet. This is what the novelist's integrity means, the measure of his scruple. If we think of *Herzog* as a severe examination of the modern orthodoxies in literature, the Wasteland myth and the arrogance of consciousness, we know at the same time that Bellow is not a smiling salesman selling toothpaste. His "positives" go no further than the propriety of silence, at this time; the illness is not miraculously cured. I would not ask him to go beyond this point. But *Herzog* is important because it reveals our whining orthodoxies for the shoddy things they are; and because it urges us to try again, and try harder. The book tells us that we are infatuated with our own illness, since we deem it the proof of our integrity. But health is better than illness, and *Herzog* points to at least one possibility.

This is what the style of the book implies: it is a prose of human size, much freer than that of *Dangling Man* or *The Victim*. The early books are rigid in their parables, they live by constriction, and they exhibit a correspondingly rigid style. The style is the parable. But according as Bellow has liberated himself, more and more deeply, from the governing orthodoxies of modern literature, he has moved into richer modes of style. There is clearly a direct relation between the possibilities he sees in life and those he has discovered in his language. The eloquence of the writing wells up from the life it exhibits, the characters, events, situations: it is not an artificially induced eloquence, a merely personal invention. In the scene in the police-station, when Madeleine comes to bring Junie home after Herzog's arrest, the graph of Herzog's feeling as he watches her is drawn with remarkable exactitude: technically, it is largely a matter of syntax, beginning with the short sentences in which Herzog registers the precision of Madeleine's movements, her command of herself, the way she knows where to drop the milk-carton even though she has just entered the room. And as the thoughts incite one another, the syntax reflects the nervous gesture, the twitches of feeling. But the feelings were there before the prose; the prose "imitates" them. Hence the change of tempo at the end, the nerves calmed; and the prose is like Mrs. Tuttle's broom, the exact and faithful answer to its occasion.

And now *Mr. Sammler's Planet,* which differs from *Herzog* more in its governing tense than in its rhetoric: the new element is the future. *Herzog* is present and past, *Mr. Sammler's Planet* is present, past, and future; present for its sense of the terrible way things are; past for its sense of history, the inescapable causes, chances, choices, the dreadful chance by which Artur escaped death while Antonina died; and now for better or worse the future, not yet a place fit for Prosperos and Calibans to inhabit.

Meanwhile, in this planetary fiction the terrestrial facts must be acknowledged. We are unhappy. Granted. Kierkegaard's true Knight of Faith, "having set its relations with the infinite, was entirely at home in the finite." Further: "Able to carry the jewel of faith, making the motions of the infinite, and as a result needing nothing but the finite and the usual." [8] We, on the contrary, seek "the extraordinary" in a world which never promised to be anything but ordinary. I am paraphrasing Artur Sammler, to whom these thoughts come as to a finite center of consciousness: he is the one who knows, because he is the one who cares most continuously. His sense of what he knows is elegiac, not satiric or sour: he lives by giving each moment its lyric due, letting his feelings bring him somehow from Monday to Tuesday, taking the harm out of accidents by redeeming them, treating them as if they could still be redeemed for use and value. Still, he is old and tired, and like nearly everybody else he wants to escape from the prison of self and desire: he thinks himself "the human being at the point where he attempted to obtain his release from being human." Bellow has always sympathized with victims of that desire, but he has tried to persuade them not to break out or cop a plea: better to hold on and meanwhile do as little damage as possible. Still, we are near the end of something—that can hardly be denied.

This marks the rhythm of *Mr. Sammler's Planet.* We have come to the end of something (History? Earth?), and now, with all systems go, we are at the beginning of something else (Fiction? Moon?). "Wasn't it the time—the very hour to go? . . . To blow this great blue, white, green planet, or to be blown from it." [9] Mr. Sammler feels that "with the end of things-as-known the feeling for new beginnings was nevertheless very strong." [10] The gloating messengers of Apocalypse will not have it all their own way, even yet: true, man "wants a divorce from

8 Saul Bellow, *Mr. Sammler's Planet* (New York: Viking, 1970), p. 62.
9 *Ibid.,* p. 51.
10 *Ibid.,* p. 278.

all the states that he knows," [11] but he is still not ready to lie down, turn over, and die. How long, O Lord, how long? Yes, Lord, but not yet: try again, a second shot. Most of this feeling in the novel is directed toward our new toy, the Moon, which Mr. Sammler thinks of as if it were the catacombs, built for a new start. "Artemis—lunar chastity." [12] On the Moon, people would have to live a simple life, work hard to breathe and stay alive; every man a priest, austere, watching and praying. This is not Gene Kelly's Moon rhyming with "tune" or "lagoon," but a remote possibility and more, a moral possibility if people are strong enough to rise to its occasion. But the possibility counts for much of the radiance of Mr. Sammler's feeling, when it is radiant, even though he does not hope to survive the death of the old world, the doomed planet.

So we come back to the old question: how to live, what to do. I bring two passages together, hoping to see them blend into one. The first: "Humankind, drunk with terror, calm itself, sober up." [13] The second, where Bellow speaks of a few persons like Mr. Sammler: "even if insulted, pained, somewhere bleeding, not broadly expressing any anger, not crying out with sadness, but translating heartache into delicate, even piercing observation." [14] Otherwise put, the rhetoric of the book says: move from pathos toward aesthetics, make your sorrows the materials of perception and appreciation. Wouldn't it be wonderful if *King Lear* were written not by Shakespeare but by King Lear, treating his own suffering as the mere content of his art? The howling tuned by the howler in the form of five acts? The early pages of *Mr. Sammler's Planet* speak of man's demands, the grotesque bill of complaint filed by every one of us, each item marked "nonnegotiable." "The old comical-tearful stuff. Emotional relationships. Desires incapable of useful fulfillment. Over and over, trying to vent and empty the breast of certain cries, certain fervencies." [15] What else can we do? There is no question of a cure, but perhaps we could "orchestrate the disorders." The same pattern, in other words: from pathos ("howl, howl, howl, howl, howl") to aesthetics ("and that's true too," Gloucester to Edgar, *King Lear,* Act V, scene ii, line 12). It is an old-fashioned kind of aesthetics, but none the worse for that. Bellow thinks of the aesthetic stance as that in which we place a certain distance between ourselves and the object of attention. We observe the decencies as much as the objects, in the sense that we stand back somewhat and take care not to lay violent hands upon the natural world. We think

11 *Ibid.,* p. 235.
12 *Ibid.,* p. 67.
13 *Ibid.,* p. 182.
14 *Ibid.,* p. 44.
15 *Ibid.,* p. 174.

of the world as something valuable to be held in trust, not as grist to our mills. So the greatest term of praise in *Mr. Sammler's Planet* is lavished upon a spirit described as "disinterested": the word reverberates through the novel as the sound of everything decent and hopeful. It is the word of silence, sounding against the noise of demands and threats. Eckhardt is quoted in its praise, with an implication that there is something divine in the state of being disinterested: "not as misanthropes dissociate themselves, by judging, but by not judging." [16]
But there is more. Mr. Sammler is thinking of the tendency of human beings, given liberty and room, to mythologize themselves: "they expand by imagination and try to rise above the limitations of the ordinary forms of common life." Going further, he asks himself:

> And what is "common" about "the common life"? What if some genius were to do with "common life" what Einstein did with matter? Finding its energetics, uncovering its radiance.[17]

Otherwise put: redeem the time. "Short views, for God's sake!" [18] It is not a question of dreaming up new symbols, but of choosing the best from those already available. "Better, thought Sammler, to accept the inevitability of imitation and then to imitate good things. . . . Make peace therefore with intermediacy and representation." [19] So the book ends with Dr. Gruner's death, and Mr. Sammler standing alone beside the corpse, saying true words about a man who "through all the confusion and degraded clowning of this life" met the terms of his contract; terms which we all know but do not meet. Mr. Sammler's planet is not the Moon, it is Earth, Stevens's "old chaos of the sun," Bellow's hospital.
The point is: if there has been a pattern, a recognizable rhythm, in Bellow's fiction from *Dangling Man* to *Herzog*, *Mr. Sammler's Planet* hasn't changed it much; it is another variation on the same theme, the hero (often poorly qualified for such a task) trying to make sense of experience in general by making sense of his own in particular: all those burdens, all that good will. Mr. Sammler is further than Herzog from the fray, the abyss, the void, for two reasons: he is older, and he is not demented. To make sense of experience, you must have had a lot of it, and you must have preserved the marks of it; and you must be ready at any moment to give it up or, a more difficult assign-

16 *Ibid.*, p. 236.
17 *Ibid.*, p. 147.
18 *Ibid.*, p. 148.
19 *Ibid.*, p. 149.

ment, to hang on to it. This is the good cause served, however differently, by Herzog's demented erudition and Sammler's soliloquies. Loyalty to the common world takes the form of interrogation, thereby disclosing its further bizarre possibilities. It is essential to Bellow's human comedy, and to his own inventiveness, that life be lived as if all were not yet lost.

The Victim

by John J. Clayton

Like Joseph, Asa Leventhal is a solitary with few friends, and a depressive. He feels burdened by a constant struggle against the world, because of a difficulty which is at once psychological and moral, as in the case of Joseph. The theme of this book is the casting-off of his self-imposed burdens by learning to accept himself and others rather than to judge and blame, by learning to have an open heart. Asa's chief burden, like Joseph's, is his pride, which is the very antithesis of true dignity. Bellow wishes to reveal the true beauty and dignity of the human being; but this beauty and dignity can be realized only by admitting that you are merely human, by accepting rather than blaming yourself and others.

The Victim also concerns the obligation of the human being to others. The book has two epigraphs. The first tells of a merchant who is confronted with a huge Ifrit brandishing a sword. " 'Stand up that I may slay thee even as thou slayest my son!' Asked the merchant, 'How have I slain thy son?' and he answered, 'When thou atest dates and threwest away the stones they struck my son full in the breast as he was walking by, so that he died forthwith.' " What are the limits of human responsibility? Is a man guilty for what he does not intend? The second epigraph is not about individual suffering but about the suffering of humanity at large. It is a passage out of De Quincey—a vision of an ocean turning into a human face, then a multitude of faces "upturned to the heavens, faces imploring, wrathful, despairing; faces that surged upwards by thousands, by myriads, by generations. . . ." Partly this is the question of *Dangling Man*—the relationship of the individual and the mass. Partly it is an image of the futility, the immensity, the helplessness of humanity's suffering. What can you do to stop all this suffering? Many are called, few are chosen; why one and not another? These precisely are the problems raised in *The Victim*.

Asa Leventhal, a city Jew of guilts and duties—the city, his job,

"The Victim" by John Jacob Clayton. From *Saul Bellow: In Defense of Man* by John Jacob Clayton. Reprinted by permission of Indiana University Press.

his brother's family are all weights on his back—blames everyone and assumes that everyone is blaming him. Kirby Allbee, another "victim" and anti-Semite, does indeed blame him, accusing Asa of having intentionally cost him his job years before, the loss of which led to poverty, his wife's death, and his degeneration.

Two plot strands develop. In the first, guilty Asa tries to deal with Allbee, to get rid of him, to understand him, to help him, to beat him up. Allbee, not revealing what he is after, insinuates himself more and more deeply into Asa's life—visiting him, following him, living with him, locking him out of his own house while Allbee has sexual relations with a pick-up, finally trying to kill Asa and himself. Asa begins by refusing to acknowledge responsibility, moves toward helping Allbee, and ends by expelling him, no longer quite so afraid of Allbee as an image of his own possible failure and a projection of his own self-hatred. As in Malamud's "Last of the Mohicans," a stranger forces the hero to see his own spiritual failings—and departs. Now Asa can call his wife, who has been South with her mother, and ask her to come home.

If Asa is healed, it is due partly to the second plot strand. Out of a sense of duty, he takes charge of his brother's family when Max is away. Partly on Asa's responsibility, Max's son Mickey is sent to the hospital, where he dies. Asa's emotional involvement here—his change from blame of Max for being away from his family to love of Max, and from duty to concern—helps make Asa aware that a man is not flawless, that in humility he must take responsibility even for what he (like the merchant in the epigraph) is hardly responsible.

The last chapter of the novel occurs years later. Asa, however, looks younger. The burden of guilt and so of struggle is lighter now. Meeting Allbee, Asa no longer sees him as the Persecutor. They have both changed: Allbee is now externally happy and semi-successful but essentially the same; Asa is externally the same but essentially changed, owing to an "expansion of the heart" and a recognition of his merely human status.

Saul Bellow's only dramatic plot—dramatic in that it is founded on an active conflict between individuals—is based directly on a novella by Dostoyevsky, *The Eternal Husband*. (What better shows that Bellow is a monologuist who longs to become a dialoguist?) This derivation has been noted by a number of critics, though none has developed the relationship in detail.[1] Bellow himself says that the

[1] For instance, Marcus Klein, *After Alienation* (Cleveland, 1964), p. 37; Harvey Swados, *A Radical's America* (Boston, 1962), p. 170. I am grateful for the assistance of Mr. James Hoffman, whose unpublished study contains a discussion of many of the parallels between *The Victim* and *The Eternal Husband*.

parallel is obvious to him now, although not at the time he wrote the novel.[2] I shall not compare the two works in depth; but I will point to a number of similarities and differences which show clearly the influence of Dostoyevsky on Bellow's early fiction—how much he was working in the Russian's moral-psychological mode—and, more important, the changes Bellow makes, changes which significantly aid him in celebrating the dignity of the human being.

The theme of Dostoyevsky's novella is the dignity of a man. Like Asa Leventhal, Alexey Velchaninov is unwell physically and burdened with guilt. To each comes a "double"—a projection of his guilty nature—whom Leventhal and Velchaninov have hurt in the past. The heroes reject these doubles as wild animals, as less than human. The "victims"—Trusotsky and Allbee—prey on the guilt-ridden heroes with a combined hatred and love. Trusotsky tells Velchaninov that he had loved him and looked up to him; he begs Velchaninov to drink with him; he kisses his hand and begs for a kiss on the lips; he cares for Velchaninov like a mother when Velchaninov is sick. Allbee wants to rub his fingers through Asa's kinky "Jew" hair (an act more homoerotic than anti-Semitic), he feels hurt that Asa is not intimate with him; finally he brings a woman into Asa's bed, not only, it seems to take Asa's place but to bind himself to Asa. Fiedler says, "Allbee . . . is Leventhal's beloved as well as his nightmare; just as Leventhal is Allbee's beloved as well as his nightmare. . . ."[3] Nightmare: for at the same time, each victim hates enough to kill; not only do Trusotsky and Allbee wish to kill their enemies, but Leventhal and Velchaninov also threaten a number of times to kill their persecutors; at the end, both antagonists indeed *try* to kill. In each case this attempt cuts the cord between the doubles. The hero is freed. But the process of becoming free is in each case more complex than this—and nearly the same: Velchaninov and Leventhal must draw close to their enemies, identify with them, pity them. Asa acknowledges his responsibility, offers help, and understands that Allbee is a suffering human, not merely his persecutor; Alexey acknowledges his kinship with Trusotsky —"We are both vicious, underground, loathsome people"[4]—and then, in humility, tells him, " 'You are better than I am! I understand it all; all. . . .' " (*EH*, p. 455). But in both cases there is the need for the attempted murder, the physical scuffle, the expulsion. Afterward each hero is healed. Velchaninov is no longer sick, no longer depressive; Leventhal's health is also improved, and he is happier, less bur-

2 "Saul Bellow," Interview with Jay Nash and Ron Offen in *Literary Times* (Chicago), Dec., 1964, p. 10.

3 Leslie Fiedler, *Waiting for the End* (New York, 1964), p. 99.

4 Fyodor Dostoyevsky, *The Eternal Husband*, in *The Short Novels of Dostoyevsky*, trans. Constance Garnett (New York, 1951), p. 443.

dened. Both encounter their doubles again, but greet them now as whole men who have regained their dignity.

In incidentals, too, the two works are alike. Both heroes are temporarily alone, deserted by a maid, a wife. It is the purgatory of summer in a great city, the first paragraph of each novel telling of the intense heat. And with the lifting of the psychological burden of each hero comes autumn coolness; each hero goes to the window for a breath of cool air. The dream figures of Allbee and Trusotsky are introduced the same way: the heroes fall asleep and are awakened by a bell: no one is there. Both show at this point evidence of guilt—Velchaninov dreams of an unknown accusation, Leventhal thinks he sees mice darting along the walls. The "victims" have been spying on, scrutinizing the heroes for some time. They wear the signs of their loss—Trusotsky a black crepe indicating the death of his wife and indicating, too, the loss of her faithfulness; Allbee the seedy clothes and disarranged look of a Bowery drunk, indicating how low he has fallen since Leventhal cost him his job. Like Trusotsky, Allbee has lost his wife, and he considers Leventhal responsible for this since she left him (and was killed in a car crash) after he ran out of money. Both pairs are complementary: Allbee is the anti-Semite Leventhal needs to justify his sense of persecution and feed his guilt, while Leventhal is the persecutor Allbee needs to be able to believe that not he but the world is responsible for his fall; similarly, Trusotsky is the projection of Velchaninov's self-accusation, Velchaninov the cuckold whom the eternal husband can't do without. Both "victims" act with aristocratic pride alternating with degenerate drinking, wild displays, and threats to a small child. Yet the heroes are doubles of the victims in the simplest sense: Velchaninov and Leventhal become drunk and sloppy, and they parallel, in imagination at least, the sexual behavior they condemn in the widowers (Trusotsky's engagement to a teenaged girl, Allbee's pick-up of the woman). In each novel a young child dies, having been taken from home on the insistence of the hero: in *Eternal Husband* it is Velchaninov's own child, in *The Victim,* the child of [Leventhal's] brother. Each novel, finally, ends in an epilogue with a bell which calls the victim-figure back to his new life.

Yet in spite of all these similarities, Bellow has written his own novel, not only in its creation of an American urban environment—where else is there so brilliant an evocation of the deadly weight of a metropolis in summer?—or in its added complexity and integration of material (the substitution of [Leventhal's] brother's family for Velchaninov's friends in the country is a fine move)—but especially in its development of the theme of human dignity.

The theme has its central expression in the two-page speech of the old Yiddish journalist, Schlossberg. It is a speech which has no parallel in *The Eternal Husband* and, like most of Bellow's important choral speeches, has no function in the plot. It is, perhaps, the central speech of Bellow's fiction.

"I try to give everybody credit," declared the old man. "I am not a knocker. I am not too good for this world."

No one contradicted him.

"Well," he said. "And what am I kicking for?" He checked their smiles, holding them all with his serious, worn, blue gaze. "I'll tell you. It's bad to be less than human and it's bad to be more than human. What's more than human? Our friend—" he meant Levanthal, "was talking about it before. Caesar, if you remember, in the play wanted to be like a god. Can a god have diseases? So this is a sick man's idea of God. Does a statue have wax in its ears? Naturally not. It doesn't sweat, either, except maybe blood on holidays. If I can talk myself into it that I never sweat and make everybody else act as if it was true, maybe I can fix it up about dying, too. We only know what it is to die because some people die, and, if we make ourselves different from them, maybe we don't have to? Less than human is the other side of it. I'll come to it. So here is the whole thing, then. Good acting is what is exactly human. And if you say I am a tough critic, you mean I have a high opinion of what is human. This is my whole idea. More than human, can you have any use for life? Less than human, you don't either."

He made a pause—and it was not one that invited interruption—and went on.

"This girl Livia in *The Tigress*. What's the matter with her? She commits a murder. What are her feelings? No love, no hate, no fear, no lungs, no heart. I'm ashamed to mention what else is missing. Nothing! The poor husband. Nothing is killing him, less than human. A blank. And it should be so awful the whole audience should be afraid positively to look in her face. But I don't know if she's too pretty or what to have feelings. You see right away she has no idea what *is* human because her husband's death doesn't mean to her a thing. It's all in packages, and first the package is breathing and then it isn't breathing, and you insured the package so you can marry another package and go to Florida for the winter. Now maybe somebody will answer me. 'This sounds very interesting. You say less than human, more than human. Tell me, please, what is human?' And really we study people so much now that after we look and look at human nature—I write science articles myself—after you look at it and weigh it and turn it over and put it under a microscope, you might say, 'What is all the shouting about? A man is nothing, his life is nothing. Or it is even lousy and cheap. But this your royal highness doesn't like, so he chokes it up. With what? With greatness and beauty. Beauty and greatness? Black and white I know; I didn't make it up. But greatness and beauty?' But I say, 'What do you know? No, tell me, what do you know? You shut

one eye and look at a thing, and it is one way to you. You shut the
other one and it is different. I am as sure about greatness and beauty
as you are about black and white. If a human life is a great thing to
me, it *is* a great thing. Do you know better? I'm entitled as much as you.
And why be measly. Do you have to be? Is somebody holding you by
the neck? Have dignity, you understand me? Choose dignity. Nobody
knows enough to turn it down.' . . ."
"Bravo!" said Harkavy. (*V*, pp. 133–35)

Notice first the authority figure: an *alte jude* who speaks in slightly
Yiddish constructions (*I'm entitled as much as you*) and rhetorical expressions like those in the fiction of Sholem Aleichem and Peretz, although these are mixed with an American idiom. So he speaks with
the weight of Jewish tradition and sets this tradition, implied in the
tone, against the cheapening or fraudulent ennobling of human life
current in America. Again and again in Bellow, wisdom comes from
the Jewish past, or at least a non-American past, often spoken by a
meshugenah, an eccentric. In *The Victim* Schlossberg and the old lady
Harkavy serve this function. Then, too, this authority figure is from
the common life, and his speech is the conscious opposite of polished
rhetoric. The responses at the end of the speech—Harkavy's "Bravo!"
and Shifcart the talent scout's "Amen and amen!"—thus establish the
quasi-comic-dramatic, quasi-religious quality of the speech. Then Shifcart offers the old man a card—and a screen test: that is, Schlossberg
himself is an actor and, according to his definition, "exactly human."
The card falls near Leventhal: that is, he is on his way to becoming
human—to understanding the wisdom of Schlossberg.

The wisdom of Schlossberg is that human life has dignity; human
life has greatness and beauty—but only on condition that it is *human*
life, not subhuman or more than human. Schlossberg's attack on the
"more than human" was seen earlier in Bellow's assault on greatness
and ideal constructions in *Dangling Man:* man tries to make himself
into a god, dehumanizing himself to remove himself from humanity
and hence from mortality. It is a perfect description of the roots of
Joseph's alienation. If this is wisdom that Asa Leventhal already possesses (it was he who pointed to Caesar as a false ideal of greatness),
he must learn how it applies to him, for, like Caesar, he rejects his
human weakness and projects it onto others. Asa lacks still more the
complementary wisdom that to be human means to feel human concern; that to be human means to be responsive to the suffering of
others.

Less-than-human, human, more-than-human is not one continuum;
a man who is more than human will also be less than human. Both
deviations involve a detachment from humanity, a refusal to admit
that one is like other men. But while there is not one continuum, the

philosophy of Schlossberg does see man as occupying a middle state traditional in Judeo-Christian theology. Being human rests on the admission of this middle state: "I am not too good for this world," Schlossberg says. I am reminded of Peretz' short story, "If Not Higher," in which Litvak, mistrustful of the rabbi of Nemirov, who disappears every Friday morning at the time of the Penitential Prayers, hides under the rabbi's bed. Early he hears the rabbi's groans of suffering for all Israel; then he sees the rabbi dress in peasant clothes and go anonymously to help a sick woman. The rabbi brings her firewood, kindles it, in spite of her objection that she cannot pay, and as the fire burns recites the prayers. The Litvak becomes the rabbi's disciple, "and ever after, when another disciple tells how the Rabbi of Nemirov ascends to heaven at the time of the Penitential Prayers, the Litvak does not laugh. He only adds quietly, 'If not higher'" (*Treasury*, p. 233). Higher not by leaving the earth but by involving himself with it; he does not remove himself from humanity but enters it, listening to and heeding its groans.

Here is the standard old Schlossberg—and Bellow—apply. By the end of this morality-novel Asa has largely succeeded in meeting it. And so, the novel is affirmative in spite of its dark tone, much more completely than *Dangling Man*. But a man has difficulties in becoming "exactly human" and thereby choosing dignity.

First, Asa, like Allbee, feels he is a victim. He is afraid that his boss, his brother's wife and mother-in-law, even his friend Williston, are against him because he is a Jew. Actually, he is never injured on these grounds; indeed, he is never persecuted at all. He fears a blacklist—there is none; he fears an attack by Elena's mother—it doesn't come. This book is not about victims. Mickey dies in the hospital, but Bellow does not inveigh against metaphysical injustice. Subtly he introduces a quick snapshot of a *real* victim of the city: "A Filipino busboy came to clear the table. He was an old man and frail looking, and his hands and forearms were whitened by immersion in hot water. The cart loaded, he bent his back low over it, receiving the handlebar in his chest, and pushed away slowly" (p. 130). Here is a victim, not Asa, eating with Harkavy, Shifcart, and Schlossberg.

It is rather Asa's sense of being a victim that we should look at— his and Allbee's too. For Allbee, the gentile and anti-Semite, feels society has become anti-gentile. "Sometimes I feel . . . as if I were in a sort of Egyptian darkness. You know, Moses punished the Egyptians with darkness. . . . When I was a boy, everything was different. We thought it would be daylight forever. Do you know, one of my ancestors was Governor Winthrop. . . . The old breeds are out. . . . It's as if the children of Caliban were running everything" (pp. 144–

45). His life has been ruined and it is none of his doing—he is a victim. "You're the one that's responsible. You did it to me deliberately, out of hate. Out of pure hate!" (p. 78).

To be a self-created victim is to lose greatness and beauty. It is to hit back, as Asa wanted to in the movie when a woman made an anti-Semitic remark. Therefore, as Opdahl says, playing the victim leads to playing the very image that the victimizer hates: Asa is in danger of becoming Allbee's *kike*.[5] Allbee, in turn, by submitting to the role of victim, has degenerated into the drunken, irrational anti-Semitic *goy* of Asa's dreams and *shtetl* tradition.

Obviously, to be a "victim" is to reject dignity. The "victim" despises himself: "I feel worthless. I know what I am. Worthless," Allbee weeps (p. 195). And Asa recognizes that he had fought with Allbee's boss (and so cost Allbee his job) not only because the man had been abusive: "No, he, he himself had begun to fear that the lowest price he put on himself was too high and he could scarcely understand why anyone should want to pay for his services. And under Rudiger's influence he had felt this. 'He made me believe what I was afraid of,' Leventhal thought" (p. 120). Again, as in *Dangling Man*, the *amour-propre* is greater the less one loves himself; self-hatred leads to ugly defensive pride. Williston tells Asa that when unemployed,

"you were fighting everybody, those days. You were worst with Rudiger, but I heard of others. . . . You should have had better judgment than to blow up."

"What, wipe the spit off my face and leave like a gentleman? I wouldn't think much of myself if I did."

"That's just it."

"What is? What I think of myself? Well. . . ." (p. 118)

Bellow does not fully go into the causes of Asa's sense of worthlessness. We know the insecurity of Asa's childhood—economic and psychological. We know his father's philosophy:

Ruf mir Yoshke, ruf mir Moshke
Aber gib mir die groschke.
(Call me Ikey, call me Moe
but give me the dough.) (p. 111)

His father walled himself off with contempt; to this extent he was less than human. Although Asa "rejected, and recoiled" from this view (p. 111), he was strongly influenced by it. "And who were his enemies?" he asks about his father. "The world, everyone. They were imaginary." Asa recognizes this about his father, but not about himself.

5 Keith Michael Opdahl, " 'The Crab and the Butterfly': The Themes of Saul Bellow," unpublished dissertation (Univ. of Illinois, 1961), p. 75.

Asa's mother, too, is another source of his insecurity, and the loss of her sanity makes him fear for his own; the loss of a home makes him fear he will never have a permanent place.

Asa's self-hatred and his role as a victim also come from present failures to live up to what he wants to be or to accept himself as he is. This is also found in the guilty Velchaninov, but Bellow greatly enlarges on the theme. Asa himself knows the process—in other people. Asa says of Allbee that he was "haunted in his mind by wrongs or faults of his own which he turned into wrongs against himself" (p. 38). And he is right: Allbee, hating himself for his degeneration and his wife's death, puts the blame first on the world or chance, and secondly on Asa. But this is just as true for Asa himself: he uses Allbee as a vindication of his picture of the anti-Semite—the anti-Semite who must hate him since he hates himself. Also, Asa uses Allbee and others as scapegoats for his self-hatred: thus, Asa is sloppy and fears sloppiness as a sign of (1) failure—the failure he could have fallen into; (2) the insecurity of a house that, unlike Williston's, is not ordered and traditional; (3) a disordered mind (his mother's madness). So, fearing sloppiness, he condemns it in Allbee and Elena but "disregards" it in himself.

A better example of his refusal to accept himself is his fear of sexual indulgence. Throughout the novel, with his wife away, Asa has sexual temptations, although he never allows them to become conscious. First, there is Elena, his brother's wife. Asa tries to keep contact between them at a minimum: "He hesitated to tell her that Mary had gone South for a few weeks to be with her mother. Elena would have insisted that he stay" (p. 11). Bellow symbolizes his vaguely sexual feelings by having Asa knock his wedding ring against a bedpost when he and Elena are alone in a hot room; later, before he remembers to call Elena, he clicks his wedding ring on his shirt buttons. Once, awakened from a nap by thunder, he looks across the street into a window: "A woman lay on a sofa, one arm bent over her eyes. At the next sound of the retreating thunder she moved her legs" (p. 138). This dreamlike sexual image is immediately followed by a call to Elena.

More important than Elena is Mrs. Nunez, the superintendent's wife. There are a number of hints of Asa's sexual feelings. Returning home one night, he sees her on the stoop—small, Indian face, full-hipped figure, high bosom, parted lips. "Mary, whom nothing escaped, had once said about Mrs. Nunez' suits, 'I don't see why she wears them. She could look very pretty in silk prints.' Till then Leventhal had scarcely noticed her. Now, when she said good evening and he nodded to her, he remembered this and had a moment of intense longing for his wife." She asks about his wife:

"Coming soon?"

"I don't think so." . . .

"Too bad," she repeated, and Leventhal, with a glance of surmise at
her small face under the white brim, wondered what hint her sympathy
might contain. There was a burst of music above them; a window was
thrown open. (p. 150)

He tells her he will be a bachelor for another month; he goes inside.
The Nunez' dog rubs up against him and Mr. Nunez tells Asa, " 'she's
crazy about you' " (p. 151). Again he remembers to call Elena. The
reader is aware that Asa has projected his own desires onto Mrs.
Nunez. Then, music—and an open window—symbolizing the rush of
passion and the hint of possibility. An association is made between
Mrs. Nunez and her dog, who is "crazy about" Asa. Mr. Nunez says
not "the dog" but "she." This animal is clearly a sexual image and,
leading as it does to the call to Elena, reminds the reader of the sexual
images Asa sees through the window at Elena's. "In one of the other
flats, a girl in a parlor chair was brushing a dog that yawned and
tried to lick her hand. She pushed its muzzle down" (p. 57). In this
way, Asa's unconscious feelings for Elena and Mrs. Nunez, both Medi-
terranean types, are tied together.

The point is not that Asa has sexual desires of which he is unconscious or only dimly aware, but that he gets rid of his guilt by
projecting these desires onto Kirby Allbee. Here again, Bellow ex-
pands on hints in Dostoyevsky. It is Allbee who should be ashamed
of looking at girls near Asa's office when "Last night he was crying for
his wife" (p. 200). It is Allbee who is "nasty, twisted, bitching dirty"
for reading the intimate postcard from Mary (p. 207). "A lot a dirty
drunk like that would know about a woman like Mary" (p. 208), Asa
grumbles. On the final night of their relationship, Asa comes home
to find the door locked and chained: Allbee is with a woman. He
smashes his way in. "There Allbee, naked and ungainly, stood beside
a woman who was dressing in great haste. . . . Her hair covered her
face; nevertheless Leventhal thought he recognized her. Mrs. Nunez!
Was it Mrs. Nunez? The horror of it bristled on him, and the outcry
he had been about to make was choked down" (p. 269). The horror
bristled because he was seeing a projection of his own unconscious
desires—seeing the scene he wanted to act out. Soon we discover how
completely it was projection: "She was a stranger, not Mrs. Nunez;
simply a woman." And Asa feels "enormously lightened." Then, when
the woman is gone, Asa yells, " 'You hypocrite! I thought you couldn't
get over your wife' " (p. 271). Seeing the image of his desires, he condemns it in Allbee—" 'You're not even human, if you ask me' "—and
throws him out. Before he does, Allbee says, "Don't you people claim
that you're the same as everybody else? That's your way of saying that

you're above everybody else" (p. 272). He is referring to Asa as a
Jew, but in his twisted way he is correct about Asa as a man. And
this is the point: by denying guilt, by hating in Allbee what he cannot
admit in himself, Asa separates himself from others—becomes less
than human in his lack of compassion because he demands to be more
than human, perfect, pure. Kirby Allbee is right when he tells Asa,
speaking of adultery, " 'Nature is too violent for human ideals, sometimes, and ideals ought to leave it plenty of room' " (p. 203).

To be human, then, means you have to confront elements inside
yourself you do not wish to see; it means you have to confront the
inhuman within and without. This idea of the *Dangling Man*'s fear
of the "unhuman in the all too human city" is vastly expanded in
Augie March and in *Henderson* as the negative side of the affirmative
joy of these novels. Here in *The Victim* the *unhuman* is an important
motif. After seeing a tanker seabound on a terribly hot day and feeling
the suffering of the men in the shaft alley by the keel, Asa imagines
that the light over the towers on the shore and water

> was akin to the yellow revealed in the slit of the eye of a wild animal,
> say a lion, something unhuman that didn't care about anything human
> and yet was implanted in every human being too, one speck of it, and
> formed a part of him that responded to the heat and the glare, exhaust-
> ing as these were, or even to freezing, salty things, harsh things, all
> things difficult to stand. The Jersey shore, yellow, tawny, and flat, ap-
> peared on the right. (p. 51)

One of the reasons we read Bellow is his ability to connect the external
environment with the heart and mind; the spot of yellow is on the
Jersey shore, in the eye of a lion (looking forward to *Henderson*), and
within human beings. It is this unhuman quality that engulfs the city
in summer heat; it is this quality he finds in the brutal scene he sees
late at night between husband and adulterous wife; when Allbee is
caught with a woman and thrown out, "a yellowish hot tinge came
over his bloodshot eyes" (p. 271). It is what Asa rejects in himself and
fears being engulfed in.

This yellow is also in the eyes of Mr. Benjamin, the insurance
broker, who argues about death with Harkavy at Libbey Harkavy's
birthday party. Death is the ground of the unhuman, and it, like the
passion and violence within each of us, must be confronted and accepted. This truth is emphasized less here than in *Dangling Man,* but
it is present, and it has no counterpart in Dostoyevsky. We have heard
Schlossberg explain that men try to be more than human in order
to avoid death, and speaking at the birthday party he says:

> Here I'm sitting here, and my mind can go around the world. . . .
> But in another minute I can be dead, on this spot. There's a limit to

me. But I have to be myself in full. Which is somebody who dies, isn't
it? That's what I was from the beginning. I'm not three people, four
people. I was born once and I will die once. You want to be two
people? More than human? Maybe it's because you don't know how to
be one. (p. 255)

To accept your self you must accept the end of yourself. To avoid
facing death is to avoid being human, to turn yourself into an abstract
entity, a "corporation" as Schlossberg puts it, and to cut yourself off
from the rest of humanity. Schlossberg has just told of the paper grass
which covered the dirt at the last funeral he attended. Now he says:
"Paper grass in the grave makes all the grass paper" (p. 256). That is,
if you try to expunge death from consciousness, you are implicitly
making life something other than what it is. But Schlossberg means
more than that the denial of death is a denial of reality—"makes all
the grass *paper*"—denial of death makes life less significant by taking
away its existential seriousness. It is a concept similar to Fernando
Molina's interpretation of Heidegger's *Sein und Zeit:* "Only the awareness of one's finitude extricates the person from the endless whirl of
pleasing himself, taking things lightly, and shirking tasks that fill
much of everyday living." [6] Confrontation of death results in living
as an "I," a particular subject, instead of living as a "they"; and it results in acknowledging yourself as a member of humanity.

"I am not too good for this world," says Schlossberg. And it is by
admitting this that one becomes good enough for it, that one becomes
human. The theme of humble acceptance of oneself is repeated again
and again in the novel. Harkavy tells Asa of a girl who found fault
with him: "All I can say is, 'Lady, God bless you, we all have our
faults and are what we are. I have to take myself as I am or push off.
I am all I have in this world. And with all my shortcomings my life
is precious to me' " (p. 88). In this easygoing character, a Jew who isn't
bothered by other people's anti-Semitic remarks, we hear the music
of Augie March—these are precisely Augie's speech patterns: the world
is possibility. This self-acceptance is echoed by Asa's brother, Max.
When he is attacked by Asa for having left his family, Max simply
agrees. " 'Yes' he said. 'I should have been here.' " And speaking of
the death of his son, he admits, " 'We must have made mistakes, too.
But what can you do? It's not like with God, you know, in the Bible,
where he blows his breath into Adam or whoever.' " He is only human (pp. 237–43).

If a man cannot accept the darkness in himself, he cannot fulfill
Schlossberg's criteria, for (1) he wishes to be more than human, and

6 Fernando Molina, *Existentialism as Philosophy* (Englewood Cliffs, N.J., 1962),
p. 109.

(2) he is less, cutting himself off from other people. As Allbee says, apologizing for having attempted to kill them both, "When you turn against yourself, nobody else means anything to you either" (p. 293). Conversely, accepting yourself, you can accept other people. Thus Max says of his mother-in-law when Asa tells him to get rid of her, "I know she doesn't like me. So what? A worn-out old woman. I feel sad, sometimes, when I look at her" (p. 241). And Max tells Asa of walking into the hospital and finding his son dead. " 'Those fools!' Leventhal exclaimed. 'Not to have somebody posted there.' " But "Max excused them with a downward wave of the hand. 'All the nurses didn't know. It's a big place' " (pp. 241–42).

Asa cannot accept what he sees in himself; no more can Allbee. Despising himself for having caused the death of his wife, Allbee uses her insurance money for drink to destroy himself, feeling that to advance himself with the money would be immoral (just as Joseph preferred to be victim rather than beneficiary). Asa too feels unworthy, largely because of guilt, afraid he has stolen his place in life and that he may end up like his brother, a common workman, or like Allbee, a derelict. He had seen bad days himself, had clerked in a hotel for "transients" on lower Broadway, and so Allbee's status was always a possibility for him. Asa dreams one night of missing a train; trying to reach a second section of it through a new gate, he is pushed out into an alley (p. 168). The anxiety that he has no right to succeed, that he has stolen his place, that he has "gotten away with it" (as a child Joseph was anxious to be found out—that the evil under his mask would be uncovered) is reinforced by the double, Allbee, to whom the Jew is an interloper, an intruder into American society. Of course Asa may reject the idea that he has taken another's place. " 'Why me?' he thought, frowning." It is the problem of the merchant and the Ifrit. "In a general way, anyone could see that there was great unfairness in one man's having all the comforts of life while another had nothing. . . . Admittedly there was a wrong, a general wrong. Allbee, on the other hand, came along and said 'You!' " (p. 79). But Allbee is a menace only because Asa sees himself as interloper. Who knows? One false move and he might be fired by Beard as Allbee was by Rudiger.

Asa's belief that he is lucky and his guilt over success make up part of a larger theme, that of causality, responsibility, and the benefit from disaster. As the bell rings to return Asa and Allbee to their seats, Asa asks, " 'Wait a minute, what's your idea of who runs things?' " (p. 294). In one way or other, this question is asked again and again. Asa wonders about Mickey's disease, "Did medicine have any idea how a thing like that singled out a child in Staten Island rather than, say, St. Louis or Denver?" (p. 64). Allbee alternates between blaming

Asa and blaming chance. In the latter mode he says " 'the day of succeeding by your own efforts is past. Now it's all blind movement, vast movement, as the individual is shuttled back and forth' " (p. 70). Asa doesn't agree: he wants to deserve. Mrs. Harkavy, with comic incongruity, points up the difficulty of determining the cause of success or failure: " 'Influence is a good thing. . . . You mustn't forget it. If you don't use it, you're left behind in the race of the swift' " (pp. 83–84). Luck, swiftness, influence: in any event, the Harkavys can accept what comes to them without having to deserve it. A rug of theirs comes from "the estate of a broker who committed suicide on Black Friday" (p. 257). And although Mrs. Harkavy says "Asa, sometimes I feel wicked still to be here at my age when children die," she adds, "But I'm not taking it away from anybody" (p. 246). Accepting herself, she accepts what comes to her.

At the beginning of the novel Asa, because he feels unworthy, is in a continual struggle to keep his place. We see him shoving through the closing subway doors, pushing into the bus. But by the end of *The Victim*, Asa is more comfortable. "The consciousness of an unremitting daily fight, though still present, was fainter, less troubling. . . . As time went on he lost the feeling that he had, as he used to say, 'got away with it,' his guilty relief, and the accompanying sense of infringement" (p. 285). Better able to accept himself, Asa is better able to accept what comes to him, whatever it be—"this was not even a true injustice, for how could you call anything so haphazard an injustice? It was a shuffle, all, all accidental and haphazard" (p. 285).

Before speaking of how this change takes place, I want to point out that Asa's categories of perception are at fault. He sees nearly everything with regard to whether it does or does not deserve blame. Elena is to blame, Allbee is to blame, Max is to blame. Complementary to this blame is the expectation of being blamed, as when Asa attends Mickey's funeral. Asa's task is to learn to see outside the categories of moral judgment, for if it is true that hatred of oneself leads to hatred of others, conversely, judgment of others leads to judgment of oneself.

This is true in Dostoyevsky's novel, in which Velchaninov is split between his "higher" and "lower" ideas, split between slandering others and being slandered by them, and it is even truer in *The Victim*. Chizhevsky shows that the elimination of abstract moral judgment and its replacement by the perception of individuals, of "I"'s, is integral to Dostoyevsky.

> In Dostoyevsky's opinion, "not to judge" is the main condition of the specific relation to people through which they become our neighbors." For Alyosha Karamazov "not judging" is the inescapable norm of

ethics. . . . Precisely because of this unwillingness to judge, Alyosha appears everywhere loving, near, and familiar; for him everybody is a neighbor in the genuine Christian sense of the word. His place—his "sphere of freedom"—is the whole moral world.[7]

Asa must move from an attitude of duty to an attitude of love in his relationship with others; he must cease perceiving people as measurable by abstract ethics and approach them instead as unique, as "thous."

But to do so means to renounce his secure isolation. To keep himself detached from Allbee and Max enables him to detach himself from failure potentially his own and from guilt. Furthermore, as Schlossberg's female counterpart Mrs. Harkavy explains, "People are bound not to take things too much to heart, for their own protection" (p. 84). One important movement in the book is his learning, in both plot strands (with Max and with Allbee), to take things to heart, to perceive others outside an abstract ethical system, to grow close to them.

Asa's relationship with his brother Max begins, naturally, in blame. Why wasn't Max here to take care of his family? Does he think he has fulfilled the duties of a father by sending home money? He decides to send Max a night letter, "the harsher the better" (p. 62). Then he becomes more and more emotionally involved with Max's family, growing to love his nephew Philip. But this closeness isn't enough to stop him from roaring out, when he learns of Mickey's death, "Where is my damned brother!" (p. 176), and he intends to meet Max in anger: "his very first word was to have been a rebuke." But seeing his actual brother rather than an abstract family-deserter,

> instead of speaking, he took in his brother's appearance, the darkness and soreness of his swollen face, the scar at the corner of his mouth from a cut received in a street fight years ago in Hartford. Outdoor work had weathered him; the loss of several teeth made his jaw longer. His suit—it was a suit such as laborers used to buy in his father's store. His new black shoes were dusty.
> "I didn't make it in time," he said.
> "I heard, Max." (p. 181)

He pities and supports his brother the rest of the afternoon. And if Asa begins by blaming Max when his brother comes to see him, he ends in love.

> "I'm going south with the idea of a new start. I paid a deposit and so on. But to tell the truth, I don't expect much. I feel half burned out already."

7 Dimitri Chizhevsky, "The Theme of the Double in Dostoyevsky," *Dostoyevsky*, ed. René Wellek (Englewood Cliffs, N.J., 1962), p. 127.

Leventhal felt his heart shaken. "Half burned?" he said. "I'm older than you and I don't say that."

Max did not reply. His large trunk was ungainly in the double-breasted jacket.

"There have been times when I felt like that too," Leventhal went on. "That's a feeling that comes and goes." His brother turned his crude, dark face up to him and his voice died. (p. 242)

Asa's heart is "shaken," but more important is that in separating himself from what his brother feels ("I'm older than you and I don't say that") he reverses himself and identifies: "There are times when I felt like that too." Bellow writes in "Distractions of a Fiction Writer": "Between the radically unlike there is no love" (p. 12). Here there is an admission of alikeness, and there is love. Asa is becoming, according to Schlossberg's standards, "exactly human." Then he takes Max to the subway:

"If you need me for anything . . ." Leventhal said.
"Thanks."
"I mean it."
"Thank you." He extended his hand. Leventhal clumsily spread his arms wide and clasped him. (p. 243)

Leaving the subway, "he felt faint with the expansion of his heart." Exactly—for it had expanded, and so had Asa. (We remember Mrs. Harkavy's warning about the danger of such expansion). "Buttoning his coat, he raised the collar, and his eyes moved from the glare of the cars ahead, *not quite steady in the immense blackness*" (italics mine). Identifying with his brother, Asa gets a taste of the darkness he has been avoiding.

In Asa's relation with Allbee, too, blame gives way to perception of a person and finally to identification. In the beginning Asa will not acknowledge his affinity with Allbee. Allbee is a bum, a drunk; Asa pigeonholes Allbee as "not a normal person, someone you would have to reckon with" (p. 37). Allbee has fallen because of his own character, different from Asa's (although Asa acknowledges that he himself might have fallen "in another way," p. 38). Later, during the conversation with Williston, he acknowledges "it was necessary . . . to accept some of the blame for Allbee's comedown" (pp. 119–20). But this legalism does not bring about Asa's transformation; what does is his growing sense of closeness to Allbee, his sense of almost physical oneness. He feels this first at the zoo where he has taken Philip.

Leventhal, in speaking to Philip, or smoking, or smiling, was so conscious of Allbee, so certain he was being scrutinized, that he was able to see himself as if through a strange pair of eyes: the side of his face, the palpitation in his throat, the seams of his skin, the shape of his body and of his feet in their white shoes. Changed in this way into his own observer, he was able to see Allbee, too, and imagined himself standing so near behind him that he could see the weave of his coat, his raggedly overgrown neck, the bulge of his cheek, the color of the blood in his ear; he could even evoke the odor of his hair and skin. The acuteness and intimacy of it astounded him, oppressed and intoxicated him. (p. 107)[8]

Momentarily Asa becomes the other; momentarily he sees himself from the point of view of the other. And he sees the other intimately. Later, during Allbee's visit, this strange perception comes to Asa again —"a feeling of intimate nearness." He is able to enter Allbee: "He could feel the weight of his body and the contact of his clothes." And he senses that "the look of recognition Allbee bent on him duplicated the look in his own [eyes]" (p. 160). Even if Asa tries to "keep alive in his mind the thought that Allbee hated him," he gives him a place to stay, lets him come to live with him. In Dostoyevsky's novella, Velchaninov *forces* Trusotsky to stay over one night to be sure he will be able to bring him to Lisa in the morning. Here Asa *offers*— not without pressure, it is true—to let this man who hates him move in. And he offers help; he feels tied to Allbee in a way that extends beyond duty and repayment. As with Max, Asa finds himself regarding Allbee "with a look of dismayed pity" (p. 196), makes coffee for him, carries him to bed, and, finally, feels himself "singularly drawn with a kind of affection. It oppressed him, it was repellent. He did not know what to make of it. Still, he welcomed it, too. He was remotely disturbed to see himself so changeable. However, it did not seem just then to be a serious fault" (p. 224). Immediately after this, Asa becomes furious when Allbee runs his fingers through his wiry, "Jew" hair. The anger may be seen as directed against the intimacy of contact as much as against the threat of anti-Semitism.

This intimate contact is hinted at by Asa's perception of the relation between Allbee and Yvonne Crane, whom he escorts to the theater where Asa meets him years later. When Allbee, true to form, quarrels with the driver for having cheated them, Yvonne Crane throws the driver a bill and they go inside; this is all Asa sees, but as he interprets the scene: "he's got that woman under his thumb" (p. 290). In other words, he projects the relationship that, as Harkavy said, Asa had had with Allbee. *He* had been under Allbee's thumb. This identification of himself with Allbee's mistress indicates the intimate nature of the relationship.

The identification which Asa comes to make between himself and

[8] Leslie Fiedler also quotes this passage in *Waiting for the End*, p. 99. Fiedler emphasizes the "passionate" nature of the relationship between Jew and mythical gentile, not the moral significance of the scene.

Allbee is largely added to what Bellow found in Dostoyevsky; there the essential relationship was complementary—cuckold to cuckolder; here it is essentially parallel—the polarity of anti-Semite/Jew merely lends irony to their similarity. And it is a similarity which grows stronger as the relationship develops. Asa becomes more slovenly; he gets drunk at the Harkavys'; he camps out, like Allbee, at another man's house. It is this new closeness that leads Asa to reject with otherwise inexplicable fury Harkavy's suggestion that Allbee is insane; Asa fears for his own sanity.

There is little intimacy in the final scene with Allbee. Perhaps the danger wrought by the closeness between them is partly responsible: Asa is no longer able to detach himself from Allbee; the awareness *I could do what he has done* is too close to consciousness. At any rate, Asa recognizes that the act of bringing in a woman to have sexual relations on Asa's bed is an act of symbolic closeness with Asa himself. Fiedler is correct in speaking of "a kind of rejection scarcely distinguishable from rape." [9] It seems that only when Asa and Allbee are wedded by the two scenes of final violence can they divorce. Asa must enter the irrational world Allbee represents to him. "He felt dimly that this disorder and upheaval was part of the price he was obliged to pay for his release" (p. 274). Then he considers the scene again, this time from the point of view of Allbee and the woman. He realizes that "Both of them . . . moved or swam toward him out of a depth of life in which he himself would be lost, choked, ended. There lay horror, evil, all that he had kept himself from" (p. 279). The point is that Asa is forced to meet the darkness from which he had kept himself. He has seen Allbee's swollen feet, he has remembered the smell of disinfectant used in hotels for transients. He is no longer protected from taking things "too much to heart." Particularly when Allbee returns to kill them both with gas, Asa is forced to confront the irrational, the something-akin-to-the-yellow-of-a-lion's-eyes: death.

Norman Podhoretz, although essentially correct, exaggerates when he writes that Asa "has not ventured into the 'depths' that he once feared would drown him; he has merely (like a successfully analyzed patient) learned something about himself that has helped him come to terms with the world and make a settlement." [10] Perhaps it is more accurate to say that because he understands that the depths he fears are within him, he does not have to be destroyed by them.

Through the growing sense of the reality of others, through his growing awareness of their kinship with him, Asa has become, in

---

[9] Fiedler, *Waiting for the End,* p. 99.

[10] Norman Podhoretz, "The Adventures of Saul Bellow," *Doings and Undoings* (New York, 1964), p. 214.

Schlossberg's terms, "human." Now he can call his wife home; he is
ready for her. That he has changed permanently we know by the final
chapter, which finds him healthier, happier, and a father-to-be. His
burdens, unlike those of Rogin's ("A Father-to-Be") are cast off. Surely
it is incorrect to say that Asa's change "grows out of the healing power
of time rather than the plot itself." [11] Rather, as we have seen, it
grows subtly out of Asa's experiences: subtly, as in life. But like
Dangling Man, The Victim moves toward a redefinition of what
human is, a definition which goes beyond Schlossberg's wisdom. In the
middle of the novel Asa's dream of expulsion from the railroad station
leads to an overwhelming sense of truth-found. "Yes, I do know it,
positively. Will I know it in the morning? I do now" (p. 169). Typically for Bellow, Asa does not hold onto it; he oversleeps, wakes up
irritated. But for a moment, he knew.

To retell the dream in greater detail: the dreamer is in a terribly
crowded station trying to get to the second section of a train he has
missed. Pushed into a corridor, he tries to go down through a newly
constructed gate to the tracks. But a contractor in a fedora stops him
—the other man, a workman, is not able to interfere with his boss—
and pushes him out into the alley; his face is covered with tears.

There is no simple relationship between this dream and the truth
that eludes Asa. It is like Asa's strange pain on awaking after the
birthday party at the Harkavys':

> He had the strange feeling that there was not a single part of him
> on which the whole world did not press with full weight, on his body,
> on his soul, pushing upward in his breast and downward in his bowels.
> He concentrated, moving his lips like someone about to speak, and
> blew a tormented breath through his nose. What he meanwhile sensed
> was that this interruption of the customary motions he went through
> unthinkingly on rising, despite the pain it was causing, was a disguised
> opportunity to discover something of great importance. He tried to
> seize the opportunity. He put out all his strength to collect himself,
> beginning with the primary certainty that the world pressed on him
> and passed through him. Beyond this he could not go, hard though he
> drove himself. He was bewilderingly moved. . . . And then the cramp
> and the enigmatic opportunity ended together. (p. 258)

Again truth approaches out of sleep. Again there is the reaching out
for some ultimate truth about the self, a truth just out of reach. Here
it is seen as a kind of birth (hence the significance of the "birthday
party")—Asa himself newborn: doubled over, unable to breathe or
cry; at the same time it is Asa *giving* birth, giving birth to the elusive
truth. Often in Bellow (as in "A Father-to-Be" or *Seize the Day*) we

11 Opdahl, p. 76.

find this un-Jewish imagery of personal rebirth, redemption into a new life.

The dream of the missed train is another moment of such transfiguration. On the surface the dream represents the defeat of the anguished dreamer by the reality principle (in business suit and fedora), a defeat analogous to death—there is no way out; one cannot cheat the rules. But far more important, Asa is able to identify himself with the runner unable to catch his train (or with Allbee, who often asks for a place on "the train"), with the rigid enforcer of the "rules" who prevents him from succeeding, and with the helpless workman (Asa's self-righteousness and conscience, his pity and sense of helpless responsibility). All are inside Asa, and thus this truth is formed: "It was supremely plain to him that everything, without exception, took place as if within a single soul or person" (p. 169). This is not solipsism but its opposite. It is a sense—a vision—of the unity of all persons, the essential alikeness of all persons, each mysteriously containing all. This is where the movement toward perception of the other as real, toward identification with others, and toward acceptance of self, of others, and of death, has been leading: toward a submergence of individuality in a transpersonal, anonymous self. It is the vision of victim and victimizer as one.

This is a truth not found in Dostoyevsky's novella, although indeed Trusotsky and Velchaninov are bound tightly together and Dostoyevsky does believe every man is responsible for every other (e.g., *Brothers Karamazov*), but this truth of unity is essential here. It is Bellow's way of reconciling the individual and the community, analogous to Whitman's magic:

> I celebrate myself and sing myself,
> And what I assume you shall assume,
> for every atom belonging to me as good belongs to you.

Now it is clear that the continual presence of crowds in the summer heat is not mere background. Maxwell Geismar speaks of "those Dreiserian and Whitmanesque masses that this highly sensitive and withdrawn artist has always yearned to link himself with." [12] Clearly, Bellow wants us to see *all* men as if they were *one* and *each* man as if he were *all*. It is his way of answering Allbee's quandary:

> The world's a crowded place, damned if it isn't. It's an overcrowded place. There's room enough for the dead . . . because they don't want anything. But the living. . . . Do you want anything? Is there anything you want? There are a hundred million others who want that very same thing. . . . It's hard to believe that my life is necessary. I guess

12 Maxwell Geismar, *American Moderns* (New York, 1958), p. 222.

you wouldn't be familiar with the Catholic catechism where it asks, "For whom was the world made?" Something along that line. And the answer is, "For man." For every man? Yes, for every last mother's son. . . . For everybody who repeats "For man" it means "For me." "The world was created for me, and I am absolutely required, not only now, but forever." (pp. 193–94)

How can the human being possess dignity among so many, all wanting as he wants? The answer: each man is everyman, All-Be: in touching Allbee, Asa touches all of humanity; indeed, he *becomes* all of humanity. Returning to the epigraphs, then, we can answer their riddles: De Quincey's vision of the human face upon the ocean is first a single face, then "innumerable faces," as the individual is at the same time all individuals, possessing the dignity not of the exceptional man but of everyman. What can a man do, looking upon this ocean, confronting all those who want? He can recognize the humanity in common between himself and the others; and he can answer one want —in this he will have responded to all.

Is he responsible to them? This brings up the parable of the slaying of the Ifrit's son. Considering the complexities of causality, one cannot say "You are guilty," but one must answer, "I am responsible." These are not the same—Asa, feeling guilt, rejects responsibility; accepting responsibility, he feels less guilt. One responds, to relieve the other's suffering. And if all are one, the other's suffering is one's own, too.

To what extent does Asa live with this truth? Bellow emphasizes that (unlike Velchaninov's complete change) Asa's change is partial. But far more successfully than Joseph the Dangling Man, Asa ends his alienation. Beginning, like Joseph, as a solitary, separated from his wife and hostile to the few friends he has, he goes much farther than Joseph in joining humanity without surrendering to society. His success heralds the overeager affirmation of Bellow's next novel, *The Adventures of Augie March.*

The Scene as Image:
A Reading of *Seize the Day*

by M. Gilbert Porter

"The New Criticism, which despite its vociferous detractors works quite well with lyric poetry, is helpless when confronted by the large irregular masses of prose fiction which we call novels." [1] So says Robert Scholes in the introduction to what is otherwise a sound anthology devoted to critical theories of the novel. The statement is unsound. It can be made at all only because the New Critics have had relatively little to say about the application of their theories to fiction. But they have not been silent. John Crowe Ransom, whose "structure/texture" approach to poetry is well known, has written about the possibilities of a formalist approach to fiction in *The New Criticism* (1941), in "The Content of the Novel: Notes Toward a Critique of Fiction" (*The American Review*, 1926), and in "The Understanding of Fiction" (*Kenyon Review*, 1950). Cleanth Brooks and Robert Penn Warren in *Understanding Fiction* (1943) and Allen Tate and Caroline Gordon in *The House of Fiction* (1950) have further advanced the cause of formalist criticism of fiction by showing its usefulness in the classroom. Mark Schorer has called attention to the unity of theme and form in fiction in "Technique as Discovery" (*Hudson Review*, 1948) and to the importance of metaphor in "Fiction and the Matrix of Analogy" (*Kenyon Review*, 1949). Allen Tate has devoted significant space to the critical problem of point of view in "The Post of Observation in Fiction" (*Maryland Quarterly*, 1944), and has acknowledged the importance of the scene in fiction:

> I should, myself, like to know more about the making of the single scene, and all the techniques that contribute to it; and I suspect that I am not asking the impossible, for this kind of knowledge is very likely the only kind that is actually within our range. It alone can be got at

[1] Robert Scholes, *Approaches to the Novel* (San Francisco: Chandler, 1961), p. v.

definitely and at particular moments, even after we have failed . . . to retain the image of the book.[2]

This brief survey of the major formalist critics who have written on fiction by no means exhausts the field, but it should suffice to refute the charge that the New Criticism is "helpless" to deal with the novel. Formalist critical methodology as applied to fiction has been strengthened recently by William J. Handy, who in *Modern Fiction: A Formalist Approach* provides the kind of analytical focusing on scene that Allen Tate called for. According to Professor Handy, the scene in fiction often functions like the image in poetry, and thus admits of the kind of analysis that the New Critics have used so successfully with poetry. The purpose of this paper is to explore Handy's thesis and to demonstrate its usefulness in a reading—a scene-as-image analysis—of Bellow's *Seize the Day*. A novel is not a lyric poem, of course, and the methods of analysis that serve for poetry cannot be applied without modification to fiction; but with some allowance for the difference in genres, the formalist methods of explicating poetic images can prove illuminating when applied to fiction. Such an analysis is especially productive in revealing Bellow's narrative strategy in *Seize the Day*, which critical opinion has judged almost unanimously to be Bellow's most tightly built novel.

Handy devotes much of one chapter to his discussion of the scene as image; his major points are these:

> These presentational units [scenes] in fiction may be viewed as being analogous to the image in poetry. That is, from an ontological point of view . . . both the image (the basic unit of presentation in the poem) on the one hand and the scene and episode (the corresponding presentational units of the story) on the other all possess the same generic characteristics:
>
> 1. *In both poetry and fiction meaning is presentational and nondiscursive.* . . .
> 2. *Both forms of presentational units* (the image of the poem, the scene and episode of the story) *comprise a single configuration of multiple meaning.* . . .
> 3. *Both forms* (poetry and fiction) *intend to formulate the particularity, the "texture" of experience.* . . .
> 4. *Both forms are directed primarily to sense perception, not to abstract intellection.* . . .
> 5. *And, finally, both forms of presentational units exceed the concept in containing more meaning than is possible of formulation in a concept.* . . .[3]

2 "Techniques of Fiction," Sewanee Review, 52 (Winter 1944), 213.

3 William J. Handy, *Modern Fiction: A Formalist Approach* (Carbondale and Edwardsville, Ill.: Southern Illinois University Press, 1971), pp. 9–12.

How the fictional scene functions to "formulate the particularity, the 'texture' of experience" in the life of Tommy Wilhelm, the protagonist of *Seize the Day*, and how these scenes approximate the poetic image provide the focus of this essay.

Ezra Pound has defined the image in poetry as "that which presents an intellectual and emotional complex in an instant of time," [4] and I. A. Richards has shown that a metaphorical image can be analyzed according to its "tenor," the idea in or the subject matter of the implied comparison, and its "vehicle," the particularity in which generality is embodied. The concept of the fictional scene developed in this essay draws on both of these observations, for it is clear that at the center of *Seize the Day* is an extended metaphor that is the integrating principle of the narrative. The metaphor, as Keith Opdahl and Clinton Trowbridge have shown, depicts human failure through the image of a drowning man.[5] Tommy Wilhelm has made a mess of his life, and now, gasping for breath and grabbing, panic-stricken, at straws (Tamkin), he sinks wearily beneath the pressures of his own making. The "tenor" of the total image that is the book is human failure. The "vehicle" in which this subject matter is embodied is the image of drowning, and each scene in the novel functions as a dimension of the total image, the "texture" of the narrative presentation. The scenes render the particularity of the diverse pressures under which Wilhelm is submerged, and function therefore to extend the central metaphor.

Pound describes the poetic image as being presented in "an instant of time," that is, in a frozen moment. The effect is a kind of timelessness. In fiction, however, characters move through time; their experience occurs in successive moments. "Works of fiction," W. J. Handy has said in another recent essay, "express man's capacity to experience his experience, not in moments merely (as reflected in the lyric poem or the painting or the sculpture), but in time." [6] The action of the novel necessarily involves the passage of time. However, Handy's em-

4 Ezra Pound, "A Few Don'ts by an Imagiste," *Poetry*, 1 (March 1913), 200.

5 Keith Opdahl, *The Novels of Saul Bellow: An Introduction* (University Park, Pa.: Pennsylvania State University Press, 1967), pp. 96–97; Clinton W. Trowbridge, "Water Imagery in *Seize the Day*," *Critique*, 9 (Spring 1968), 62–73. Both Opdahl and Trowbridge have provided provocative insights into the dominance of water imagery in the novel, but Trowbridge seems interested mainly in the affective functions of language and tone, and Opdahl seems content to provide an adumbrated description of the images, pointing to representative ones but not examining in detail their cohesive function in the novel as a whole. Neither writer concerns himself with the skillful use Bellow makes of the scene as image in *Seize the Day*.

6 William J. Handy, "Criticism of Joyce's Work: A Formalist Approach," in *James Joyce: His Place in World Literature*, Proceedings of the Comparative Literature Symposium, 2 (Lubbock, Texas, 1969), 62.

phasis on the scene as the basic presentational unit of fiction suggests that *within* scene, time functions in a manner not dissimilar to Pound's concept of an "instant of time." What fiction achieves in the successful treatment of time and space within scene is what Joseph Frank has called "spatial form," the arrangement of action and setting in accentual levels of presentational unity. He illustrates his theory with an examination of the scene in *Madame Bovary* in which Rodolphe woos Emma with sentimental rhetoric while below them on the street a country fair is in progress, the mobs being addressed by both local politicians and a livestock auctioneer. Frank's analysis is worth quoting at length:

> As Flaubert sets the scene, there is action going on simultaneously at three levels, and the physical position of each level is a fair index to its spiritual significance. On the lowest plane, there is the surging, jostling mob in the street, mingling with the livestock brought to the exhibition; raised slightly above the street by a platform are the speechmaking officials, bombastically reeling off platitudes to the attentive multitudes; and on the highest level of all, from a window overlooking the spectacle, Rodolphe and Emma are watching the proceedings and carrying on their amorous conversation, in phrases as stilted as those regaling the crowds.
>
> . . . "Everything should sound simultaneously," Flaubert later wrote, in commenting on the scene: "one should hear the bellowing of the cattle, the whisperings of the lovers and the rhetoric of the officials all at the same time."
>
> But since language proceeds in time, it is impossible to approach this simultaneity of perception except by breaking up temporal sequence. And this is exactly what Flaubert does: He dissolves sequence by cutting back and forth between the various levels of action in a slowly-rising crescendo until—at the climax of the scene—Rodolphe's Chateaubriandesque phrases are read at almost the same moment as the names of prize winners for raising best pigs. . . .
>
> This scene illustrates, on a small scale, what we mean by the spatialization of form in a novel. *For the duration of the scene, at least, the time-flow of the narrative is halted: attention is fixed on the interplay of relationships within the limited time-area.* The relationships are juxtaposed independently of the progress of the narrative; and the full significance of the scene is given only by the reflexive relations among the units of meaning. In Flaubert's scene, however, the unit of meaning is not, as in modern poetry, a word-group or a fragment of an anecdote, but the totality of each level of action taken as an integer; the unit is so large that the scene can be read with an illusion of complete understanding, yet with a total unawareness of the "dialectic of platitude" (Thibaudet) interweaving all levels, and finally linking them together with devastating irony. In other words, the struggle towards spatial form in Pound and Eliot resulted in the disappearance

of coherent sequence after a few lines; *but the novel, with its larger unit of meaning, can preserve coherent sequence within the unit of meaning and break up only the time-flow of narrative.*[7] (my italics)

"Cutting back and forth between the various levels of action" in time-present enabled Flaubert, as Frank has demonstrated, to present movement within scene with a kind of simultaneity that approximates Pound's concept of an "intellectual and emotional complex in an instant of time."

Bellow performs a similar feat in *Seize the Day.* Tommy Wilhelm moves through time, from his prebreakfast appearance outside his hotel room to his attendance at the funeral of a stranger in mid-afternoon; but the narration renders this successive movement in a series of eight stills, or scenes. Instead of cutting back and forth between levels of action in time-present, as Flaubert does, Bellow's omniscient narration most often cuts back and forth between time-present and time-past in the mind of Tommy Wilhelm. The setting and time-present form the frame that contains Wilhelm's reflections on time-past and its effect on his current situation. Because Wilhelm's mind is the integrating agent of time and place—and also of action—his mood is the primary device for establishing the limits of individual scene. Juxtaposing time-past and time-present within the context of setting and through the mind of the protagonist has the effect of, if not actually arresting time, at least rendering it in slow motion, so that "spatial form" is achieved and the focus falls on the intrareferential relation among the parts that make up scene (language, action, character, mood, and so forth) and, finally, that contribute cumulatively to the total image that is the book. Slow motion is appropriate to *Seize the Day* because it suggests the movements of a man under water.

Though it is usually easy for the critic to determine where one scene ends and the next begins, it is not always easy for him to explain his rationale for such division. The difficulty probably lies in the eclectic nature of the scene in fiction. Like drama, the scene commonly involves action based on conflict. Other characters are therefore involved, and the action occurs in time and in a given place. The arrival or departure of a character, or a shift in time or place, is likely to entail a shift in scene—but not necessarily; for, like poetry, fiction can present attitudes or emotions in almost pure states, through dreams, say, or through omniscient narration, stream-of-consciousness, or any of several other techniques. Therefore, the mood of the protagonist or the central intelligence must be considered of major im-

[7] Joseph Frank, "Spatial Form in Modern Literature," *Sewanee Review,* **53** (1945), 230–32.

portance in determining the limits of scene. If a mood is sustained through several shifts in setting and characters, the scene must usually be judged continuous. The pace of a scene must also be considered, and narrative bridges (summaries, descriptive passages, and so on) must be accounted for. In practice, these matters seem less complicated because the individual scene, like the whole work, creates a dominant impression and has an internal consistency of its own if it has been built skillfully. To discover this internal consistency, the critic must allow the scene to dictate from within the key to its analysis. Hopefully, the rationale behind the division of scenes in *Seize the Day*[8] will become clear in the discussions of each of its eight scenes.

Scene I (3–26) begins with an archetypal descent. Wilhelm emerges from his hotel room on the twenty-third floor and goes down to the lobby. Water imagery begins immediately. "The elevator sank and sank" and the carpet in the lobby "billowed toward Wilhelm's feet" (3); "French drapes like sails kept out the sun," and, outside, resembling an anchor chain is a "great chain that supported the marquee of the movie house directly underneath the lobby" (4). The Ansonia Hotel across the street looks "like marble or like sea water, black as slate in the fog." Its image is reflected in the sun as though "in deep water" (5). Wilhelm walks to the newsstand, which provides the setting for the first scene. In the glass cigar counter Wilhelm sees his reflection, but not clearly, because of "the darkness and deformations of the glass" (6), a watery reflection. Three times in this scene he refers to himself as a "hippopotamus," an ungainly water creature. Wilhelm lights a cigar, buys a Coke and a newspaper, and exchanges small talk with Rubin, the newsstand operator. He lingers at the newsstand to avoid entering the dining room to join his father, Dr. Adler, for breakfast because he fears that the day holds something ominous for him:

> Today he was afraid. He was aware that his routine was about to break up and he sensed that a huge trouble long presaged but till now formless was due. Before evening he'd know. (4)

As Wilhelm fidgets at the newsstand, Rubin's casual remarks in time-present spark Wilhelm's reflections on time-past. Rubin remarks perfunctorily that Wilhelm is looking "pretty sharp today." Wilhelm reflects ruefully that once such an observation was accurate, but that now he has gone to seed. Other casual remarks by Rubin lead Wilhelm into three extended reflections, each of which reveals some aspect of his past that has contributed to his present discomfort.

There is, first, his stock-market investment with Dr. Tamkin, the glib, semiliterate pseudopsychologist. "With all this money around,"

8 Saul Bellow, *Seize the Day* (New York: Viking Press, Inc., 1956). Page numbers appear in parentheses in the text.

Tamkin had told him enthusiastically, "you don't want to be a fool while everyone else is making" (9). On the strength of this recommendation and in desperation, Wilhelm had entrusted the remainder of his savings to Tamkin. Though he sees himself as a porcine hippopotamus, Wilhelm perversely allowed his money to be invested in lard. Now he justifiably fears for his investment. But Tamkin is more to Wilhelm than a financial long shot. Despite his obvious flaws, he is a surrogate father: "At least Tamkin sympathizes with me and tries to give me a hand, whereas Dad doesn't want to be disturbed" (11).

The reflection on Tamkin leads by association into a reflection on Dr. Adler. Wilhelm's father is a retired physician, respected, wealthy, and gracefully aged. He wishes only to spend his autumn years in the peace and security that he feels he has earned. The father is clearly a self-centered, uncompassionate old man, but Wilhelm is far from a blameless son. He has been, he knows, a great disappointment to his father: he was a college dropout, a bungling father, a misfit at last in the business world, and has become an unhygienic "slob." Unlovable though he knows he is, he yearns still to be loved. Two lines of poetry occur to him as he reflects on his father: ". . . . love that well which thou must leave ere long," from Shakespeare's Sonnet 73, is the attitude that Wilhelm feels his father should take toward his declining son; this line leads to another, even more elegiac in nature, Milton's "Sunk though he be beneath the wat'ry floor . . ."—a line from *Lycidas* that extends the water imagery and reflects Wilhelm's moribund personality. Wilhelm then recalls another element in his personal history that might account in part for his father's attitude: when Wilhelm left college to go to Hollywood, he had changed his name from Wilhelm Adler to Tommy Wilhelm:

> He had cast off his father's name, and with it his father's opinion of him. It was, he knew it was, his bid for liberty, Adler being in his mind the title of the species, Tommy the freedom of the person. (25)

Acknowledging this earlier rejection of his father leads Wilhelm to retrace the circumstances surrounding that event, and into his consciousness lumbers the figure of Maurice Venice, agent for Kaskaskia Films.

Water imagery continues in this reflection. Venice, whose name suggests water, occupies an office in the midst of the sides and roofs of buildings—"sheer walls, gray spaces, dry lagoons of tar and pebbles" (17–18). Wilhelm remembers him as a relative of Martial Venice the producer and, thus, as "the obscure failure of an aggressive and powerful clan" (20). In describing for Wilhelm the condition of those nameless faces that make up movie audiences, Venice really describes his own condition: "Listen, everywhere there are people trying hard, miserable, in trouble, downcast, tired, trying and trying. They need a break, right? A breakthrough, a help, luck or sympathy" (22). Venice knows what he is talking about, for he too is a drowning man; he speaks with difficulty in a "choked, fat-obstructed voice"; he is an objectification of failure whose warning Wilhelm fails to heed. To Venice, Wilhelm is the type of person who is "stood up." He casts Wilhelm appraisingly as a loser, and Wilhelm's screen test shows Venice to be a prophet. Wilhelm goes to California without Venice's backing, but his efforts to become an actor are futile. Wilhelm takes no pleasure in learning later that Venice has been arrested for pandering, and that his true love, the bathing beauty Nita Christenberry, has been sentenced to three years for prostitution. There is a wry turn in the narrative here through allusion. The nebulous relative of "aggressive and powerful" Martial (Mars) whose last name is Venice (Venus) becomes a mock-Cupid at last in his touting of love, failing to retain the happiness he thought he had found in his water nymph.

Having reviewed in his mind some of his major mistakes of the past, Wilhelm summarizes them in a kind of self-flagellation:

> He wanted to start out with the blessings of his family, but they were never given. He quarreled with his parents and his sister. And then, when he was best aware of the risks and knew a hundred reasons against going and had made himself sick with fear, he left home. This was typical of Wilhelm. After much thought and hesitation and debate he invariably took the course he had rejected innumerable times. Ten such decisions made up the history of his life. He had decided that it would be a bad mistake to go to Hollywood, and then he went. He had made up his mind not to marry his wife, but ran off and got married. He had resolved not to invest money with Tamkin, and then had given him a check. (23)

The pressures generated by this mental recital cause Wilhelm extreme depression and anxiety. The scene ends with his silent prayer for succor:

> "Oh God," Wilhelm prayed. "Let me out of my trouble. Let me out of my thoughts, and let me do something better with myself. For all the time I have wasted I am sorry. Let me out of this clutch and into a different life. For I am all balled up. Have mercy." (26)

This is the drowning man's appeal for assistance from a divine source. Several times in this scene reference is made to Wilhelm's "panting laugh," a sound suggesting both panic and frantic exertion to stay afloat. The anguished prayer that Wilhelm delivers silently at the end of the scene grows out of the cumulative effect of his reflections within time-present—his reflections on past mistakes, bad luck, and weakness in character, all of which culminate in his current condition. All of these reflections are unified in a "single configuration of mean-

ing" in the presentational form of the scene. The movement from his
room to the newsstand, then, is really a single movement unified by
the implied metaphor of drowning and by the introspective, foreboding mood of the central character. This strategy establishes the
pattern for the scenes that follow.

Scene II (26–30) is very brief. Wilhelm picks up his mail from the
desk clerk, realizing as he does so—as much from the desk clerk's
accusing attitude as from the day of the month—that his morning
mail contains a bill for his rent, a bill that he cannot pay because
all his money is tied up in his venture with Tamkin. Stimulated by
the bill for his rent and by his own shortage of funds, Wilhelm begins
mentally to accuse his father of selfishness in knowing that his son is
in trouble and refusing to offer him assistance. As if to corroborate
his charge, Wilhelm then recalls the scene in which his father revealed
to him that he had forgotten the date of his wife's—and Wilhelm's
mother's—death. For a moment, his father's selfishness is established
and Wilhelm appears in a sympathetic light.

Almost immediately, however, the narrative strategy changes, and
the focus of narration shifts. The omniscient narrator reveals Wilhelm
as he appears in the eyes of his father: an overweight, jittery, whining,
unkempt bungler. And then, from a still more detached view, Wilhelm's actions are described as he stands musing on his father's continued indifference:

> Unaware of anything odd in his doing it, for he did it all the time,
> Wilhelm pinched out the coal of his cigarette and dropped the butt in
> his pocket, where there were many more. (28)

Suddenly, the sympathetic light in which he has just appeared dims,
for he shows himself no longer entitled to claim, as he did earlier,
that "from his mother he had gotten sensitive feelings." Wilhelm's
misery is too real to be negated by the revelation of such character
traits, but the empathy that the reader develops regularly for Wilhelm
is vitiated by this strategy. Such distancing through point of view—
and it occurs repeatedly in the book—adds realistic dimension to
Wilhelm's characterization and prevents his suffering from becoming
maudlin.[9]

His attention returning to the mail in his hand, Wilhelm finds a
letter from his wife, who protests the recent postdated check he sent
her and demands that he pay the enclosed premiums on the boys' educational insurance policies. One of his most painful problems comes
clearly into focus—money:

9 For this perception into the achievement of aesthetic distance through a carefully shifting focus of narration, I am indebted to Professor Ron Billingsley, Department of English, University of Colorado at Boulder.

They were his kids, and he took care of them and always would. He had planned to set up a trust fund. But that was on his former expectations. Now he had to rethink the future, because of the money problem. Meanwhile, here were the bills to be paid. When he saw the two sums punched out so neatly on the cards he cursed the company and its IBM equipment. His heart and head were congested with anger. (30)

This scene documents at least two of the major pressures that are pushing Wilhelm under: the estrangement between Wilhelm and his father and between Wilhelm and his wife, and it insists on the immediacy of his financial problem. His mood throughout the scene is one of anger resulting from a sense of persecution. In accordance with the controlling metaphor of drowning, Wilhelm's head and heart are "congested" at the end of the scene, and in this condition he enters the dining room, putting an end to his long delay in meeting his father for breakfast.

Scene III (30–41) takes place entirely in the dining room. The mood at breakfast is casual and, at times, almost lighthearted, at least on the surface. Water imagery pervades the scene, occasionally in mildly comic fashion. Wilhelm sees his father sitting in a "sunny bay" where "water glasses" cast light patterns on the tablecloth, and the white enamel on the window frames is "streaming with wrinkles" (30–31). Seated by Dr. Adler in this aquatic circumambience is, appropriately, Mr. Perls. Wilhelm immediately dislikes the fishy Mr. Perls: "Who is this damn frazzle-faced herring with his dyed hair and his fish teeth and this drippy mustache?" (31) The faintly humorous suggestion here seems to be that one who sits down before Perls runs the risk of being classified as a swine. This is especially true of one who has invested his savings in lard and who refers to himself frequently as a hippopotamus. The initial humor in this suggestion is lost, however, in the truth of its application to Wilhelm and in his awareness of its truth.[10] Narrative summary in the scene has revealed, for example, that Wilhelm is a careless, insensitive driver, that his car is filthy, that he does

---

[10] Cf. Keith Opdahl's comments on humor in *The Novels of Saul Bellow*, pp. 114, 176. Opdahl sees the humor in *Seize the Day* as an attribute of the caricature of Tommy Wilhelm and a reflection of Bellow's ambivalent attitude toward the transitory truth of human experience; it provides Bellow with aesthetic distance from the convictions inherent in Wilhelm's experience. It seems to me, however, that what little humor there is in the book is always undercut by the genuine and intense suffering of Wilhelm. His responses necessarily condition the reader's responses. For example, when Mr. Perls and Dr. Adler laugh at the schemes of Tamkin, Wilhelm laughs with them, but his heart is not in it: "Wilhelm could not restrain himself and joined in with his own panting laugh. But he was in despair" (41). Clearly, laughter does not function in *Seize the Day* as a comic mask of personal defense, a posture of survival, as it does in *Augie March, Henderson the Rain King,* and *Herzog.*

not wash his hands before meals, that he uses an electric razor to avoid touching water (the hydrophobia of a drowning man), and that he lives in a room with "worse filth than a savage" (36–37). Furthermore, when conversation turns to money, Wilhelm finds to his disgust that he is lying about his financial condition to please his father and to impress Mr. Perls, even though in his mind he has just condemned both of them for their transparent greed. He feels dirtied by his pandering to their values, and his reaction is the usual one: he experiences "congestion."

When the conversation turns to the dubious credentials of Dr. Tamkin, Wilhelm joins halfheartedly in the laughter while experiencing despair in his heart because the object of their ridicule is the man in whom Wilhelm has foolishly invested all his immediate financial hopes. His laugh is again his characteristic "panting laugh," an expression of panic and exhaustion. The weight of his misery provokes Wilhelm to see himself as a heavily laden leviathan: "The spirit, the peculiar burden of his existence lay upon him like an accretion, a load, a hump" (39). The scene ends as Wilhelm thinks anxiously of the imminent opening of the stock market and of what the day's trading may portend for him.

Unlike the previous two scenes, in which reflections were dominant, this scene conveys its meaning mainly through dialogue. The dominant impression of the scene is the intensity of Wilhelm's self-disgust. When Mr. Perls excuses himself from the table, the mood changes and the next scene begins.

Scene IV (42–55) continues to rely heavily on dialogue in a kind of verbal-emotional fencing match between Wilhelm and his father. Wilhelm attempts to engage his father, to thrust through his defenses and turn up some form of deep feeling or genuine concern for the suffering of his son. Dr. Adler attempts to evade the emotionalism that Wilhelm imposes on him; finally he strikes back at his son with feeling, but the emotion he displays is anger, not sympathy, and it is provoked by selfishness, not paternal love. When Perls leaves their table, Wilhelm begins to gorge himself on the remaining food, causing Adler to reflect again on his son's obesity and slovenly ways. While Adler observes his son, Wilhelm again feels "congested," partly from the vast amount of food he has just eaten but mainly from the pressure of suppressing his desire to discuss his problems with his father. The subject matter of each man's reflections reveals the distance between them: Wilhelm is concerned about his own emotional condition and his father's indifference to it; Adler is concerned about Wilhelm's physical condition and his son's indifference to it.

When they speak to each other, these differences become more explicit. Adler recommends the "baths" to his son, then exclaims that

the "Gloriana has one of the finest pools in New York," but Wilhelm
is repulsed by the "odor of the wall-locked and chlorinated water"
(43). But Adler presses his point. "There's nothing better," he says,
"than hydrotherapy when you come right down to it. Simple water
has a calming effect and would do you more good than all the bar-
biturates and alcohol in the world" (44). With unwitting irony, Adler
plays Hardhearted Hannah to Wilhelm's drowning man. One does not
prescribe hydrotherapy to a drowning man, unless, of course, one is
totally indifferent to the conditions of others. It is clear from the
exchange that selfish indifference is indeed Adler's condition. On the
level of dramatic irony, however, Adler prescribes with more wisdom
than he knows, for Wilhelm's final symbolic death by water—Adler's
hydrotherapy—is necessary to restore him to psychic health.

That Wilhelm is a drowning man becomes clearer and clearer. Having overcome his feeble attempts to suppress the expression of his
feelings to his father, Wilhelm explains what Margaret is doing to
him, accompanying his description with an appropriate choking gesture:

> "Well, Dad, she hates me. I feel that she's strangling me. I can't catch
> my breath. She just fixed herself on me to kill me. She can do it at
> long distance. One of these days I'll be struck down by suffocation or
> apoplexy because of her. I just can't catch my breath." (48)

But Adler is unmoved; he accuses Wilhelm of victimizing himself by
allowing his wife to dominate him and by expecting from the marriage
a perfection that marriage cannot provide. The old man even accuses
Wilhelm of contributing to his marital difficulties through extra-
marital affairs with both men and women. Wilhelm feels the pressure
of this unjust accusation in conjunction with the pressure of his wife's
persecution. He struggles for breath, becomes "choked up and congested," and thinks: "Trouble rusts out the system" (52). "Wilhelm
had a great knot of wrong tied tight within his chest, and tears ap-
proached his eyes but he didn't let them out" (53). Finding himself
sinking beneath the wrongs piled upon him, Wilhelm cries out for
assistance:

> He felt as though he were unable to recover something. Like a ball in
> the surf, washed beyond reach, his self-control was going out. "I expect
> *help!*" The words escaped him in a loud, wild, frantic cry and startled
> the old man, and two or three breakfasters within hearing glanced their
> way. (53)

This cry for help (the hapless swimmer's plea for assistance) directed
toward his earthly father parallels the silent prayer for aid that
Wilhelm directed toward his heavenly father at the end of Scene I,
but the intensity is greater here. In response, his father again offers

him advice he cannot use: "I want nobody on my back. Get off! And
I give you the same advice, Wilky. Carry nobody on your back" (55).
A drowning man, of course, is not likely to carry anyone on his back
—though Wilhelm realizes later that Tamkin has been riding on his
back, another pressure pushing him down (105). Adler's indifference
to his son's need confirms the validity of the sense of persecution that
emerges as Wilhelm's dominant feeling in this scene. This estrangement of son from father as a result of the father's self-centeredness is
established dramatically here as a condition of long standing, a major
contributing factor to Wilhelm's present problems.

Swearing silently at himself for breaking down in front of his father,
Wilhelm moves into the lobby, where Scene V (55–77) begins. Wilhelm's chest aches and he smells "the salt odor of tears in his nose"
(56). He thinks again of the line from *Lycidas*—to "sink beneath the
watery floor"—and suddenly he encounters Tamkin, for whom references in earlier scenes have made dramatic preparation. With the
appearance of Tamkin, Wilhelm feels himself "flowing into another
channel" (57). They exchange greetings and Wilhelm attempts, skeptically, to discover through cogitation if Tamkin is all he purports to
be. Wilhelm remembers his own penchant for self-destructive choices
and recalls how he thought five days ago, when closing the deal with
Tamkin, that "when he tasted the peculiar flavor of fatality in Dr.
Tamkin, he could no longer keep back the money" (58). Tamkin had
told him to invest some money in order to learn the stock market
because "to know how it feels to be a seaweed you have to get in the
water" (61). Now, Wilhelm senses fearfully, he is "in the water" deeper
than he had anticipated.

Much of this scene—which moves immediately from the lobby back
to the dining room, where Tamkin eats his breakfast—deals with
Wilhelm's vacillating attitude toward Tamkin. Wilhelm's suspicions
are aroused when Tamkin uses bad grammar, when he brags of his
fantastic international financial deals, or when he reveals the details
of his many "cases": the epileptic blonde, the eccentric nudist-dentist,
the transvestite general. However, when Tamkin shows concern for
human suffering, Wilhelm is drawn back to him. He believes that
Tamkin reveals true insight into human aspiration when he declares:
"only the present is real—the here-and-now. Seize the day" (66). Wilhelm responds from the heart when Tamkin describes the lonely
person "howling from the window like a wolf when night comes"
(67). And Wilhelm thinks he finds a key to understanding his own
problem in Tamkin's analysis of the two major souls in man:

> "In here, the human bosom—mine, yours, everybody's—there isn't
> just one soul. There's a lot of souls. But there are two main ones, the

real soul and a pretender soul. Now! Every man realizes that he has to
love something or somebody. He feels that he must go outward. 'If thou
canst not love, what art thou?' Are you with me?"

"Yes, Doc, I think so," said Wilhelm listening—a little skeptically
but nonetheless hard.

" 'What art thou?' Nothing. . . . In the heart of hearts—Nothing! So
of course you can't stand that and want to be Something, and you try.
But instead of being this Something, the man puts it over on everybody instead. You can't be that strict to yourself. You love a *little*. Like
you have a dog" (Scissors.) "or give some money to a charity drive. Now
that isn't love, is it? What is it? Egotism, pure and simple. It's a way
to love the pretender soul. Vanity. Only vanity, is what it is. And social
control. The interest of the pretender soul is the same as the interest of
the social life. Oh, it is terrible! Terrible! You are not free. Your own
betrayer is inside of you and sells you out. You have to obey him like a
slave. He makes you work like a horse. And for what? For who?"

"Yes, for what?" The doctor's words caught Wilhelm's heart. "I
couldn't agree more," he said. "When do we get free?"

"The purpose is to keep the whole thing going. The true soul is the
one that pays the price. It suffers and gets sick, and it realizes that the
pretender can't be loved. Because the pretender is a lie. The true soul
loves the truth. And when the true soul feels like this, it wants to kill
the pretender. The love has turned into hate. Then you become dangerous. A killer. You have to kill the deceiver." (71)

Wilhelm sees in Tamkin's theory an explanation of his past action:
in going to Hollywood, changing his name, marrying against his better
judgment, and investing hastily in the stock market, Wilhelm realizes
he was serving his "pretender soul," the agent of social control, and
now he is enduring the bondage of his own creation. That this false
self must be destroyed he is not yet ready to admit, nor is he comfortable with the knowledge that Tamkin has been "treating" him
on the sly. "I don't like being treated without my knowledge," Wilhelm declares; "I'm of two minds" (73)—that is, of two minds as well
as two souls.

Tamkin too, it seems, is of two minds and two souls, and he demonstrates this dramatically when he hands Wilhelm the stock market
receipts along with one of his poems, evidence of his pretender soul
on the one hand and, apparently, his true soul on the other. The
poem, of course, is an anachronistic, ungrammatical, hypermetric piece
of, in Wilhelm's words, "mishmash" and "claptrap." The bad quality
of the poem throws Wilhelm into a panic again as he assesses the
credentials of the man who represents his economic survival. "Kiss
those seven hundred bucks goodbye," he says, "and call it one more
mistake in a long line of mistakes" (75). Wilhelm feels "choked and
strangled" (76). In explicating his poem, Tamkin assures Wilhelm that

in the conflict between *"construct* and *de*struct" money is *"destruct"*
but nature is "creative": "It rolls the waters of the earth" (77). The
scene ends with Wilhelm's portentous vision of these waters as destructive: "The waters of the earth are going to roll over me" (77).
With the introduction of Tamkin into the narrative, the pace of the
novel increases. The movement from place to place accelerates, and
greater emphasis is placed on action and dialogue as more characters
are admitted into each scene. In accordance with the developing metaphor of the novel, Wilhelm is being swept faster by the currents that
are carrying him to the center of his personal maelstrom.

Scene VI (77–90) begins with Wilhelm and Tamkin "crossing the
tide of Broadway traffic" (77) to enter the brokerage office. Here, everything is strange to Wilhelm: he is flooded with impressions of an
impersonal, rapacious, money-mad world. Man's staples—wheat, rye,
lard, eggs—are reduced in this place to flashing lights and whirring
tumblers on a giant electric board. On his right and left sit secretive
old men whose withered lives are devoted entirely to the pursuit of
money, and all around him Wilhelm feels confusion:

> That sick Mr. Perls at breakfast had said that there was no easy way to
> tell the sane from the mad, and he was right about that in any big city
> and especially in New York—the end of the world, with its complexity
> and machinery, bricks and tubes, wires and stones, holes and heights.
> And was everybody crazy here? What sort of people did you see? Every
> other man spoke a language entirely his own, which he had figured out
> by private thinking; he had his own ideas and peculiar ways. (83)

Wilhelm is clearly at sea here, bewildered and frightened, and his
fear sparks two reflections. In the first he escapes in his mind to a
farm he once owned in upstate Roxbury—where the chickens and the
eggs were real—and for a moment he imagines the peace and quiet
of a country day. In the second, he recalls an experience he had in an
underground corridor beneath Times Square:

> In the dark tunnel, in the haste, heat, and darkness which disfigure
> and make freaks and fragments of nose and eyes and teeth, all of a
> sudden, unsought, a general love for all these imperfect and lurid-
> looking people burst out in Wilhelm's breast. He loved them. One and
> all, he passionately loved them. They were his brothers and his sisters.
> He was imperfect and disfigured himself, but what difference did that
> make if he was united with them by this blaze of love? And as he walked
> he began to say, "Oh, my brothers—my brothers and my sisters," bless-
> ing them all as well as himself. (84–85)

Though the feeling he then had soon passed, Wilhelm concludes as
he remembers his experience that "there is a larger body, and from

this you cannot be separated" (84). These two reflections provide Wilhelm with momentary respite from his immediate discomfort—and his transcendental vision prepares the way for the ambivalent final scene—but the insistence of the flashing lights and clicking wheels of the exchange board call him abruptly back to the feverish activity of the stock market.

Though the brokerage is strange to Wilhelm, it is familiar to Tamkin, who moves knowingly from place to place and from group to group in the room. His appearance and movements suggest to Wilhelm a bird of prey, perhaps a sea hawk: "a rare, peculiar bird he was, with those pointed shoulders, that bare head, his loose nails, almost claws, and those brown, soft, deadly, heavy eyes" (82). Appealing to Tamkin to sell their rye in order to cover their losses in lard, Wilhelm finds himself chided by Tamkin for his faintheartedness. Tamkin recommends that Wilhelm try *"here-and-now* mental exercises" to compose himself:

> "Nature only knows one thing, and that's the present. Present, present, eternal present, like a big, huge, giant wave—colossal, bright and beautiful, full of life and death, climbing into the sky, standing in the seas. You must go along with the actual, the Here-and-Now, the glory——" (89)

As Tamkin drones on to the end of the scene—advocating through his water imagery focusing on the present, recognizing opportunity, seizing the day—Wilhelm recalls a chest condition he once had and how Margaret read to him the melancholy lines from Keats's *Endymion:*

> Come then, Sorrow!
> . . . .
> I thought to leave thee,
> And deceive thee,
> But now of all the world I love thee best.

Margaret's voice from the past forms a counterpoint to Tamkin's voice in the present; both are appropriate to Wilhelm's condition. The combined effect of the two voices—Tamkin's water imagery and Margaret's elegiac tone—produce in Wilhelm a mood of resignation. His plight is too desperate, his strength inadequate, and the forces opposing him too strong for him to resist much longer. The waters are bearing him down. On this note of resignation to fate the scene ends.

Scene VII (90–105) finds Wilhelm and Tamkin at lunch in a cafeteria with a gilded front. The scene is developed by what a composi-

tion teacher might call statement and amplification. Taking his cue
from Wilhelm's comments about how his estranged wife mistreats him,
Tamkin provides the central statement in the scene:

> "Why do you let her make you suffer so? It defeats the original ob-
> ject in leaving her. Don't play her game. Now, Wilhelm, I'm trying to
> do you some good. I want to tell you, don't marry suffering. Some
> people do. They get married to it, and sleep and eat together, just as
> husband and wife. If they go with joy they think it's adultery." (98)

"One hundred falsehoods," Wilhelm thinks, "but at last one truth.
Howling like a wolf from the city window" (98). Wilhelm knows,
furthermore, that he is one of the compulsive sufferers that Tamkin
has described:

> True, true! thought Wilhelm, profoundly moved by these revelations.
> How does he know these things? How can he be such a jerk, and even
> perhaps an operator, a swindler, and understand so well what gives?
> I believe what he says. It simplifies much—everything. People are
> dropping like flies. I am trying to stay alive and work too hard at it.
> That's what's turning my brains. This working hard defeats its own
> end. At what point would I start over? Let me go back a ways and try
> once more. (99)

Tamkin's statement is central in this scene, and Wilhelm establishes
its validity through his reflections. The remainder of the scene provides dramatic corroboration of the fact that Wilhelm is "married to
suffering"; however it is his suffering that defines his humanity at
last, and enables him to break out of his imprisoning self.

As Tamkin and Wilhelm return to the brokerage, an old violinist
singles out Wilhelm from the crowd, pointing his bow and exclaim-
ing, "You!" in testimony to Wilhelm's status as a victim, a mark. On
the sidewalk outside the brokerage, old Mr. Rappaport grabs Wilhelm's arm and insists that he be guided to the cigar store across the
street. Begrudgingly, yet still passively, Wilhelm allows himself to be
used. Rappaport delays Wilhelm, intensifies his anxiety over the
status of his investment in lard, bores him with a senseless story about
Teddy Roosevelt, and causes him to be separated from Tamkin at a
crucial moment. When Wilhelm finally escapes the old man and enters
the brokerage, he discovers that both the lard and the rye have
dropped drastically. He is wiped out, and Tamkin has disappeared.
The scene has demonstrated his bad judgment and passiveness and
the resultant suffering. At the conclusion of the scene, Wilhelm, with
"unshed tears" rising in his eyes, looks "like a man about to drown"
(104).

In Scene VIII (105–18), the final scene, Wilhelm does drown, but
not without thrashing about futilely before surrendering to his fate.

The pace in this scene is very fast, and the water imagery is overwhelming. Wilhelm dashes to Tamkin's room at the hotel, but is greeted only by a maid, an empty room, and the "mop water smell" of the "brackish tidal river" (106). Wilhelm then begins his final symbolic descent. Seeking his father, he goes downstairs to the health club, past the swimming pool, and finds him in the misty massage room. He asks his father for assistance, describing his condition in desperate terms: "I just can't breathe. My chest is all up—I feel choked. I just simply can't catch my breath" (109). But again his father is deaf to his cries for help. Wilhelm dashes to a phone booth and calls Margaret, asking her to give him some financial relief. The booth is oppressively close; he breaks into a sweat and warns Margaret that he is "suffocating" (113). He yells at her—or to her—and she hangs up with the assertion "I won't stand to be howled at" (114)—and in her metaphor reverberates the cry in the night that Tamkin attributed earlier to the archetypal lonely person. Wilhelm now is painfully that person.

Rushing out into the street in a panic, Wilhelm encounters "the inexhaustible current of millions of every race and kind pouring out" (115). "The sidewalks," to Wilhelm, "were wider than any causeway" (115). Thinking he sees Tamkin nearby, Wilhelm becomes caught in the crush of a crowd and finds himself in the "dark and cool" of a Jewish funeral home where "the stained glass was like mother-of-pearl" (116). In the press of people Wilhelm is maneuvered alongside the casket and is engaged suddenly and totally by the face of the strange corpse. He feels a "splash of heartsickness" (117), and the tears he has held back so long begin quietly to fall:

> Standing a little apart, Wilhelm began to cry. He cried at first softly and from sentiment, but soon from deeper feeling. He sobbed loudly and his face grew distorted and hot, and the tears stung his skin. A man —another human creature, was what first went through his thoughts, but other and different things were torn from him. What'll I do? I'm stripped and kicked out. . . . Oh, Father, Paul? My children. And Olive? My dear! Why, why, why—you must protect me against that devil who wants my life. If you want it, then kill me. Take, take it, take it from me.
>
> Soon he was past words, past reason, coherence. He could not stop. The source of all tears had suddenly sprung open within him, black, deep, and hot, and they were pouring out and convulsed his body, bending his stubborn head, bowing his shoulders, twisting his face, crippling the very hands with which he held the handkerchief. His efforts to collect himself were useless. The great knot of ill and grief in his throat swelled upward and he gave in utterly and held his face and wept. He cried with all his heart. . . .
>
> The flowers and lights fused ecstatically in Wilhelm's blind, wet eyes;

the heavy sea-like music came up to his ears. It poured into him where
he had hidden himself in the center of a crowd by the great and happy
oblivion of tears. He heard it and sank deeper than sorrow, through
torn sobs and cries toward the consummation of his heart's ultimate
need. (118)

This is Wilhelm's death by drowning, and every scene in the book
has pointed toward this culminating moment. The salt water of his
tears is the medium of his suffocation. Wilhelm cries for the failure
that he has been, for the death-in-life that he has experienced. He
cries for the pretender soul, now put to rest, whose misplaced values
caused him to be married to suffering in all aspects of his existence.
He cries for the time he has wasted and the mistakes he has made.
His tears are tears of grief.

He cries also, however, for mankind, for those millions—like himself—who have howled like wolves in anguish and loneliness from
city windows at night. He cries for all men who must suffer and die;
he cries for what Virgil called the *lacrimae rerum*, the tears in things.

Because he is able to transcend his personal grief, Wilhelm's tears
are also tears of joy. In destroying the pretender soul, Wilhelm prepares for the coming of the true soul, which will not lead him to
torture himself because of an unworthy father, which will not persuade him to go to Hollywood or marry unwisely or seek a quick
fortune with a charlatan. In the termination of his marriage to suffering, Wilhelm's fragmentary glimpse in the underground corridor of
a transcendental "larger body" comes to fruition in his ability to find
refuge "in the center of a crowd by the great and happy oblivion of
tears." Where there has been alienation, there is now the possibility
of communion. Wilhelm's drowning, then, is also a baptism, a rebirth.
It is clearly a sea change, demonstrating that, as St. John of the Cross
stated, the way down is also the way up.

The unity of effect achieved in *Seize the Day* results from the skillful
blending of all the elements of fiction in tightly constructed scenic
units functioning very much like poetic images built around a controlling metaphor. Each scene extends the central image of Wilhelm's
drowning by embodying a particular aspect of his life that has contributed to the pressure that finally overwhelms him in literal failure
and symbolic death and rebirth. Unity is enhanced further by cross
references between scenes. Wilhelm's appeal to his heavenly father
in Scene I is paralleled by his two subsequent appeals (in Scenes IV
and VIII) to his earthly father. Adler's advice to Wilhelm to "carry
nobody on [his] back" in Scene IV is given ironic significance in Scene
VIII when Wilhelm declares that Tamkin was "on [his] back." Tamkin's comparison of loneliness to a "howling wolf" (Scene V) is picked
up in Wilhelm's reflection (Scene VII) on truth "howling like a wolf

from the city window" (98) and again in Margaret's assertion (Scene VIII) that she will not be "howled" at. The dramatic irony in Adler's prescription of "hydrotherapy" for Wilhelm (Scene IV), Wilhelm's gesture of self-strangulation (Scene IV), Tamkin's theory of the necessary death of the pretender soul (Scene V), and Wilhelm's vision of transcendental love in the underground corridor all coalesce in Wilhelm's symbolic drowning in Scene VIII: it is "hydrotherapy," self-induced, that destroys Wilhelm's false self and opens his heart to true values and to communion with nature and man, ending his long alienation. "Spatial form" in a larger sense is achieved, then, both within and between scenes.

Not every novel, of course, lends itself to the kind of analysis employed here. The "New Novel" from France and much recent Black Humor fiction, for example, are probably too convoluted and open ended to reward scenic analysis. Stream-of-consciousness novels too frequently lack sufficient dramatic form to be divided into traditional presentational units, and very long novels present problems either of tedium or of severe selection. The critic must always be guided by the nature of the novel he is examining, allowing the work to dictate from within the critical focus appropriate to it. When the nature of the novel so dictates, the scene-as-image approach can be a very useful methodological tool.

The Ambiguous Assault
of Henderson and Herzog

by Richard Pearce

After Henderson introduces himself to the Arnewi children by setting a bush on fire with his Austrian lighter, he is greeted by a girl, not much older than his daughter Ricey, who bursts into loud tears. "What's eating this kid?" Henderson asks. Assured that he is not to blame, he responds with abandon:

> "She's coming to me for help. I feel it. Maybe a lion has eaten her family? Are there man-eaters around here? Ask her, Romilayu. Say that I've come to help, and if there are killers in the neighborhood I'll shoot them." I picked up my H and H Magnum with the scope sights and showed it to the crowd. With enormous relief it dawned on me that the crying was not due to any fault of mine, and that something could be done, that I did not have to stand and bear the sight of those tears boiling out. "Everybody! Leave it to me," I said. "Look! Look!" And I started to go through the manual of arms for them, saying, "Hut, hut, hut," as the drill instructors always did.

Eugene Henderson is a gigantic and pugnacious buffoon—"Six feet four inches tall. Two hundred and thirty pounds. An enormous head, rugged, with hair like Persian lambs' fur. Suspicious eyes, usually narrowed. Blustering ways. A great nose." He stalks the wilds of Africa in his T-shirt and jockey shorts. An inveterate intruder, he invades the primitive world with his urban manners, his demotic tongue, his tropism for disaster. A hyperbolic schlemiel, whenever he "goes among people . . . there's the devil to pay." A paranoiac egoist, he takes personal responsibility for social and natural calamities.

And yet Henderson achieves heroic stature and singular dignity. His speech is more often formal, even archaic, than it is colloquial. He is attuned to beauty, and he vibrates in response to the primeval sunrise, the palms of the Arnewi hands—that looked as though they had "played catch with light"—the "saffron swelling" of Queen Mtalba's huge and aged belly. He has a deep and instinctive sympathy for the vulnerable, the suffering, the lonely. He "cannot stand still under blows," whether they fall on him or others. And he responds to insult, injustice, and calamity with reckless impulse, utilizing his great physical prowess as well as his military training.

If Henderson is a descendant of the *miles gloriosus*, the braggart soldier of classical comedy, or the *alazon*, the impostor and intruder, he is also a descendant of Sophocles' Ajax—who, deceived and humiliated by the gods when they turned him from a heroic warrior into a clownish butcher, remained a hero.[1] And if *Henderson the Rain King* wavers between the mock-heroic and the heroic, Bellow weights the balance toward the latter. The underlying epic formality of Henderson's speech and the archetypal pattern of his quest withstand the incongruous colloquialism and the mocking parody. Henderson's innocence, his conscience, his sense of responsibility, his capacity for feeling and acting, as well as his pride, his impulsiveness, and his vengefulness —all of his character traits—are extraordinary, beyond conventional measure, and certainly beyond moderation. Also beyond conventional measure is his awareness and acceptance of an absurd situation. On the opening page of the novel Henderson says:

> "When I think of my condition the facts begin to crowd me. . . . A disorderly rush begins—my parents, my wives, my girls, my children, my farm, my animals, my habits, my money, my music lessons, my drunkenness, my prejudices, my brutality, my teeth, my face, my soul! I have to cry, 'No, no, get back, curse you, let me alone!' But how can they let me alone? They belong to me. They are mine. And they pile into me from all sides. It turns into chaos."

Henderson's exuberance, the sheer quantity of all he reaches for and internalizes, and the catholicity of his taste, as well as the openness of his style and the rhetorical patterns of his speech that encompass the colloquial and the mundane, lead us to think of the epic persona of "Song of Myself." Yet there is a signal difference in the ways Henderson and Whitman encounter the contradictions of their worlds. Whitman embraces reality and merges with it. He breathes in fragrances that are fair and foul. He ingests the landscapes of gently rolling hills, rugged mountain peaks, seashores, urban streets. He "weaves" the song of himself out of contraltos, carpenters, children, pilots, deacons, lunatics, machinists, quadroon slave girls, immigrants, presidents, prostitutes, and virgins. He becomes each object that he looks upon, and

---

1 For a discussion of Henderson's relation to the classical comic tradition, see my *Stages of the Clown: Perspectives on Modern Fiction from Dostoyevsky to Beckett* (Carbondale, Ill.: Southern Illinois University Press, 1970). For a discussion of Sophocles' Ajax as existential hero, see Jan Kott's *Eating of the Gods: An Interpretation of Greek Tragedy* (New York: Random House, 1973).

that object becomes a part of him. But Whitman's embrace ultimately
denies the singularity and separateness of others. Despite his celebration of multiplicity, his long catalogs undermine uniqueness and
translate quality into quantity. Despite his enthusiasm for contradic-
tion, his parallel phrases and coordinate clauses tend to level out differences. Despite his call for the individual reader to travel his own
road, the only individual who emerges from "Song of Myself" is that
of the persona. Indeed, Whitman's embrace is implicitly acquisitive
and self-aggrandizing. And it will lead to the imperialistic posture of
"Years of the Unperform'd," where he celebrates the American who

> . . . colonizes the Pacific, the archipelagoes;
> With the steam-ship, the electric telegraph, the newspaper, the
>   wholesale engines of war,
> With these, and the world-spreading factories, he interlinks all
>   geography, all lands.[2]

Henderson also embraces reality—"I am a true adorer of life, and
if I can't reach as high as the face of it, I plant my kiss somewhere
lower down." Yet his embrace is more aggressive than Whitman's. And
it is only part of the response of this "soldierly temperament" to a
world he both loves and hates, accepts and rejects. Henderson fills his
handsome farm buildings with pigs and infuses the genteel neighborhood with the stink of swill and dung. While drunk, he falls off his
tractor, runs over himself, and then stamps around for months "with
the bulk of a football player and the color of a gipsy, swearing and
crying out and showing my teeth and shaking my head—no wonder
people got out of my way." Henderson's aggressive response to the
flatness of his suburban world is essentially the same as his response
to the Arnewi plague of frogs—dynamiting the cistern—and to the
Wariri insult—carrying out the heavy corpse that was planted in his
tent. This response is epitomized in his agon with Mummah, the
heavy wooden goddess, who resisted the strongest Wariri tribesmen:

> As I came closer I saw how huge she was, how over-spilling and form-
> less. She had been oiled, and glittered before my eyes. . . . Never hesi-
> tating, I encircled Mummah with my arms. I wasn't going to take no
> for an answer. I pressed my belly upon her and sank my knees some-
> what. She smelled like a living old woman. Indeed, to me she was a
> living personality, not an idol. *We met as challenged and challenger,
> but also as intimates.* And with the close pleasure you experience in a
> dream or on one of those warm beneficial floating idle days when every
> desire is satisfied, I laid my cheek against her wooden bosom. I cranked

2 See Henry Nash Smith's essay "Walt Whitman and Manifest Destiny" in his
Virgin Land: The American West as Symbol and Myth (Cambridge, Mass.: Harvard
University Press, 1950).

down my knees and said to her, "Up you go, dearest. No use trying to make yourself heavier; if you weighed twice as much I'd lift you anyway." The wood gave to my pressure and benevolent Mummah with her fixed smile yielded to me; I lifted her from the ground and carried her twenty feet to her new place among the other gods. (italics mine)

Henderson and Mummah meet "as challenged and challenger, but also as intimates." Henderson's aggressive response to the world, unlike Whitman's embrace, is an affirmation—and evocation—of separateness, uniqueness, and vital reciprocity. Indeed, Henderson's posture might owe less to Whitman than it does to Melville. For Ahab's assault, far more than Whitman's embrace, affirms the contradictory nature of reality and the uniqueness of others. Ahab responds to the senseless violence and injustice of a world that is also splendid and enriching. His obsessive assault on the white whale may turn him into a lonely monomaniac, and he may turn himself and his crew into destructive and self-destroying instruments, but in the process Ahab grows in humaneness and in his capacity to love. In the end, he fully recognizes the separateness and the unique value of persons as different from one another as Pip and Starbuck and the other members of his variegated crew. In the end, that is, Ahab's assault is less possessive than Whitman's embrace, and comparison leads us to a clearer evaluation of Henderson's "soldierly temperament" and to a sharper description of his posture. Henderson's aggressive response to the world, like Ahab's, is an assault on reality. But it is an ambiguous assault, for, unlike Ahab's, it contains an element of tenderness. Indeed, it contains the Whitmanesque embrace.

In *Herzog*, Bellow once again creates a character of extraordinary stature, but whereas Henderson's measure is substantially physical, Herzog's is entirely mental. On the train between Grand Central Station and Woods Hole he fires a burst of twenty-four letters to most of his personal acquaintances, as well as to: a Polish historian, a Bowery minister, the credit department of Marshall Field, a specialist on the Gold Pore theory, an Indian utopianist, the President of the United States, Martin Heidegger, a U.S. Public Health official, Adlai Stevenson, Nehru, Martin Luther King, Police Commissioner Wilson, an alderman, Secretary of the Interior Udall, and Professor Shapiro, with whom he discusses Joachim da Floris, Proudhon, Spengler, and the history of Western civilization.

That Herzog's letters remain unsent and even unfinished may lead us to describe Herzog as an alienated intellectual, inert and solipsistic. His ultimate posture—lying in a hammock on his dilapidated Ludeyville estate while chronicling his failures—might confirm such a conclusion. But the power of the novel and the palpable drive of its energy should prompt us to look further. And if we do, we find that Herzog's letters are his assault on reality. Herzog attempts to seize reality as Henderson seized the huge wooden goddess—but with language—and the agon is just as strenuous, and just as ambiguous: "Perhaps I'd like to change it all into language, to force Madeleine and Gersbach to have a *Conscience*. There's a word for you. I must be trying to keep tight the tensions without which human beings can no longer be called human. . . . And I've filled the world with letters to prevent their escape."

Nor is Herzog's attempt to "keep tight the tensions" the same as Whitman's urge to contain the world within himself. For each letter takes up the challenge of otherness and is an expression of Herzog's "soldierly temperament." Herzog repudiates the President's new tax program, mocks the pretentiousness of Heidegger's "fall into the quotidian" ("When did the fall occur? Where were you standing?"), exposes Emmett Strawforth's "Philosophy of Risk" and the inevitable threat of political leaders, chides Adlai Stevenson for his unproductive display of "old-fashioned intensity," illuminates the inadequacy of Commissioner Wilson's police force, questions the blasting of polar ice caps to produce more oil, and derides the "foolish dreariness" of Spengler's "canned sauerkraut," just as he attacks his in-laws, psychiatrist, and lawyer for betraying him with Madeleine. His assault varies from bold contention and incisive argument to polite exchange and self-parody.

Yet Herzog's letters also include praise and admiration for Nehru, Martin Luther King, and a utopian activist in India; they include a brotherly concern for Asphalter, the biologist who tried to save his tubercular monkey with mouth-to-mouth resuscitation; they include a tender apology for leaving Ramona; and they stimulate a wide range of positive as well as negative recollections from Herzog's past. Indeed, Herzog's attempt to "keep tight the tensions" while attacking injustice and irrationality is, like Henderson's assault on reality, an affirmation and evocation of pluralism—the separateness and the diverse energies of others.

Even though Henderson's assault leads to comic and calamitous failures, his action does effect change. Herzog's letter writing, on the contrary, makes no difference in the course of his life or in the course of history. Moreover, as Henderson's story ends he is running in circles around his homebound plane on the frozen runways of Newfoundland; the ending is joyous and open and the energy level is high. Herzog, on the other hand, comes full circle at the end, for he has never actually left his hammock in Ludeyville. He has come to terms with his failures, but his energy is drained. He is satisfied to "remain in occupancy," with "no messages for anyone. . . . Not a single word," and we experience a feeling of inertia and entropy. The difference between these successive novels may be explained by the fuller and more consistently comic conception of Henderson, but even more by Bellow's shift from a hyperbolic, mythic, and oblique approach to one that deals with modern life more directly and personally. That is, though Herzog remains in a heroic mold and retains something of Henderson's "soldierly temperament," his decisions are more like those of a real person—Bellow himself—living in the modern world.

There is still another reason for the difference between the two novels, which we can begin to see by focusing on a singular conflict of forms within *Herzog.* Herzog comes to realize the inherent purpose of his letter writing—that he wants to change reality into language—just before the melodramatic sequence that ends in an automobile accident, Herzog's arrest for illegal possession of a handgun, and his confrontation with Madeleine in the police station. At this point, language-bound recollection, introspection, and speculation yield to fast-paced action, and a baroque style of narrated and interior monologue, complicated by the random and incomplete letters, yields to a relatively straightforward third-person narrative.

The melodramatic sequence is precipitated by Herzog's visit to the New York City courthouse, where he experiences a Dostoyevskian nightmare of misery, perversion, and legal injustice. And he responds: "How long can I stand such inner beating? The front wall of this body will go down. My whole life beating against its boundaries, and the force of balked longings coming back as stinging poison. Evil, evil, evil . . . ! Excited, characteristic, ecstatic love turning to evil." His thoughts then turn outward as he witnesses the trial of a woman who beat her child to death while her lover lay smoking on a bed nearby. Herzog recreates the scene: "The child screamed, clung, but with both arms the girl hurled it against the wall. On her legs was ruddy hair. And her lover, too, with long jaws and zooty sideburns, watching on the bed. Lying down to copulate, and standing up to kill. Some kill, then cry. Others, not even that." At this point in the novel, Herzog's inner and outer worlds are joined, and he becomes a man of action. Impulsively, he flies to Chicago, steals an old revolver that had belonged to his father, peers through his wife's window to witness her lover gently bathing their daughter Junie, and takes Junie on an outing to the Museum of Science and the aquarium. But although the revelation of Gersbach's tenderness to Junie has freed Herzog of the desire to murder him and Madeleine, the momentum of this narrative sequence drives toward an obligatory climax: the collision, the arrest for illegal possession, and the confrontation with Madeleine in the police station.

Herzog derives much of its power, suspense, and direction from a

linear dynamic of inevitable and impelling forward motion. The linear
dynamic peaks in the melodramatic sequence. But it begins to build
its momentum early in the novel, as Herzog's taxi presses through the
traffic toward Grand Central Station. And, as the train hurtles toward
Woods Hole, it impels Herzog's furious letter writing; indeed, it forms
an ironic or contrapuntal contrast to the discontinuity and random
direction of Herzog's letters: "Quickly, quickly, more! The train
rushed over the landscape. It swooped past New Haven. It ran with
all its might toward Rhode Island. Herzog, now barely looking
through the tinted, immovable, sealed window felt his eager, flying
spirit streaming out, speaking, piercing, making clear judgments, ut-
tering final explanations, necessary words only."

The linear dynamic of inevitable and impelling forward motion
does not, however, dominate the novel as a whole, any more than it
does the sequence on the train. Rather, our total experience of *Herzog*
arises from the conflict between the linear dynamic and the random
dynamic of Herzog's letters and reminiscences. Inasmuch as Herzog
assaults reality with language, let me describe this conflict—or Herzog's ambiguous assault—as a conflict of traditional grammar with a
grammar of energy. For it is with traditional grammar that Herzog,
the rational humanist, tries to harness the random social, political,
and psychological energies of the past and present. And it is with a
grammar of energy that Herzog, the man of passionate feeling, perceives the world and its history.

In the traditional grammar, the Ludeyville frame of the novel is
Herzog's present tense—the "now" from which he reflects on the action
line that has led to his present "occupancy." The action line is Herzog's past tense—beginning with his decision to flee New York and
Ramona, and leading through his abrupt departure from Martha's
Vineyard, his evening with Ramona, his visit to the New York City
courtroom, and the melodramatic sequence—the final scene of which
drives Herzog to Ludeyville. But the past-tense line of action is continually broken by Herzog's jumbled and disconnected recollections
of events that took place even earlier. The event line, which no matter
how jumbled or disconnected is easily and inevitably reconstructed by
the reader, is Herzog's past perfect.

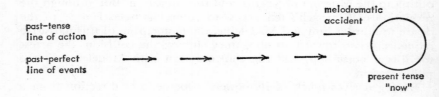

Although the narrative is driven by its traditional grammar, there is a counterdynamic that can only be described by a grammar of energy or forces. Herzog's letters are like vectors, spinning off the past-tense line of action, aiming in various directions but, due to all the countervailing forces in the field, never completely toward the past or present. Due to their high energy level, the obliqueness of their directions, and their incompleteness, they have the effect of fracturing the novel's traditional grammar.

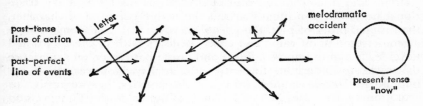

We are impelled by the forward motion of the novel's dynamic. We are anxious to find out what happens to Herzog—what will happen in Martha's Vineyard, whether Herzog will come to terms with his family, what he will do with the gun, whether he will face down Madeleine, what will become of his relationship with Ramona, whether he will ever integrate his historical speculations and complete his book. But at the same time, we are driven centrifugally in the random directions of his unsent letters and his disconnected reminiscences.

Henderson assaults reality physically. Bellow's remarkable achievement in *Henderson the Rain King* is to create an ambiguous hero, sensitive and blustering, intelligent and buffoonish, reflective and impulsive, in touch intellectually with the main currents of modern life and pugnaciously anti-intellectual. Furthermore, it is to bring Henderson's complex agon with the modern and primitive worlds almost entirely into the physical realm. In *Herzog*, Bellow's achievement is almost the reverse: it is to endow the mental agon of an intellectual buffoon with physical energy. Through what I have tried to describe as a conflict of grammar, Bellow evokes uniquely and palpably the heroic agon of a man who would change reality into language, who struggles to "keep tight the tensions without which human beings can no longer be called human."

Herzog assaults reality with language. He attempts to harness the random political, social, and psychological energies of the past and present with sentences, paragraphs, and letters that proceed logically from salutation to signature. The ambiguity of Herzog's assault derives from an agon between consciousness and grammar—between reality as it is perceived phenomenologically and the order required for making sentences. This is the same order that is required in making a traditional novel; and Saul Bellow is engaged in an agon very much like that of his protagonist. Herzog, despite his personal experiences of failure and despair, and despite his awareness that history is driven irrationally by the violent clashing of egos, continually affirms his faith in rational humanism. Bellow, despite his restless experimentation in narrative forms, and despite his lessons from Joyce in subjectivity and discontinuity, continually affirms his faith in the traditional novel. He continually affirms the heroic potential of character, the rational order of plot, the possibility of attaining wisdom through an understanding of cause and effect. Bellow's faith in the traditional novel leads him to impose a linear and causal pattern on an experience that seems to undermine linearity and causality. However, the linear impulse in *Herzog* cannot, with any authenticity, be progressive or evolutionary. Nor does Bellow succumb to the deterministic regression of naturalism—the domino effect of an inescapable causality that, with increasing momentum, strips a character of his humanity. Hence, the narrative line in *Herzog* follows the path of entropy: Herzog moves to a state of maximum consciousness, which is also a state of inertia, and the novel comes full circle to a point where all its energy is spent, not because this is Bellow's comment on the modern condition but because of his allegiance to the traditional novel.

Still, the narrative line is only one component of *Herzog's* structure. And the conflict between the novel's linear impulse and its irrational energies expresses the heroic agon of a bold and honest writer as he ambiguously assaults the contradictions of Western history, the human psyche, and the modern experience.

Herzog, or, Bellow in Trouble

by Richard Poirier

Bellow's most important cultural essays—"The Thinking Man's Wasteland" (1965), his talk to the PEN Conference in 1966 (as it later appeared in *The New York Times Book Review*), and, in 1971, "Culture Now: Some Animadversions, Some Laughs"—address themselves directly, and with often startling crudity of mind, to the cultural issues which came to dominate his fiction after *Seize the Day*. In particular, *Herzog* in 1964 and *Mr. Sammler's Planet* in 1968 are efforts to test out, to substantiate, to vitalize, and ultimately to propagate a kind of cultural conservatism which he shares with the two aggrieved heroes of these novels, and to imagine that they are victims of the cultural debasements, as Bellow sees it, of the sixties.

The fact that some of his best work—*The Victim, Dangling Man,* and *Seize the Day*—are generally regarded as distinguished contributions to the literature of the Waste Land tradition would not in itself invalidate his disparagements of that tradition or of the academic promotion of it. Other writers, including Mailer, have managed to live within some such complex of attitudes to their own and to our profit. The difference in Mailer's case is that he has a confidently zestful appetite for, and an assurance in his capacities to cope with, the cultural obscenities which might otherwise force him into those feelings of self-righteous victimization so crippling to Bellow's work. Without knowing it, Bellow is far more alienated than Mailer. It shows in his writing; or rather in the evidence that the act of writing, and the promise of cultural mastery which might be engendered by it, is not in his case sufficient to save him from the feelings of victimization visited on his heroes. And yet he likes continually to imagine that it is. Thus when he speaks out in the PEN address against "the disaffected, subversive, radical clique," he doesn't seem to recognize there, anymore than in his novels, that he is exposing his own "disaffection," poorly disguised by bad jokes:

"Herzog, or, Bellow in Trouble" by Richard Poirier. This is a revision by the author of his essay, "Bellows to Herzog," which first appeared in *Partisan Review* (Spring 1965). Used by permission of the author.

On the one hand these teachers, editors, or cultural bureaucrats have absorbed the dislike of modern classic writers for modern civilization. They are repelled by the effrontery of power, and the degradation of the urban crowd. They have made the Waste Land outlook their own. On the other hand they are very well off. They have money, position, privileges, power. They send their children to private schools. They can afford elegant dental care, jet holidays in Europe. They have stocks, bonds, houses, even yachts. With all this, owing to their education, they enjoy a particular and intimate sympathy with the heroic artistic life. Their tastes and judgments were formed by Rimbaud and D. H. Lawrence. Could anything be neater?

There is a random vulgarity in the superficial notations of this passage which is but one evidence of Bellow's effort to blind himself to the fact that he is no less "repelled" by such things as "the degradation of the urban crowd." This has been, after all, a theme in all his work; it is responsible for some of its most powerful descriptive efforts; and one is forced into the embarrassment of supposing that the essential difference between Bellow and the people he is here criticizing is that he, but not they, deserves "elegant dental care," etc., etc., etc. Bellow's problem in the sixties is that the imagined forces of dissolution are not, in this passage or elsewhere in his writing during the period, substantially enough evoked, are indeed too trivially evoked, to teach him, in Empson's phrase, "a style from a despair."

Despite some surface differences, the style of *Herzog* and of *Mr. Sammler's Planet* projects the same authorial presence: of a man nursing imagined betrayals, a man who chooses to retaliate by historical pontifications which, given his own sense of the wastes of history, are intellectually barren, and who nonetheless tries to validate what he says by a species of comic evasion. The comedy, that is, is a way of convincing us that because he himself presumably knows he's being rhetorically banal, the banality must therefore illustrate not the deprivations of his imagination but the bankruptcy of contemporary culture. No one who does not hopelessly confuse culture with literature and both of these with the limits set by the accomplishments of Saul Bellow is apt to be convinced by this procedure.

The test is all in the "doing," as James said long ago, and it is peculiar that those who share Bellow's cultural conservatism have failed to ask themselves whether or not his performance as a writer, as distinct from his opinions as a would-be thinker, contribute to the vitalization either of literary culture or the language. On any close inspection, Bellow's rhetorical ambitions are seen to be disjointed from those aspects of his later fiction which are most compelling—the brilliance of detailed, especially of grotesque, portraiture, and a genius for the rendering of Yiddish-American speech. In *Herzog* in particular, his writing is most alive when he writes as a kind of local colorist. And yet, in the language of analysis and Big Thinking with which he endows his hero, and it is, again, of a piece with the canting style of Bellow's essays, he wants to be taken as a novelist of civilization, especially the civilization of cultural degeneracy as it affects the urban-centered Jew in the American sixties.

That he tries to localize these immense concerns within essentially Jewish material is not the problem. After all, the Jewish writer in the American city is potentially as well situated within the tensions of a great cultural conflict as was Faulkner in the Mississippi of the Snopses, the Faulkner of the middle period when he was writing out of what a similarly beleaguered writer—Yeats in Ireland—called his "ill luck." Bellow feels threatened in his role as public defender of two distinct yet historically harmonious cultural inheritances: of the Jew as poor immigrant, the outsider whose native resources save him from the bitterness of alienation, and of the Jew as successful *arriviste* in American society, enriched and burdened all at once by traditions of high culture. Now a kind of insider looking out, he yearns for those cultural supports which, since World War II, have been commercialized by the society at large if not submerged entirely under the tidal waves of mass produced taste. All differences allowed, a similar combination of inheritances is precisely what fired the genius of Faulkner and Lawrence and Yeats, all of whom were also at the crossroads where high and what might be called native culture find themselves both threatened and courted by the commercialized culture of the middle.

This is a difficult position for a writer to be in; it is also an extraordinarily profitable one. Bellow has so far shown himself unequal to them. Because if contemporary culture is so corrupt and corrupting as he makes it out to be, then the very rhetoric he so glibly uses in his essays and in the essayistic meditations of Herzog and Sammler is more discredited than he dares admit. In the writings of this century where there is a disposition about the state of the culture similar to Bellow's, there is also a kind of stylistic and formal complication generally missing from his work. This complication is not "academic" or faddish or willful. Instead it reflects a confirmed sense of the enormous effort required both to include, with any kind of human generosity, and then to correct, by the powers of style, the preponderant influences of pop culture and of a ruined education system. Some of the consequences to Bellow's work of the essential timidity of his effort— like all timidity it tends to be both self-pitying and vindictive—have been noticed by Morris Dickstein and Richard Locke and by a few of the reviewers of *Mr. Sammler's Planet*. But *Herzog*, while being universally praised, was nonetheless equally flawed, an indication of what was later to become more evidently the matter.

With what Bellow tells brilliantly, the career of Herzog, many are probably now familiar: a twice married sometime professor of English, author of *Romanticism and Christianity* and of a child in each of his marriages, Herzog has recently been divorced, at 47, by his second wife Madeleine. She, in his recollections, shows unusual competence in disposing of her body, other people's ideas, and Herzog's schedule, thus taking, unobserved, his best friend and confidant, Valentine Gersbach, to her bed. It is a story of betrayals, and of a mind so fevered that it remembers them with an attention luridly bright and constantly shifting: to his lawyer, to his psychiatrists, to his colleagues, to his family, to his various women, especially Ramona, middle ageing, generous, loveable and nonetheless made a bit ridiculous, as is everyone in Herzog's account except children and a few other minor characters. Everything we know about these people we know from Herzog's mind. They are confined to the jumble of his recollections as he lies alone in the run-down house he bought for Madeleine in the Berkshires, cheated in this, too. He returns there at the end of the novel, which is also the conclusion of the actions about which he begins to reminisce on page one. The enclosed, self-protective quality of the book is thus formally sealed: its end is its beginning.

Given Bellow's ambitions so much to exceed the confined circumstances of his hero's life and to make it a "representative" modern one, his method seems, on the very face of it, disastrously claustrophobic. Normally we'd wonder how the author is to operate freely within such a book, much less manage to puff it up. Of course he makes himself felt in the ordering of things, so that the fragments of the story as they flash through Herzog's mind are comically, sometimes critically juxtaposed with his intellectual theorizings. And the very first line, "If I am out of my mind, it's all right with me, thought Moses Herzog," is a joke about the hero's "rightness" and about his "thinking" that maybe we're expected to carry like a comic tuning fork through the rest of the book. The evidence increases as one reads, however, that Bellow is in the novel whenever he wants to be simply by becoming Herzog, the confusions at many points between the narrative "I" and "he" being a blunt and even attractive admission of this. But the identification of hero and author is apparent in other, ultimately more insidious ways. Thus Herzog is allowed to characterize himself in a manner usually reserved to the objectivity of the author: the letters he writes, and never mails, to the living who betrayed his love, to the dead thinkers who betray his thinking, to the living great who betray him politically are, he says, "ridiculous." (He does not himself betray the book by also admitting that the letters, for all the parroted praise the reviews have given them, are frequently uninventive and tiresome.) He claims also not to like his own personality.

Bellow's novelist skill is here seen most adroitly at the service of his larger intellectual and, too obviously, of his more personal motives. Allowing no version of the alleged betrayals other than Herzog's, Bellow still must protect his hero's claims to guiltlessness by a process all the more ultimately effective for being paradoxical: he lets Herzog's suffering issue forth less as accusations against others than as self-contempt for his having been cozened by them. There could be no more effective way to disarm the reader's scepticism about the confessions of such a hero within so protective a narrative form. Bellow can thus operate snugly (and smugly) within the enclosure of his hero's recollections, assured, at least to his own satisfaction, that he has anticipated and therefore forestalled antagonistic intrusions from outside. He really does want Herzog's mind to be the whole world, and the hero's ironies at his own expense are only his cleverest ruse in the arrangement. No wonder, then, that Herzog's talk about himself and about ideas is, in passages that carry great weight, indistinguishable from the generalized Bellovian rhetoric by which here, as in Bellow's other novels, "victims" become "modern man," their situation the World's: "He saw his perplexed, furious eyes and he gave an audible cry. *My God! Who is this creature? It considers itself human. But what is it? Not human in itself. But it has the longing to be human.*"

The recurrence of such passages in Bellow's work is only one indication of how straight we are to take them, of how much he tends to summarize himself in the pseudo-philosophical or sociological or historical expansions of the otherwise parochial situations of his heroes. Perhaps the most lamentable result of Bellow's complicity at such points is that he loses his customary ear for banality of expression or for the fatuity of the sentiments. I don't know another writer equally talented who surrenders so willingly to what are by now platitudes about his own creations. Seldom in Faulkner, even less in Joyce, and far less frequently in Lawrence than people who can't listen to his prose like to believe, do we find what the literary ragpickers call key passages. Where such passages obtrude in writing that asks us to be discriminating about style, as they do in Fitzgerald and Hemingway as well as in Bellow, there is always a lack of assurance in what Bellow has himself called "the sole source of order in art": the "power of imagination." And he distinguished this from "the order that ideas have." "Critics need to be reminded of this," he remarks in "Distractions of a Fiction Writer."

His alertness in the matter is understandable. Between his evident intellectual ambitions and the fictional materials he thinks congenial to them there is in *Herzog*, as in *Henderson the Rain King* and in *The Adventures of Augie March,* a gap across which these novels never successfully move. Sections of the present book read like a lesser *Middle-*

march, the longest of the "ridiculous" letters offering pretty much what Bellow-Herzog want to say about "modern" life. Herzog's interest in romanticism is itself an expression of a familiar concern of Bellow: the effort to preserve individuality during a period of economic and scientific acceleration with which it is supposedly impossible for the human consciousness to keep pace. Henry Adams, among others, gave us the vocabulary; George Eliot predicted the condition; Bellow the novelist is victimized by it. What I call the gap in his novels between their intellectual and historical pretensions, on one side, and the stuff of life as he renders it, on the other, prevents me from believing that he is himself convinced by his snappy contempt for "the commonplaces of the Waste Land outlook, the cheap mental stimulants of Alienation." Quoted from a letter of Herzog's these are obviously identical with Bellow's own attitudes. My objection isn't merely that Bellow would replace the "commonplaces" of alienation with even more obvious commonplaces about "the longing to be human." I mean that his works, the truest and surest direction of their energy, suggest to me that imaginatively Bellow does not himself find a source of order in these commonplaces.

Lawrence, who would have found Bellow interesting, was right: "Never trust the artist. Trust the tale. The proper function of the critic is to save the tale from the artist who created it." Imagine such a critic's response to Bellow's connivance at his hero's self-promotion as Your Ordinary Striver:

> Just then his state of being was so curious that he was compelled, himself, to see it—eager, grieving, fantastic, dangerous, crazed and, to the point of death, "comical." It was enough to make a man pray to God to remove this great, bone-breaking burden of selfhood and self-development, give himself, a failure, back to the species for a primitive cure. But this was becoming the up-to-date and almost conventional way of looking at any single life. In this view the body itself, with its two arms and vertical length, was compared to the Cross, on which you knew the agony of consciousness and separate being. For that matter, he had been taking this primitive cure, administered by Madeleine, Sandor, et cetera; so that his recent misfortunes might be seen as a collective project, himself participating, to destroy his vanity and his pretensions to a personal life so that he might disintegrate and suffer and hate like so many others, not on anything so distinguished as a cross, but down in the mire of post-Renaissance, post-humanistic, post-Cartesian dissolution, next door to the Void. Everybody was in the act. "History" gave everyone a free ride. The very Himmelsteins, who had never even read a book of metaphysics, were touting the Void as if it were so much salable real estate. This little demon was impregnated with modern ideas, and one in particular excited his terrible little heart; you must sacrifice your poor, squawking, niggardly individuality—which may be nothing

anyway (from an analytic viewpoint) but a persistent infant megalo-
mania, or (from a Marxian point of view) a stinking little bourgeois
property—to historical necessity. And to truth. And truth is true only
as it brings down more disgrace and dreariness upon human beings, so
that if it shows anything except evil it is illusion, and not truth. But
of course he, Herzog, predictably bucking such trends, had characteristically, obstinately, defiantly, blindly but without sufficient courage or
intelligence tried to be a *marvelous* Herzog, a Herzog who, perhaps
clumsily, tried to live out marvelous qualities vaguely comprehended.

Though Bellow is among the most intelligent of contemporary
American writers, I can't find in this glib presumption to Thought
any difference between his and Herzog's presence. Distinction of intellect is of course not necessary to fiction; but what is most bother-
some about the passage is Bellow's failure to acknowledge the comic
preposterousness of the kind of mental activity going on in it, a pretension that might itself characterize the hero were he not at this point
indistinguishable from the author. Nothing but nothing in Herzog's
career—are we to think of his surrender of his wife's diaphragm to her
messenger Gersbach?—suggests that his self-hood or self-development
has been "this great bone-breaking burden." Such terms describe nothing in the book. They refer instead to a literary historical commonplace about the self to which Bellow wants his book attached. "Species," "primitive cure"—the vocabulary continues to mythologize a
life that has been shown to be at most pitiably insipid. Typically, even
the effort at inflation gets blamed on the times: Herzog abuses himself
for thinking in a way so "up-to-date and almost conventional." When
does it end! Betrayed by someone in the way he thinks of how someone
has betrayed him! Having therefore rejected a place on the Cross (actually by 1964 so worn a piece of literary furniture as to be ready, like
Art Nouveau, for sentimental revival) he momentarily settles "down
in the mire of post-Renaissance, post-humanistic, post-Cartesian dissolution, next door to the Void." Alas, another neighborhood too
fashionable for honest H. The process of correction and mockery by
which these successive placements are given up involves, of course, the
wholly unacceptable assumption that the novel has made Herzog in
some way suitable for them. Not every hero in modern literature is
allowed uncritically to try on for size so many distinguished roles and
then to say not that they don't fit but that they are too much in season.
By the end of the passage Herzog is our culture hero "predictably
bucking such trends," though how, where, with whom and in what
sense he does any "bucking," how he might even ironically call himself "marvelous Herzog," the things that happen in the novel and that
get said in it, this passage being a sample, don't and cannot show.
Yes, the terms of the passage are those of an English professor whose

book is being stolen from him as mysteriously (if you think like Herzog) as was his wife. But they are also Bellow's terms despite his little ironies, Audenesque in the double take of their direction. What is missing is any indication that Bellow is aware of the *essential* irrelevance, the *essential* pretension and shabbiness of the self-aggrandizing mind at work in, and for, the hero.

To a considerable degree the novel does work as a rather conventional drama of alienation, though this is precisely what Bellow doesn't want it to be. It is about the failure of all available terms for interpretation and summary, about the intellectual junk heap of language by which Herzog-Bellow propose dignities to the hero's life and then as quickly watch these proposals dissolve into cliché. A similar process goes on in *Augie*, against the competition of an anxious and often phony exuberance, and it was there that Bellow began to fashion a comic prose which could bear the simultaneous weight of cultural, historical, mythological evocations and also sustain the exposure of their irrelevance. His comedy always has in it the penultimate question before the final one, faced in *Seize the Day*, of life or death—the question of what can be taken seriously and how seriously it can possibly be taken. The result, however, is a kind of stalemate achieved simply by not looking beyond the play of humor into its constituents, at the person from whom it issues, at the psychological implications both of anyone's asking such questions and of the *way* in which he asks them.

It seems to me that Bellow cannot break the stalemate with alienation implicit in his comedy without surrendering to the Waste Land outlook and foregoing the mostly unconvincing rhetoric which he offers as an alternative. That is why his comic style in *Herzog,* even more than in *Henderson* or *Augie,* is less like Nathanael West's than like that of West's brother-in-law, S. J. Perelman. Both Perelman and Bellow raise the question of "seriousness" by piling up trivial detail, by their mock submission to the cheery hope of redemption that people find in the ownership of certain "things," in certain styles, in certain totemic phrases: "I am thirty-eight years old," begins one of Perelman's sketches, "have curly brown hair and blue eyes, own a uke and a yellow roadster, and am considered a snappy dresser in my crowd. But the thing I want most in the world for my birthday is a free subscription to *Oral Hygiene,* published by Merwin B. Massol, 1005 Liberty Avenue, Pittsburgh, Pa." And in another piece, to the remark of a West Indian maid, "You mus' be crazy," he allows the reply " 'But aren't we all?' I reminded her with a charming smile. *'C'est la maladie du temps*—the sickness of the times—don't you think? *Fin-de-siècle* and lost generation in a way.' " Compare to the first Herzog's purchases of summer garb or Ramona's dedication to shrimp Arnaud,

New Orleans style; compare to the second a lot of Herzog's intellectualizing; and for an equivalent to Perelman's high "theatric" mode see Madeleine's bitch performance when she makes her switches "into the slightly British diction [Herzog] had learned to recognize as a sure sign of trouble."

Bellow has greatly increased the range of such comedy, from the clutter of "things," a post-Depression comedy, to the clutter of ideas and culture, a comedy after affluence. But he is still anxious to stay within that comedy. He doesn't dare ask any questions about it or about the characters from whom it emerges. That's why the comparison to Perelman is an apt one. And I mean no criticism of Perelman, whose intentions are not those of a novelist, particularly of novelist-as-thinker. I mean to say that Bellow's failure to ask tough questions about where he *himself* wants to be taken seriously, a failure of his ruined recent play, *The Last Analysis*, doesn't allow me to take him seriously when he chooses to talk about Herzog's struggle for self-development or when, after the scene in court, he allows reference to "the unbearable intensity of these ideas." In question are such ideas as: "If the old God exists he must be a murderer. But the one true God is death." Sophomoric tag-lines don't deserve the status of "ideas." Whatever they are they're really as comfortable as old shoes, especially when you can so believe in their "unbearable intensity" that you can lie down. And it is from that position that the story is told.

The Schlemiel as Liberal Humanist

by Ruth R. Wisse

Schlemiels abound in Bellow's fiction, even in the stories he chooses to translate and anthologize.[1] Bellow is concerned, throughout his literary development, with the diminished stature of the individual in everyone's perception but his own:

> It's obvious to everyone that the stature of characters in modern novels is smaller than it once was, and this diminution powerfully concerns those who value existence. I do not believe that the human capacity to feel or do can really have dwindled or that the quality of humanity has degenerated. I rather think that people appear smaller because society has become so immense.[2]

The diminution of the hero is only a matter of perspective; the actual ratio of aspiration to human accomplishment has not appreciably altered.

Bellow's considerable achievement as a writer has been to portray, against the unquestionably dwarfing forces of modern society, the honest, often successful struggle of the individual striving to define himself as a man within a narrowing range of active possibilities.

The most Jewish of Bellow's heroes, his most typical schlemiel, and most entertaining humorist, is Moses Elkanah Herzog, who is provided with a far more detailed personal history and more substantial biography than such characters usually receive, even in the author's other works. It is only when reading the evocative descriptions of Herzog's

---

[1] Saul Bellow, ed., *Great Jewish Short Stories* (New York, 1963). The volume includes at least ten schlemiel tales, among them Grace Paley's "Goodbye and Good Luck," Isaac Bashevis Singer's "Gimpel the Fool" (in Bellow's translation), Philip Roth's "Epstein," Sholom Aleichem's "On Account of a Hat," and Bernard Malamud's "The Magic Barrel." Bellow is also the translator of Sholom Aleichem's "Eternal Life" in *A Treasury of Yiddish Stories,* ed. Howe and Greenberg (New York, 1953).

[2] Stanley Kunitz, ed., *Twentieth Century Authors,* First Supplement (New York, 1955), p. 73.

childhood and the ample information on his professional and personal life that we realize, by contrast, how poorly documented are the lives of our other characters and how thinly their roots have been sketched. Schlemiel portrayals that emphasize economic or social insecurity have no need for such sensuous background: in fact, the very thinness of personal history brings out in bolder relief the uncertainty of the character's position and destiny. But *Herzog*, which explores the psychology of the schlemiel, necessarily dips into childhood to explain the responses of the adult.

His father, Herzog candidly recalls, was an urbane Menahem Mendl:

> In 1913 he bought a piece of land near Valleyfield, Quebec, and failed as a farmer. Then he came into town and failed as a baker; failed in the dry-goods business; failed as a jobber; failed as a sack manufacturer in the War, when no one else failed. He failed as a junk dealer. Then he became a marriage broker and failed—too short-tempered and blunt. And now he was failing as a bootlegger, on the run from the Provincial Liquor Commission. Making a bit of a living.[3]

At the same time, this is the father, "a sacred being, a king." And as for Herzog's mother, she pampered and over-protected the children. The daughter must have piano lessons. Her precious Moses must grow up to be a great *lamden*—a rabbi. She pulled him on a sled, sacrificing her strength to her children. Moses, the Jewish immigrant child, "dear little Yingele," was the traditional repository of parental dreams. Center of the universe, he experienced, as he tells us, "a wider range of human feelings than he had ever again been able to find." The boy is the focus of love, but the failing father gives ominous warning of things that might lie ahead. Here, on the familial level, is the theological paradox, domesticated: the Jew as the repository of God's Torah, His hope, living in the temporal world as one of a persecuted, despised minority. The Jewish son, like Herzog, experiences the paradox in his own home. Elected to embody all the unfulfilled aspirations of his parents, he knows before he sets out that he will never achieve them: his father's presence tells him so. Yet, as in the national idea of election, the warmth and love given to the child communicate a sense of importance, an idea of worth and a framework of meaning that are never entirely eradicated in spite of all subsequent battering. Herzog writes his unfinished, unposted letters. He is nonetheless able to say: "*I* am Herzog. I have to *be* that man. There is no one else to do it."

The family relationship has been singled out as crucial in establishing the basic psychodynamics of Jewish humor. It is claimed that

---

[3] Saul Bellow, *Herzog* (New York, 1964), p. 137. The other extended quotations are from pages 230, 104–5, 170, 238, 119–20, 86, and 77.

the Jewish comic, or schlemiel, remains a "boy-man" even when fully
grown, largely because of "the Jewish mother's destructive domination,
her demands for love and success from her son which are linked to
her refusal to grant him the independence required for manhood." [4]
Recent American Jewish literature supplies sufficient testimony on
this subject, from the lowbrow *How to Be a Jewish Mother* through
the black humor of Lenny Bruce and Bruce Jay Friedman, to *Portnoy's
Complaint* by Philip Roth. But the example of Herzog would lead us
to temper this generalization somewhat, since it suggests that demands
for love and success may be constructive as well as the opposite. Most
works emphasize the uses of love as a means of domination, and the
exaggerated expectations of success as a catalyst to failure. Bellow is
one of the very few American Jewish writers to consider and present
another interpretation of the same observable phenomena: that love
and those expectations explain why Herzog "characteristically, obstinately, defiantly, blindly but without sufficient courage or intelligence
tried to be a *marvelous* Herzog, a Herzog who, perhaps clumsily, tried
to live out marvelous qualities vaguely comprehended." The family
situation, smothering the boy in more love than he would easily find
again; endowing him with greater importance than his peers would
concede him; placing him at the center of a comprehended circle,
whereas he would subsequently find himself floating around some ill-
defined circumference; all this blesses the child with a secure sense
of self even as it bedevils his later abilities to "get along." Herzog is
a "heart's hog," [5] attempting the marvelous, even as he makes an
ironic, schlemiel's progress toward it; and for this his childhood is,
as he knows, largely responsible.

Herzog's final self-acceptance has been attacked, and vehemently,
as a "fatty sigh of middle-class intellectual contentment." [6] The resolution of the book has been assailed, even by friendly critics, as offering either too little or too much. Harold Fisch, writing on "The
Hero as Jew," concurs with the widespread acceptance of *Herzog* as
"an attempt to reach beyond mere victim-literature to some more
positive ground of hope" but finds that actually "Herzog does not
go anywhere." "The book does not ultimately offer salvation, and in

---

[4] Albert Goldman, "Boy-man Schlemihl: The Jewish Element in American Humor," p. 8. (In *Explorations*, pp. 3–17, eds., Murray Mindlin & Chaim Bernant,
London: 1967.
[5] G. P. Elliot, "Hurtsog, Hairtsog, Heart's Hog?," *Nation*, October 19, 1964, pp.
252–54.
[6] John W. Aldridge, "The Complacency of *Herzog*," in *Saul Bellow and the
Critics*, ed. Irving Malin (New York, 1967), p. 210.

that sense it fails as a twentieth-century epistle from the Hebrews." [7]
Theodore Solotaroff, by contrast, complains that the conclusion is too
affirmative: "The elegiac prose of the closing section is so naturally
luminous and moving that one tends to overlook the fact that it is
quietly burying most of the issues that earlier had been raised in connection with its relations to society." [8] And in fact the general critical
tendency has been to find fault with its ability to resolve at all: "Herzog is finally as arrogantly complacent in his new-found affirmative
position . . . as Bellow dares to allow him to be." [9]

From the standpoint of schlemiel-literature, this criticism is entirely
beside the point. Insofar as the schlemiel is a comic hero, he is promised a "happy ending," if not in the normal sense, then at least in his
own self-appraisal. Along the way we may expect the sacrifice of male
initiative, pride, dignity and socioeconomic achievement—and all of
these expectations are fulfilled—but the conditions of the sacrificial
game require that at least one runner, wisely-chastened, optimistic,
self-accepting, must reach base. When Herzog says (to the horror of
critics), "I am pretty well satisfied to be, to be just as it is willed, and
for as long as I may remain in occupancy," he is within the same convention as virtually all the figures we have previously discussed. In
every conceivable empirical test the schlemiel may fail, but he never
fails in his final self-acceptance; otherwise the whole premise of the
loser-as-victor would be destroyed.

Then, too, criticism of Herzog's complacency does not seem to take
into account the degree to which Herzog is an ironic hero, still in the
schlemiel tradition. The ironic smugness is present in the very first
sentence, for the man who says "If I'm out of my mind, it's all right
with me" already appears to be "pretty well satisfied to be just as it
is willed." On the other hand, Herzog can go further in self-criticism
than even the severest of his critics, and he is usually more unsparing,
as well as wittier, in pointing up his own flaws. As he sits, for example, in the city courthouse:

> Herzog discovered that he had been sitting, legs elegantly crossed,
> the jagged oval rim of his hat pressed on his thigh, his striped jacket
> still buttoned and strained by his eager posture, that he had been
> watching all that happened with his look of intelligent composure, of
> charm and sympathy—like the old song, he thought, the one that goes,
> "There's flies on me, there's flies on you, but there ain't no flies on

[7] Harold Fisch, "The Hero as Jew: Reflections on *Herzog*," *Judaism* 18, no. 1
(Winter 1968): 52.
[8] Theodore Solotaroff, "Napoleon Street and After," *Commentary* 38 (December
1964): 66.
[9] Aldridge, "The Complacency of *Herzog*," p. 210.

Jesus." A man who looked so fine and humane would be outside police jurisdiction, immune to lower forms of suffering and punishment.

Herzog is under no prolonged illusion about his Christlike goodness. He recognizes that his sympathy is socially meaningless and morally fattening, and he mocks it. So too his multifaceted importance to the human race:

> The mirror of the gum machine revealed to Herzog how pale he was, unhealthy—wisps from his coat and wool scarf, his hat and brows, twisting and flaming outward in the overfull light and exposing the sphere of his face, the face of a man who was keeping up a front. Herzog smiled at this earlier avatar of his life, at Herzog the victim, Herzog the would-be lover, Herzog the man on whom the world depended for certain intellectual work, to change history, to influence the development of civilization. Several boxes of stale paper under his bed in Philadelphia were going to produce this very significant result.

Or again, here is Moses as he sees himself in the frequent role of lover:

> And Herzog thought . . . is this really possible? Have all the traditions, passions, renunciations, virtues, gems, and masterpieces of Hebrew discipline and all the rest of it—rhetoric, a lot of it, but containing true facts—brought me to these untidy green sheets, and this rippled mattress?

Surely Solotaroff is right when he says that irony here "takes on the status of an ontological principle." Even the final affirmation follows a crisis of self-doubt: "But this intensity, doesn't it mean anything? Is it an idiot joy that makes this animal, the most peculiar animal of all, exclaim something? And he thinks this reaction a sign, a proof, of eternity?" If Herzog does ultimately accept himself, he does so in the spirit of compromise.

The ending is also typical of schlemiel conclusions in that the character's salvation, not his benevolence, is its exclusive concern. The saint is concerned for others and is canonized for his ability to affect attitudinal or substantive change. While he too, like our hero, risks being thought a fool, his glory is invariably recognized, perhaps posthumously, but without equivocation. Salvation for the schlemiel, to the contrary, is always partial and personal. He does not affirm the objective presence of goodness, but merely the right and the need to believe in it as one component of the human personality. Herzog is always being exposed to social evils, yet always, by his own admission, as a spectator whose concerns are his own feelings and his own conscience. It may be, as Norman Mailer has complained, that with *Herzog* the reality of the novel has coagulated into mere moral earnest-

ess. This is the limitation of all schlemiel works, a seemingly inevitable quality of the genre. What once appeared in the novel as the
individual's interaction with his society has now narrowed to a study
of the individual's reaction to society. The modern novel of sensi-
bilities does not appear to be a suitable medium for what Mailer calls
"cutting a swath across the face of society," [10] for society is present
only insofar as it cuts a swath across the face of the protagonist.
Herzog is, to the dismay of activists, predicated on a certain in-
eluctable unsatisfactoriness in the environment. Had the novel presented serious possibilities for ameliorative social action, then Herzog's
reflective intelligence and his irony would have been a crime. But
Herzog is neither judge, counsel, nor defendant. In the critical courtroom sequence he appears as simply one of the millions who must
share his place in the city with a woman capable of beating her child
to death. If Herzog's pain were the result solely of Madeleine's in-
fidelity and Gersbach's deceit, the "problem of evil" might have
seemed chimerical or paranoiac. Had Herzog's knowledge of evil come
from his readings, it would have seemed abstract, intellectual. As observer in the courtroom, Herzog becomes a witness to horrors far
greater than any in his own experience, and more deeply personalized
than those of history or the daily news. He is exposed to life-size bar-
barians, his neighbors, in a brutal challenge to his apple-cheeked
humanism.

> I fail to understand! thought Herzog, . . . but this is the difficulty
> with people who spend their lives in humane studies and therefore
> imagine once cruelty has been described in books it is ended. Of course
> he really knew better—understood that human beings *would* not live so
> as to be understood by the Herzogs. Why should they?

Having witnessed the trial, Herzog blindly stumbles away, into the
path of a cripple whose "eyes, prominent, severe, still kept him standing, identifying him thoroughly, fully, deeply, as a fool. Again—silently—*Thou fool!*" The events of the sequence remind us of Nathanael West,[11] except that Bellow takes pains to keep Herzog decidedly unrealistic. When he is finally alone, Herzog goes over in
his mind what he has seen and tries to salvage some human meaning
for the murdered boy. It is hardly accidental that the murder drama-

10 Norman Mailer, "Modes and Mutations: Quick Comments on the Modern
American Novel," *Commentary* 41 (March 1966): 39. Mailer's own Sam Slovoda, in
"The Man Who Studied Yoga," might have been a rather lovable (slob, slovenly)
schlemiel had the author not imposed on his character a sour intelligence and the
longing to be a hero. As it is, he is "a man who seeks to live in such a way as to
void pain, and succeeds merely in avoiding pleasure."
11 See Leslie Fiedler, *Love and Death in the American Novel* (New York, 1960),
p. 464, for a discussion of *Miss Lonelyhearts* as schlemiel-everyman.

tized for Herzog is just the sort of murder from which no shred of meaning can be extracted, one which like Auschwitz stands outside the scope of rational thought. Herzog "experienced nothing but his own *human feelings,* in which he found nothing of use." The only resolution he draws—and that irrationally—is to protect his own child.

The courtroom drama is a "play within a play," exploring the subject's relation to what is basest in the modern world. These are horrors that cannot qualify as economic or social problems. Nothing *can* be gained for the murdered boy, no symbolic assurance that the world will be better for his death, no religious murmurings, no personal revelations. Nothing is learned from the murder of this child or from the murders of millions of such children. Now Herzog is a kind, thoughtful humanist, and what is he to do with the anguish dumped on his doorstep? His response is not effective, merely affective. When his life touches the uncomfortable, he struggles to understand it. He does not, however, give up his life to it. The irony merely intensifies as Herzog continues to worry about his soul (*his* soul!) on a trip through Hades. Herzog knows this is petty (petit) and knows also it is necessary because that is his function as a human being. "The strength of a man's virtue or spiritual capacity measured by his ordinary life."

Elsewhere Bellow has written: "We make what we can of our condition with the means available. We must accept the mixture as we find it—the impurity of it, the tragedy of it, the hope of it." [12] It is just this emphasis on *mixture* that distinguishes Herzog and other Jewish schlemiels from the meek Christians like Melville's Billy Budd or Faulkner's fabled corporal. Schlemiels are not creatures of the Manichean imagination: even Charlie Chaplin's *The Great Dictator* divides the alternatives of civilization too sharply between innocence and guilt to be an authentic part of the genre. Though the moral dilemma must always be presented as a confrontation between opposites, its tone is determined by the implied purity of each faction. Herzog and his comic forebears are themselves a little tainted; never having known the primal innocence of Eden, they do not pull up their skirts in outrage at the appearance of villainy, and having no ascetic inclinations, their own chances of "staying clean" are slight. The otherworldly purity of the saints, products of the Christian literary imagination, is best suggested by their silence or stuttering: holiness beyond speech. The stained humanity of the schlemiel pours out in obsessive verbosity. Yet to say that the polarization between good and evil is less extreme is not to imply that the moral concern is any the less acute. In an article written concurrently with the last parts of *Herzog,* Bellow puts the proposition as follows:

> either we want life to continue or we do not. If we don't want to continue, why write books? The wish for death is powerful and silent. It respects actions; it has no need of words.
> But if we answer yes, we do want it to continue, we are liable to be asked how. In what form shall life be justified? That is the essence of the moral question. We call a writer moral to the degree that his imagination indicates to us how we may answer naturally, without strained arguments, with a spontaneous, mysterious proof that has no need to argue with despair.[13]

Herzog is such an attempt at proof.

What sets Herzog apart from the characters previously discussed is his intelligence, and more particularly, his self-consciousness. In *Menahem Mendl,* Sholom Aleichem juxtaposes the life-styles of two characters for ironic effect, but here the protagonist juggles his own distinct levels of existence. Not only does Herzog elucidate his opinions and clarify his feelings, he is able, as an intellectual and a professor of history, to relate those opinions and feelings to the broader flow of Western thought. Thus we find Herzog raising many of his own questions on the nature of the fool:

> he insisted on being the ingénu whose earnestness made his own heart flutter—*zisse n'shamele,* a sweet little soul, Tennie had called Moses. At forty, to earn such a banal reputation! His forehead grew wet. Such stupidity deserved harsher punishment—a sickness, a jail sentence. . . . Still, extreme self-abuse was not really interesting to him, either. . . . Not to be a fool might not be worth the difficult alternatives. Anyway, who was that non-fool? Was it the power-lover, who bent the public to his will . . . the organizational realist? Now wouldn't it be nice to be one? But Herzog worked under different orders—doing, he trusted, the work of the future. The revolutions of the twentieth century, the liberation of the masses by production, created private life but gave nothing to fill it with. This was where such as he came in. The progress of civilization—indeed, the survival of civilization—depended on the successes of Moses E. Herzog.

Is the fool escaping his adult responsibilities, or is he alone fulfilling them? If the only alternatives are the Ayn Rand objectivists and Herzogian innocents, may the progress of civilization not indeed depend upon him?

Not the author or reader, but the character himself raises these questions. Maynard Mack has written that comedy depends on our remaining outside, as spectators, in a position from which we may

---

[13] Saul Bellow, "Writer as Moralist," *Atlantic,* March 1963, p. 62.

notice the discrepancies between the facades of personalities as they present themselves, and these personalities as they actually are. "The point of view that ours must be continuous with in comedy is not the character's but the author's." [14] Though true for classical comedy, this description does not fit *Herzog*. Bellow has deliberately—how deliberately only a careful study of syntax will reveal—written the entire book from the character's own point of view, allowing him to observe and note all the discrepancies, and thereby making him the conductor of humor. Because comedy does depend on discrepancies between surface and substance, Herzog is allowed at least two modes of observation: the letters, a direct means of externalizing his concerns; and indirect narration, also reflecting the protagonist's point of view, but permitting a wider inclusion of conversation and event. The rapid transition from one to the other sometimes accounts for the comic tone, as when Moses, fleeing from the sex-priestess, Ramona, writes political kudos to Stevenson and Nehru while his unsteady thoughts hurtle him back and forth to and from his personal involvements. More often, within the indirect narration itself, Herzog reveals the self he admires side by side with the self he scorns:

> The house in Ludeyville was bought when Madeleine became pregnant. It seemed the ideal place to work out the problems Herzog had become involved with in *The Phenomenology of Mind*—the importance of the "law of the heart" in Western traditions, the origins of moral sentimentalism and related matters, on which he had distinctly different ideas. He was going—he smiled secretly now, admitting it—to wrap the subject up, to pull the carpet from under all other scholars, show them what was what, stun them, expose their triviality once and for all. It was not simple vanity, but a sense of responsibility that was the underlying motive. That he would say for himself. He was a *bien pensant* type. He took seriously Heinrich Heine's belief that the words of Rousseau had turned into the bloody machine of Robespierre, that Kant and Fichte were deadlier than armies. He had a small foundation grant, and his twenty-thousand-dollar legacy from Father Herzog went into the country place.

The irony of "It seemed" and "He was going" in the second and third sentences derives from the superimposition of Herzog's present knowledge of himself over past hopes. He mocks both his unfulfilled expectations and the very substance of his ideas. The recognition that he is a "bien pensant type" is like his perception, cited earlier, that he is like the old song "There's flies on me, there's flies on you, but there ain't no flies on Jesus." He is ironic about his would-be goodness, suspicious of its motives, and scornful of its inutility. Looking back

14 Maynard Mack, *"Joseph Andrews* and *Pamela,"* in *Fielding: A Collection of Critical Essays,* ed. R. Paulson (Englewood Cliffs, N.J., 1962), p. 58.

on the ambitious scholar he was, he smiles at his boy-scout meritoriousness. And the final juxtaposition of his sources of income is the unkindest cut of all, the small foundation grant with the big legacy, the earnings of the great intellectual overshadowed by the rewards of the dutiful boy. Here the character, aware and amused by the dismal gap between "is" and "would have been," makes himself his own comic butt.

Herzog's internalization of irony sets him apart from Bloom, from whose saga his name alone is lifted: in *Ulysses*, Joyce has placed in apposition "the persuasive surfaces of personalities as they see themselves, and these characters as they are," even when he seems to be offering a stream of consciousness. The very form of the mock epic imposes the shadow of his heroic predecessor over a dwarfed Bloom. Joyce called his work *Ulysses*, but Herzog casts his own little light. In *Herzog*, the protagonist is endowed with the complexity of mind and ironic vision that in *Ulysses* remains the prerogative of the author. The result is not an ironic exposure of life, but rather an ironic life, exposed.

Herzog is finally the character who lives according to a twofold perception of himself in relation to the world, both giant and dwarf, alien and center of the universe, failure and success, cuckold and great lover, intellectual and schlemiel. The single reality of the naturalists is for him insufficient. To Sandor Himmelstein, the deformed lawyer, he protests:

> "And you think a fact is what's nasty."
> "Facts *are* nasty."
> "You think they're true because they're nasty."

To James Hoffa, who shares this "angry single-mindedness," he considers saying: "What makes you think realism must be brutal?" Herzog fights the Wasteland rhetoricians, "The vision of mankind as a lot of cannibals, running in packs, gibbering, bewailing its own murders, pressing out the living world as dead excrement." He points out how corrupting is the effect of this mode of perception on both the individual and on society. Even as he is insisting on the need for the pumping heart, for "moral realities," he jibes at himself:

> Do not deceive yourself, dear Moses Elkanah, with childish jingles and Mother Goose. Hearts quaking with cheap and feeble charity or oozing potato love have not written history.

Time and again he makes fun of his search for love and belief in love as a female pursuit, which in the terms of this novel is no flattering tribute. Yet, finally, when all is said and written, Herzog addresses himself seriously, if not earnestly, to his and, as he sees it, the world's situation: "We must get it out of our heads that this is a doomed time, that we are waiting for the end, and the rest of it, mere junk from fashionable magazines." The intellectual rejection of pessimism is ultimately coupled with a psychological readiness to accept, even bless, the future. The ironic life accepts itself. "Anyway, can I pretend that I have much choice?"

Because Herzog's irony is internalized, there is less than the usual ironic distance between author and character. This opens the book to charges of sentimentality, since modern literature and literary criticism are very much concerned with distances and masks, and we are frankly unaccustomed to committing our disbelief to the hands of a reliable narrator. In this work, the author's position or point of view is not noticeably different from the protagonist's. Herzog steers his pumping heart between the Scylla of Madeleine ("Feel? Don't give me that line of platitudes about feelings") and the Charybdis of Valentine, the false commercialized whirlpool of a heart. He controls the novel even when he is not yet in control of himself. Bellow has written a humanist novel, presenting one individual's life—a life by all standards a near-failure—which in its intelligence and energy commands our attention and affection. *Herzog,* a study of irony as a modern form of moral vision, is the more *engagé* because of Saul Bellow's minimal irony about his subject.

The Battle of the Sexes in
Three Bellow Novels

by Victoria Sullivan

Saul Bellow is not a sexist. The women in his novels are like the men, a sad, crazy, mixed-up lot. They fall into two basic categories: the victims and the victimizers, the latter tending to be more colorful. If they appear less three-dimensional than the men, and if they are certainly less sensitive than Doris Lessing's heroines, this is the natural consequence of novels in which the protagonist tends to be a middle-aged Jewish male with a world view to match his ethnic bias. Women are very important to him, but he often finds them strange, illogical, and disturbing. They represent one more pressure on his already over-burdened psyche. He is a man who finds it difficult to love; his marriages fail; he is a weekend father. His relations with the opposite sex are fraught with tension and pain. Because the narrative method is one that filters women through his consciousness, women possess reality only as they act upon him. However, even such a limitation in point of view does not usually produce the Henry Miller type of distortion or Philip Roth fantasy figures, because the Bellow protagonist recognizes, at the least, that women are complex. He does not underestimate his antagonists in the battle of the sexes.

Misery is the common state of the Bellow "hero"; some, such as the comic rain king Henderson, struggle against this, and others, such as Tommy Wilhelm, just give up. But however down and out the "hero" is, there is still, somewhere, a willing female who ministers to his needs. And he has many needs: he is vain; he fears aging; he has difficulty maintaining his pride in a hostile environment; even his clothes don't suit him. Because he is decidedly heterosexual, he must also worry about his appeal to women. To make life still more difficult, there is a counterpart to the willing female: the castrating wife. This woman feeds on human flesh, preferably her husband's. She is either a hysteric or a cold fish, sometimes both. The hero's journey through life is shaped to a great extent by his encounters with these various females. Like Odysseus, he attempts to subdue the wily Circes; unlike Odysseus, he rarely succeeds.

Despite their easy categorization into two basic types—the destructive ones who victimize the hero, and the nurturers who tend to be his victims—Bellow's women are not merely sex objects. Each is an individual with a full range of idiosyncracies. They all have souls and they all suffer. Because their only roles in the novels are those they play in the protagonist's life, they are all girl friends, wives, or mothers. They have no other role, such as friend, colleague, doctor, or lawyer. Certainly, their sexual attractiveness is among their most salient features, or, as in the case of ex-wives, their lack of attractiveness. For some reason, almost all Bellow ex-wives wear bangs and have cold eyes and cold voices; maybe this is the essence of ex-wives. They are also lethal on the telephone. Wilhelm almost passes out in a phone booth talking to Margaret—his "ex-wife" in the sense that he has separated from her; just listening to her voice, he has difficulty breathing—the Medusa effect over the wires.

The sexual battle rages in Bellow's novels, with small losses and gains experienced on both sides. There are few real armistices, only temporary holding actions. The men and women bear many scars, for it is a wearing battle. A novel about a man who is willing to risk all, such as Henderson, may end with the hope of happiness, the hint of conjugal pleasure. But for the player who is a loser, such as Wilhelm, there is little hope. The norm is probably Herzog, victim of one voracious female but in easy control of several others. The message of Bellow's novels is clear: don't seek happiness in love; it is a mine-laden battlefield.

I

The Jewish penchant for noisy suffering reaches its zenith in Moses Herzog, who drags his battered ego across Europe, into the Berkshires, out to Chicago and back, and on a brief and ludicrous trip to Martha's Vineyard. Always there are women to tend to him, sweet creatures of the flesh who seek to heal the wounds inflicted by life in general but also by the virulent Madeleine, Herzog's second wife. In Poland there is plump, pink Wanda. Once there was delightful Japanese Sono, a sort of built-in Greenwich Village geisha, with her steaming hot baths, her massages, and her bad English. Finally, on the Upper West Side of Manhattan, there is dark, sensuous Ramona, probably in her late thirties (she keeps her age a secret) and therefore a little shopworn by middle-aged male standards, but still eager to give of herself.

After the abortive Martha's Vineyard sojourn, Ramona is desperate
to see herself as involved in Herzog's speedy return:

> Ramona said, "Perhaps some lovely woman scared you on the train,
> and you turned back to your Ramona."
> "Oh . . ." said Herzog.
> Her theme was her power to make him happy. Thinking of Ramona
> with her intoxicating eyes and robust breasts, her short but gentle legs,
> her Carmen airs, thievishly seductive, her skill in the sack (defeating
> invisible rivals), he felt she did not exaggerate. The facts supported her
> claim.[1]

Herzog never really falls for Ramona; perhaps she is too kind, too
giving, too available. As an intellectual and a man of the world, he
is fascinated by her elaborate seductive rituals—the gourmet shrimp
dishes, the fine expensive wine, the erotic Middle Eastern music on
the phonograph, and the ultimate in black lace underwear—but he
manages to maintain his objectivity toward her at all times:

> Ramona had Moses' complete sympathy—a woman in her thirties, suc-
> cessful in business, independent, but still giving such suppers to gen-
> tlemen friends. But in times like these, how should a woman steer her
> heart to fulfillment? In emancipated New York, man and woman, gaud-
> ily disguised, like two savages belonging to hostile tribes, confront each
> other. The man wants to deceive, and then to disengage himself; the
> woman's strategy is to disarm and detain him. And this is Ramona, a
> woman who knows how to look after herself. (p. 232)

But does she really know how to look after herself, or is this Herzog's
blindness speaking? What she wants is love, security, respect; what she
receives is half-amused admiration of her "skill in the sack." She takes
care of him, she protects him, but ultimately, for all her efforts, Ramona never touches Herzog as deeply as the ball-breaking Madeleine,
the true savage. For Herzog, men and women really do come from
"hostile tribes," and he relishes most those confrontations that prove
most hostile.

Madeleine is a flesh-and-blood, walking, talking male fantasy of a
femme fatale, an eternal Eve. Of course she is beautiful. She is also
cunning, unprincipled, sexy, cold, dependent, undependable, fiercely
intellectual, totally unsympathetic—but still a woman whom Herzog's
lawyer Sandor Himmelstein characterizes as "some dish." Even before
their marriage her love-hate response to Herzog is perfectly clear:

> She wanted him there at night. She would even, half with rancor, take
> his hand and put it on her breast as they were falling asleep. But in

[1] *Herzog* (Greenwich, Conn.: Fawcett Publications, 1964), p. 187. All quotations
are from this paper edition and are cited parenthetically in the text by page number only.

the morning she would have liked him to disappear. And he was not used to this; he was used to being a favorite. (p. 140)

Her ambivalent sexual attitude is an obvious character trait. Why then does this little boy-man who wants to be taken care of, this suffering Herzog, seek out such a woman? Why does he pursue her to the very steps of the Catholic Church (to which she has converted in a typically hysteric reaction to her unhappy Jewish childhood)? The pleasures provided are surely perverse. Madeleine is a masochist's delight. After making love with her husband,

> she turned on the light, picked up one of those dusty Russian folios, put it on her chest, and started to read away. As I was leaving her body, she was reaching for the book. Not a kiss. Not a last touch. Only her nose, twitching. (p. 78)

It is apparently her bitchiness—and she is a classic bitch—and her inviolate egotism that excites him. She cuckolds him with his best friend; she throws him out of the house for which he has just signed a lease; she tries to prevent him from seeing his daughter; she tells her aunt that he's no good in bed; and still he can't stop being obsessed with her. Madeleine keeps him wallowing in bathos, and this is her secret power: she recognizes his need to suffer, and she feeds it. Meanwhile, poor Ramona, with her endless patience, must sit and listen to Herzog's monologues about the malevolent Madeleine:

> "Madeleine's greatest ambition, I think, is to fall in love. This is the deepest part of the joke about her. Then there's her grand style. Her tics. To give the bitch her due, she is beautiful. She adores being the center of attention. In one of those fur-trimmed suits she struts in, with her deep color and blue eyes. And when she has an audience and begins spellbinding, there's a kind of flat pass she makes with the palm of her hand, and her nose twitches like a rudder, and by and by one brow joins in and begins to rise, rise." (p. 235)

Totally involved in compiling this meticulous, resentful catalogue of her mannerisms, Herzog is insensitive to the needs and feelings of the woman he is with, Ramona.

This is perhaps the essential trait of the self-involved Moses Herzog type: insensitivity toward others. Dr. Karen Horney maintains that in the neurotic, "the ability to love is greatly impaired," [2] and certainly Herzog illustrates this point. His self-absorption leaves him capable of infatuation or obsession, but hardly of love. Thus, for Herzog, women necessarily fall into the category of either victim or victimizer; he can have no other relationship with a woman, for sympathetic women don't understand his need to be kicked in the groin, and the Made-

[2] *Self-Analysis* (London: Routledge & Kegan Paul, 1942), p. 20.

leines who do kick him are cold, blue-eyed bitches. Of course, he refuses to see the logic of his life pattern, and can therefore be free to indulge himself in great bouts of self-pity. In one of his frequent moments of musing on life, he writes:

> Will never understand what women want. What do they want? They eat green salad and drink human blood.[3] (p. 56)

A fine image, but hardly more accurate than Esther Greenwood's perceptions about men in *The Bell Jar*:

> And I knew that in spite of all the roses and kisses and restaurant dinners a man showered on a woman before he married her, what he secretly wanted when the wedding service ended was for her to flatten out underneath his feet like Mrs. Willard's kitchen mat.[4]

The problem in both cases is similar: a paranoid anxiety that the world is designed to make one miserable, and only fast footwork and constant vigilance can prevent one from being exploited endlessly in sexual combat. Esther and Herzog share an ironic world view; they are not without humor in their characterizations of others, but their own insecurities lead them to place people in boxes too narrow to be just. They become convinced that they are the only truly sensitive souls. With such an attitude, members of the opposite sex become part of the general conspiracy.

II

Tommy Wilhelm (*Seize the Day*) is another protagonist with a persecution complex, but in his case it is quite justified. Measured by any standard of success, he is a failure. Wilhelm lives in the Hotel Gloriana, home of aging Upper West Side Broadway types whom life has passed by, but being younger than they—he is only in his forties—he ought not to belong there. He has left his wife, but she won't divorce him. He has no job. He is a massive disappointment to all who know him: his father, a doctor, who won't lend him money when he needs it most; his mother, now dead, who still occasionally haunts his memory; his wife, who does everything possible to thwart him, even refusing to file a joint tax return; and his mistress, Olive, a rather shadowy figure in the novel, who supposedly wants to marry him.

---

[3] Interestingly, Herzog shares this confusion with Sigmund Freud, who wrote in a letter to Marie Bonaparte: "the great question that has never been answered and which I have not been able to answer, despite my thirty years of research into the feminine soul, is 'What does a woman want?' " Quoted in Ernest Jones, *The Life and Work of Sigmund Freud*, vol. II (New York), p. 421.

[4] Sylvia Plath, *The Bell Jar* (London: Faber & Faber, 1966).

Wilhelm is the tragicomic ineffectual modern American husband, the cartoon husband of the fifties, victim of the rise of what has been labeled American Momism. His wife Margaret, with her Mamie Eisenhower bangs, is cold, hard, and disagreeable. She sucks the life from Tommy, and he is dying of suffocation. But she is still a model mother who stays home with the kids, refusing to work even though Tommy is out of a job. She is righteously indignant at his even raising the issue: "Absolutely not. I'm not going to have two young children running loose." [5] She is exactly in the tradition of the feminine mystique. When Tommy points out that the boys are not exactly babies—one is fourteen and the other, almost ten—she quickly responds with the specter of teen-age gangs. Margaret has all the *Ladies Home Journal* replies at hand; she is not going to be maneuvered into a position she does not want. So Tommy the suffering male must bear the burden of totally financing this domestic establishment, the comforts of which he no longer partakes.

Margaret is depicted as a cunning sadist:

> Margaret would tell him he did not really want a divorce; he was afraid of it. He cried, "Take everything I've got, Margaret. Let me go to Reno. Don't you want to marry again?" No. She went out with other men, but took his money. She lived in order to punish him. (p. 94)

Clearly, this is Wilhelm's interpretation of her life motivation; what Margaret might tell us is a story we never hear. As he tells it, she deprives him of home, hearth, children, and even the family dog, which he loves:

> Four years ago when we broke up I gave her everything—goods, furniture, savings. I tried to show good will, but I didn't get anywhere. Why when I wanted Scissors, the dog, because the animal and I were so attached to each other—it was bad enough to leave the kids—she absolutely refused me. Not that she cared a damn about that animal. (p. 47)

She is obviously a wretched woman, a certified ball-breaker, and more than a match for poor Tommy. A Mailer hero would sodomize her, toss her out the window, and be done with her. But Wilhelm's reaction is one of impotent rage. In one of the final scenes of the novel he is on the phone with her, begging for understanding and mercy:

> "You must realize you're killing me. . . . Margaret, go easy on me. . . . I'm at the end of my rope. . . . How can you treat someone like this whom you lived with so long. Who gave you the best of himself. Who tried. Who loved you." (pp. 112, 113, 114)

[5] *Seize the Day* (New York: Viking, 1956), p. 113. All quotations are from the paper edition.

Her reply cuts through his bathos like an icy knife: "How did you imagine it was going to be—big shot? Everything made smooth for you?" Wilhelm is reduced to shrieking and crying, and in a final castrating gesture, Margaret asks him to call her when he has "something sensible to say." In absolute frustration, he tries to tear the phone from the wall.

Of course, to balance Margaret there is the "other woman," Olive, but she does not provide very formidable opposition. Small, dark, and Catholic, she appears too weak to save anyone, though her mere existence in his life is doubtless of value to him in his struggle to avoid going under totally. Ultimately, Olive is dominated by other, more powerful men in her life: her father and her priest. For Wilhelm, this provides further embarrassment: "Up in Roxbury he had to go and explain to the priest, who was not sympathetic." (p. 94) Olive gives sexual solace and affection, but she seems as victimized by life as Wilhelm:

> When she would get up late on Sunday morning she would wake him almost in tears at being late for Mass. . . . he would rush her to church and drive in second gear in his forgetful way, trying to apologize to calm her. She got out a block from church to avoid gossip. (p. 94).

She wants to nurture him—she is that sweet sort of woman—but she possesses no really potent weapons in the battle against the powerful Margaret. Even her willingness to marry outside of the Church is thwarted by Margaret's refusal to divorce Tommy. Olive's role in the novel is slight; at most, she is a pathetic footnote to the detailing of Wilhelm's demise. The man is too weak to win the struggle with Margaret. She will win; from what we see of her, she has a stronger stomach and more sheer survival capacity than her indecisive husband. Such men are frequently the casualties of modern marriage—they have too much honor to just run away from the situation, but too little self-confidence to carve a successful new life.

III

Perhaps the most obviously successful Bellow "hero" is Eugene Henderson, the mad, gargantuan African rain king. Despite the failure of his first marriage and the shakiness of his second, he is a comic man. He is also a chaotic man, and of course he is a great sufferer even though he is not a Jew. What he seeks is some sort of meaning in life, and for this he runs away to Africa. Like Herzog, he is pursued by his own internal demons. He is also pursued by women. What is it that makes these Bellow men irresistible to women? In Henderson's case it is a genuine mystery, even to himself.

His first wife, Frances, is "a remarkable person, handsome, tall, elegant, sinewy, with long arms and golden hair, private, fertile, and quiet. None of her family can quarrel with me if I add that she is a schizophrenic, for she certainly is that." [6] Marrying a withdrawn schizophrenic is a typical Henderson act; insanity clearly attracts him. He is a collector of oddities and extremes. He is also quite genuinely zany, and perhaps this is the source of his appeal—the sheer outrageousness of the man. The major female character in the novel and in his life is his second wife, Lily, a large woman who pursued him with boundless energy and passion before their marriage. It is she who seduced him when he was still married to Frances. It is she who chased him across Europe and cornered him in France, where, like Ramona, she insisted upon her special ability to satisfy his need:

> "You think you can live without me, but you can't," she said, "any more than I can live without you. The sadness just drowns me." (pp. 17–18)

Sentimentality and moralizing are her forte. But she discovers after the fact that actually living with Henderson is tantamount to walking straight into a surreal nightmare. He plagues her any way he can: in one scene the fifty-five-year-old Henderson sits on an expensive resort beach with a slingshot, roaring drunk, his leg in an enormous dirty cast, shooting stones at bottles and watching them shatter—a practice frowned upon by the beautiful people. It is his wife to whom they complain.

Lily, with her big white face, is herself no prize. Like most Bellow women, she is a touch crazy, a touch perverse, and, as Henderson points out on several occasions, her hygienic habits are questionable. She doesn't change her underwear as often as she might, and as superintendent of his home, she can be mightily deficient:

> she herself was not very cleanly, and for one reason or another we couldn't get anyone from the neighborhood to do the cleaning. Yes, she swept up once in a while, but towards the door and not out of it, so there were mounds of dust in the doorway. (p. 31)

This reminds us of Madeleine Herzog, whose house was also disorderly and dirty, littered with the dusty folios and assorted paraphernalia of a serious graduate student in medieval Russian studies, as well as with "eggshells, chop bones, tin cans under the table, under the sofa . . ." (*Herzog*, p. 77). It seems that these passionate women are

[6] *Henderson the Rain King* (New York: Viking, 1959), p. 4.

slovenly, that they have too much inner fire to make truly fine domestics. In contrast, Herzog's first wife, Daisy, with her straight stocking seams, had been "an utterly steady, reliable woman, responsible to the point of grimness" (*Herzog*, p. 271).

Henderson discovers, as the years pass, a voice inside him shouting "I want, I want, I want," and although he tries to divert it, it will not cease. Marrying Lily has merely suppressed it for a while, but its restless insistence, its demand for unspecified satisfaction reasserts itself. His first analysis of the voice is that it is the cry of lust. But it is not lust. Big, beautiful, dirty Lily with her trembly lips and her boarding-school mumble clearly satisfies Henderson sexually. He loves her mismatched breasts. No, the need is deeper, more basic, and it is his recognition of this that drives him to mythic Africa, land of primal urges. Into the heart of darkness goes Henderson and a native guide Romilayu, whose promise is: "Me tek you far, far" (p. 44). Indeed, the choice turns out to be wise, because Henderson is cleansed by his traumatic experiences there.

He meets fat old Queen Willatale, full of wisdom and strange powers that emanate from her belly, where Henderson must place a sticky kiss. For her he tries to kill a pestilence of frogs, but instead he blows up the only cistern in this arid region and is forced to flee in disgrace. Further into the wilds, he encounters a magnificent king and becomes a king himself, against his will, the king of the magical rain ceremony. He suffers greatly (but not because of some woman, as is the usual case with the Bellow protagonist), and in the course of his adventures the old, crazy, selfish Henderson is broken on the rack of experience, so that he returns home newly compassionate. He has learned wisdom: "I don't think the struggles of desire can ever be won. Ages of longing and willing, willing and longing, and how have they ended? In a draw, dust and dust" (p. 285).

What makes Henderson special among Bellow protagonists becomes clear in the course of the novel: his ego is not based on sexual conquest, and he is thus saved from the energy-draining need to brave the bedroom battle continuously. While on his African quest, he is celibate. Perhaps his age is a factor.[7] Not that he has reached an age of abstinence—he marries and fathers twins in his fifties—rather, the mere act of sex is no longer so competitive. Wilhelm and Herzog are both in their forties, a time when American men frequently suffer a crisis in self-esteem. One common cure for this malady is an affair with

---

[7] Certainly, the fact that Artur Sammler of *Mr. Sammler's Planet* (1970) is in his seventies removes him from the victories and humiliations of the sexual battlefield. He is free to operate his life inside a totally different context of limitations, though not all the characters in that novel are so free.

a younger woman, which occasionally leads to divorce and remarriage, as in the case of Herzog and Madeleine. The word "cure" must be used advisedly, for the action taken is more often a flight from a painful self-confrontation than a true attempt to deal with the problems of middle age. Though vanity is fed, the crisis is merely postponed.

By not seeking to avoid pain, Henderson is able to purge himself. His relationship with King Dahfu and his lovely consort, the underground lioness Atti, is marked by the most extreme experiencing of pity and fear:

> I started to call to him, "King, King, wait, let me go in front of you, for Christ's sake."
>
> "Spring upward," he called back to me. But I was clumping and pounding after him trying to pass him, and sobbing. In the mind's eye I saw blood in great drops, bigger than quarters, spring from my skin as she sank her claws into me, for I was convinced that as I was in motion I was fair game and she would claw me as soon as she was within range. Or perhaps she would break my neck. I thought that might be preferable. (p. 263)

This trial by lioness is quite ludicrous, Henderson racing about the room in his stained jockey shorts, transparent green silk pantaloons, and pith helmet, convulsed with fear. But for him it is a moment of truth; his admiration for the king is without bounds, and in some not totally rational fashion, their friendship leads Henderson toward a deeper understanding of himself. Writing home to Lily, he can make tangible plans for the future (something most Bellow heroes cannot do):

> "Well, Lily, everything is going to be different from now on. When I get back I am going to study medicine. My age is against it, but that's just too damn bad, I'm going to do it anyway. You can't imagine how keen I am to go into the laboratory." (p. 284)

He even asks her to apply to various medical schools for him, so that his future will be arranged when he returns. And in the same letter, he expresses honest commitment to this woman who is his wife:

> "Lily, I probably haven't said this lately, but I have true feeling for you, baby, which sometimes wrings my heart. You can call it love. Although personally I think that word is full of bluff." (p. 284)

It may be distance that allows him to put this sentiment into words, but the new tone of gentleness is also the product of his suffering while he was absent from her. He does have "true feeling" for her now. The battle for power between them is over. He can love her and also be true to himself; after almost a year away, he looks forward to seeing Lily because he no longer needs to visit his frustrations upon her or to hurt her to feel his own self-importance. His value is now inside himself.

IV

Henderson escapes the vicious circle that Herzog cannot: the attempt to define oneself by someone else's values, which so frequently ends in rejection by the person one attempted to please. One way this pattern may occur is illustrated most painfully when Herzog quits his university job and moves to the Berkshires with Madeleine in order to be free to write his great opus. The plan is hers, but it is she who quickly becomes tired of the rustic life, she who insists they leave for Chicago, and she who steers their marriage toward the rocks by taking Valentine Gersbach for her lover. Even at the end of the novel, when Herzog is warily picking up the pieces of his life—he is once more living in the broken-down Berkshire home, only now he waits for another woman, Ramona—he still cannot break free from his obsession to analyze all actions as part of the "hostile tribes" theory of male-female relations. He is picking flowers to decorate the table, when he stops because:

> it struck him that he might be making a mistake. . . . Picking flowers? He was being thoughtful, lovable. How would it be interpreted? (He smiled slightly.) Still, he need only know his own mind, and the flowers couldn't be used; no, they couldn't be turned against him. So he did not throw them away. (p. 415)

Now this may look like a sign of health, the assertion that "he need only know his own mind," but to accept this statement at face value would surely be a mistake. For he follows this seemingly honest self-assessment with the perception, "they couldn't be turned against him," once more sinking into the trap of strategy and tactics. The man can do nothing straight, nothing unself-consciously.

This raises the issue of where Saul Bellow stands. Does he know that one of his specialties is setting up confrontations that are ultimately dissatisfying to both men and women? Is he aware that the very concept of a battle between the sexes is self-defeating, for in that war there are no winners, only greater or lesser losers? Of course, he does not use the war metaphor specifically, as Norman Mailer does,[8]

---

[8] War langauge is used so consistently by Mailer to describe the relations between the sexes that it almost ceases to be a metaphor. Stephen Rojack regularly conceives of his marriage in military terms: We had been married most intimately and often most unhappily for eight years, and for the last five I had been trying

but the male-female dialectic in his fiction clearly involves a power struggle. Marriage is his usual field of battle, and bad marriages are the norm. Women are generally perceived, either consciously or unconsciously, as "the enemy" by the protagonist, or at least as the opponent in a rather deadly sporting event. When Madeleine comes to the police station in Chicago, Herzog sees her as trying to score a few crucial points in the contest. Tommy Wilhelm is slowly suffocating as a direct result of his wife's sadistic screw-tightening. He says to his father:

> "Well, Dad, she hates me. I feel that she's strangling me. I can't catch my breath. She just has fixed herself on me. She can do it at long distance. One of these days I'll be struck down by suffocation or apoplexy because of her. I just can't catch my breath." (p. 48)

Margaret is the Great Bitch Wife, removing oxygen from the environment by her very existence. Wilhelm is a victim-type, one of society's losers of whom everyone takes advantage, and one would not wisely identify Bellow with Wilhelm.

Considered as a group, the novels *Seize the Day, Herzog,* and *Henderson the Rain King* exhibit certain perceptions and concerns that recur in Bellow's fiction. Male-female relations are an area of life that causes much pain. They tend to be spiritually debilitating. There are almost no instances of successful couples. The crazy scientist Luke Asphalter seems to be more or less happily involved with the graduate student Geraldine Portnoy, but we never meet her; besides, Asphalter is so bizarre (a forty-five-year-old bachelor famous for giving mouth-to-mouth respiration to his dying, tubercular monkey, Rocco) that their relationship can hardly be cited as an instance of Bellow's affirmation that love is possible. Nor does Wilhelm's pathetic affair with the small, dark Olive from Roxbury provide much comfort; it is rather sweet, but it is also doomed.

Again and again, these three novels make clear that women cause pain. Men may cause pain too, but we are left to infer this from the action for we are never allowed a subjective view of the woman's experience. Women are characters in the movie that flashes through the protagonist's head. Bellow does not attempt to penetrate their skulls; they have no monologues. The only self that they reveal is that which the protagonist perceives. We never see Madeleine's point of view. Nor Ramona's. Nor Daisy's. Nor Margaret's. Nor Lily's. Because the common denominator of the three male protagonists is their ability

---

to evacuate my expeditionary army, that force of hopes, all-out need, plain virile desire and commitment which I had spent on her. It was a losing war, and I wanted to withdraw, count my dead, and look for love in another land, . . . (*An American Dream* [New York: Dell, 1964], p. 16).

to suffer, it is clear that the women who leave the greatest marks on their lives are those who produce the most suffering. The patient types are lost by the wayside, and only the truly insidious females are allowed to feed on the hero's entrails like tapeworms. Henderson breaks free of this syndrome by running away to Africa and wrestling with real, live demons instead of those that lurk within, making a man seek pain instead of pleasure. Of course, Lily never fit into the super-bitch category that Madeleine and Margaret fill with such style, but Henderson was managing to turn her into a very unsatisfying wife all the same. What becomes clear is that if a man is neurotic enough, he can kill any relationship, and if he is really eager to mess up his life, he invariably chooses a woman who is happy to cooperate in this project.

Whether Bellow creates such patterns because he believes they are the only ones possible or because he is engaged in charting a modern American phenomenon is difficult to determine. These relationships are consistently neurotic, but they are not aberrations. According to Rollo May, the lack of the ability to love is a major characteristic of modern life; he suggests that contemporary man separates sex and love to his own detriment:

> What underlies our emasculation of sex is the separation of sex from eros. Indeed, we have set sex over against eros, used sex precisely to avoid the anxiety-creating involvements of eros. . . . The threat of the loss of one's own being in falling in love comes from the dizziness and shock of being hurled into a new continent of experience.[9]

Schizoid personalities, alienation, and fear of emotion are widespread in our culture. Sex is no longer the problem; the problem is love. None of these three Bellow males has difficulty getting laid (though Herzog occasionally suffers from premature ejaculation); what proves difficult is sustaining a warm feeling. Herzog may be the archetypal twentieth-century product: the intellectual who can analyze any situation with devastating precision and irony, but who is incapable of almost all simple pleasures—acutely aware and acutely unhappy simultaneously. Is he Saul Bellow in a thin disguise? I do not know. He certainly has much in common with the middle-class, middle-aged American Jewish male intellectual as artist—the Philip Roths, Norman Mailers, Leslie Fiedlers, and others. Doris Lessing gives us a fine example of the type in her character Saul Green in *The Golden Notebook*. Before she even meets him, Anna says to her friend Molly:

> "If he's an American on the loose in Europe, he'll be writing the American epic novel and he'll be in psychoanalysis and he'll have one of

9 *Love and Will* (New York: Dell, 1969), pp. 65, 83.

those awful American marriages and I'll have to listen to his troubles
—I mean problems." [10]

Anna is absolutely correct in her analysis, and she falls for him anyway. Neurotic men of this variety are not unappealing.

If Bellow takes sides in the battle of the sexes, he is only making
the natural alliance with his sex that one would expect. He is not
very hopeful about satisfaction. His talent lies in his precision in
chronicling frustration and pain. He can locate the wound; he cannot
cure it. Clearly, his sympathies lie with his protagonists, a not unusual
situation in the history of the novel. First-person narratives (and Bellow's are all more or less of this variety) are always likely to suffer from
bias; in this case, it is not a bias that mitigates truth.

[10] *The Golden Notebook* (New York: Ballantine, 1962), p. 543.

Bummy's Analysis

by Irving Malin

In his preface to *The Last Analysis,* Bellow informs us that the Broadway production "neglected" the "mental comedy" of his characters. He does not define the phrase, although he feels strongly about it. "Mental comedy" seems redundant. Doesn't all comedy—even slapstick!—depend upon the consciousness of the observer who, seeing a pie strike a face, contrasts "before" and "after," "normality" and "abnormality"? Bellow is certainly such an observer (and creator) of situations. His heroes tend always to be aware of shades, nuances, and tensions. Perhaps I strain here, but it is curious that Bellow says *"mental* comedy" rather than merely "comedy."

He also writes that his play's "real subject is the mind's comical struggle for survival in an environment of Ideas—its fascination with metaphors, and the peculiarly literal and solemn manner in which Americans dedicate themselves to programs, fancies, or brainstorms." The fact that he alerts us to the "real subject" suggests again that he is afraid of misreadings, various false interpretations. He offers *his* intentions, *his* truths. The ironies begin. Bellow is introducing here in a didactic, pedagogical manner a play that, according to him, attacks all theoreticians. Is he joking? Does he want us to extend our awareness of the comedy to include his own "sins"?

Bellow has always "had a weakness for autodidacts"—he admits this in the next few lines of his preface—and his weakness enables us to grasp the ironies of the preface and, moreover, to recognize his very "presence" in his clownish hero. Although *The Last Analysis* is apparently far removed from the sophisticated ironies of *Herzog* and *Mr. Sammler's Planet,* it shares with these—and all of the other fictions—a sense of play, of mirror images, of secret fun.

The following analysis—and the previous paragraphs—will be intensive and theoretical. I explain details that appear somewhat unimportant. I read the text closely, even perhaps more closely than it deserves. Such reading adds to the fun. I am an "amateur philosopher" writing about an "amateur philosopher" writing about an "amateur philosopher."

In the stage directions, Bellow indicates that the action of his play occurs in a "two-story loft in a warehouse. . . ." The setting seems perfectly ordinary. Is there, however, an additional meaning? Can we see the symbolism of the physical facts? The play, as we shall learn, deals with the various stories told (or retold) by the hero. These stories are "double" in effect because he needs in his present condition to create (or recreate) a new self—to shed his skin. He tells *certain* stories for his own mental well-being. "Loft." *Luftmensch* (remember Augie March). Left. I free-associate, but I think Bellow does the same. Surely, his play is about the "upper depths"—the phrase is his—and it ends, we should note, with a raising of the "arms in a great gesture." How can his hero *rise and fly?* What should he *leave* behind? These questions are at the heart of *The Last Analysis*.

There are other curious, interesting details in the setting. Bellow writes that the stage is "hung with bright fabrics, although they are by no means new." Note the contrasts between old and new, dark and light. Such metaphors are, as I will indicate, increasingly important; they recur frequently. The next lines also stress contraries—a "barber chair" and an "elegant old sofa such as an analyst of the Vienna school might have used. . . ." There are *old* posters and *new* television equipment. Obviously, the clutter symbolizes "eccentricity."

At curtain we discover Bummidge, the hero, "lying in the barber chair, completely covered by a sheet." Is he dead or alive? Will he be spruced up or embalmed? (Remember the endings of *Seize the Day* and *Mr. Sammler's Planet.*) We do not know right away. In this crazy environment, we cannot be certain of anything!

It is significant that the first words are spoken by an intruder, Winkleman, Bummidge's cousin. They are: "Imogen, where's my cousin?" Again, we sense symbolic meaning. This shrewd businessman (and keeper of the "law") does not know how to react to his location. It is, after all, loony. And, of course, Bummidge—called "Bummy" affectionately—does not really know where *he* is; he is looking for his true self.

Winkleman notes the television equipment, saying that it's "not the real thing." It is only "closed-circuit"—an interesting choice of words, which underlines the hero's sense of enclosure and his relative obscurity. Once, Bummy was "king of the networks"—the idea of royalty is introduced comically—and when he played this role, he also helped his cousin to rise financially.

Winkleman continues to belittle Bummy. He calls him fool, theoretician, "mental climber." He accuses him of acting insanely, hiring a "secretary who used to be a bunny in the Playboy Club and a collaborator who used to be a ratcatcher," and of attempting to be untrue to himself. Thus, Winkleman's tirades help us to view Bummy as an outcast, a misfit, a "has-been," but because the lawyer is not a very pleasant person—he is a petty tyrant—we begin to sympathize with his adversary.

Winkleman's soliloquy gives him away. He informs us that he uses people; he is, to employ one of Bellow's favorite metaphors, a parasite. He thinks only of "jobs to be done." He exits, "holding his nose like a swimmer." He refuses to rise; he merely submerges his identity into amateur role playing.

Bummy enters just after his cousin departs. He continues to speak of dreams, mysteries, and obscurities. He retells a dream he had the previous night: "A huge white animal climbed into my bed. I thought, 'A polar bear.' I looked again and saw pigs feet. A white sow." Bummy tries to analyze its meaning. Is the animal Mother or Father? Is the fatness meaningful? Surely, Bummy is funny here because he applies Freudian formulas rigidly; he attempts to inhibit shifting transformations. He destroys the texture of the dream. (He is a parody of literary critics and psychiatrists who drown all nuances.) But there is more to his first analysis. The very fact that he tries to understand his "tiny psychosis"—each dream is one, he tells us—means that he is somehow more alive than his cousin who refuses to "let go."

Bummy *laughs* during his soliloquy. He laughs, we are told, in several keys, "assuming various characters." He resembles the changing animal of the dream; he refuses to stay in one place. Even in the dream he "puffed up with rage like a squid." He "almost levitated from the bed." He spoke in many tongues. These details demonstrate his ability to change erratically. Of course, his changes are so wild that he longs for *one* solution, *one* fixture of meaning.

Bummy is comedian *and* analyst. When he looks at himself in the mirror—certainly, the entire proceedings are a kind of mirror: dream mirrors reality (and vice versa); the cousins mirror each other; the "action" mirrors the soliloquies—he shrewdly wonders: "Can people accept my message of sanity and health if I look like death or madness?" It is too early for decent answers. But he already reaches for "everyone" and "everything": "Heart, reason, comic spirit." He knows that he has to perform his own act despite the fact that the "enterprise is bigger than me."

Now the plot "thickens." His relatives and friends arrive, and even without realizing it sometimes, they pretend to be something. They act (as does Bummy), but they do not grasp the nature of their enterprises. They settle for easy victories, hollow triumphs. Madge, Bummy's sister, tries to be the conservative "matron from New Rochelle"; she proclaims common sense. She really hates her brother for his failure to live up to his financial success (and to help her with her schemes). Bummy tugs with her. When he touches her slip, he tries not only to remember the past—"my unconscious is trying to tell me something"—but to crack her defenses. He wants to free her from her normal routine. He recreates her: "Madge, look deep! Infinite and deep!"

And as she becomes once more the "sordid," bitchy person she was (and is)—the past is never dead—she is "inspired." She shakes: "Who *am* I, anyway?" What about Bummy? He is her analyst, but he participates in her act. He is, if you will, an active observer.

Bummy enjoys this "mental comedy." He realizes that by purging Madge—that is, by unmasking her—he can help discover his own longings, fears, and dreams. But he cannot gain complete freedom. He must have more consultations, more laughs, before he can be reborn.

When he returns—after we learn that Winkleman and Madge are in "hot water" and need money to protect their social parasitism—Bummy plays an even more difficult role. He is both patient and analyst; he wears glasses as analyst and removes them as patient. (The glasses suggest the distortions of the play itself.) As patient, he recounts dreams about swimming pools, old gentlemen; as analyst, he gives standard, trite readings of symbols. But these interpretations are limited because they fail to account for quirky differences. The point is clear: there must be more than "breast castration, anxiety, fixation to the past." Bummy (as patient) screams: "I am desperately bored with these things, sick of them."

What can he do? He must recreate his ambivalences; he must *become his dreams.* Therefore, he again "carries himself away"; he flies away from the present as he relives his childhood hostility toward his father: "You attacked all my pleasure sources. But I fought. I hid in the cellar. I forged your signature on my report card. I ate pork." Obviously, he is after bigger game than pigs (remember his previous dream) or prisons. He tries to get at the "bottom" of things. He is funny, of course, but he strangely echoes the heroic plights of Oedipus and, later, Christ—as well as Bellow's earlier and later protagonists.

It would be easy to claim that Bummy has never grown up, nor mastered his feelings toward "Papa" (also the analyst). He surely acts childishly toward his own money-oriented, selfish son, Max. What is he? At times with Max he shows reasoned authority, asserting that "Your father is only flesh and blood. Reason is your only help." He also behaves irrationally, shifting his tone: "Ha, he, ha, I'm an imposter. Can't you see? Catch me please." Bummy moves beyond conventional role playing into a world of his own. He splits into fragments, but at least they are "authentic" (unlike the institutionalized ones of the business world). He always departs; he leaves the stage to prepare for more personalized, creative entrances.

Now we can understand that the chatter of the others in his absence is purposeful. Bellow slows the action; he submerges us, as it were, in banal analysis. Madge claims that "Bummy's got to get us off the hook." Winkleman is worried. Pamela, Bummy's girl friend, says: "I'll find out what he's got in the bag." These flat notations, these stereotyped characters reinforce the superior playfulness of the "star"; they maintain his comic inventiveness.

Bummy emerges as an artist. (Surely, there is a parallel between him and Bellow the playwright.) His art is crude—to say the least!—but it is in touch with realities. He holds a child's potty and says: "We were all *body* once." He listens to the free association of his stomach noises. He builds on such mundane foundations, recognizing that he must somehow have "wings" yet move "on foot like a goose." *He flies with earthy metaphors.*

Bummy lives with symbols. Though he says at one point that the sagging floor is a "mere symbol," he appreciates the "mental comedy." Here, he is seeing symbols of animals (goose, pig), of prisons, of flight, and condemning "mere symbols"! Afterwards, he indulges in heightened speech: "You have filled my life with stench and noise; dogged me night and day; lived on me like green fungus on pumpernickel." Bummy moves from speech to epic theater. He becomes Christ; he stretches out his arms. Perhaps this performance is his salvation. He knows that all actors move beyond easy symbols and create timeless, spiritual ones. But he is still incomplete—as the curtain falls, he asks: "What comes next?"

We soon find out. Act Two begins minutes later—Bellow doesn't allow us or his hero to stay at rest—and the others go through their usual acts. Max continues to think about money; Madge and Winkleman (actually, he is referred to more fittingly as "Winkie") conspire; Bella, Bummy's shrewish wife who was introduced earlier, calls people "dogs": "The government should label people the way it does meat—prime, choice, and dog food."

When Bummy enters, he is excited by an infant. He adores the "state of Nature"; he exclaims that "everything loathsome about the human species is forgiven time after time, and with every child we begin again." He reinforces beginnings—after all, he is preparing to be reborn.

Despite the desire of the others to use him—the parasite image is again underlined—Bummy exerts his sly strength and "directs" them. He "ad libs" their lines, not for materialist gain but for comic expression. He presents a play within the play. He has them perform roles that are, in a sense, more representative of their souls than their usual petty conspiracies.

Bummy is "on." He first addresses the closed-circuit audience of analysts (and agents): "Sixty-one years ago I was literally nothing. I was merely possible. Then I was conceived, and became inevitable. When I die, I shall be impossible. Meanwhile between two voids, past and future, I exist." The words are grand, sublime, somewhat overdone; yet they convey the "dangling man" existing between two voids. They do more: they suggest that only by performing truly can he gain identity. He creates meanings for past and future, self and nonself. It is, as he says, "my personality, my mind! My mind has a will of its own." His mind bridges the voids, fights the death wish, recognizing that "we are what we are owing to our morbidity."

Bummy's "mental comedy" is linked to death: "Organisms without death have no true identity." By laughing at our small, unnatural roles (as he does at his past efforts), we "leap beyond repression." We reclaim "freedom by acting." (Note the metaphors of flight.) His comic task is to liberate the others—we remember his Christ routine at the end of Act One—by forcing them to laugh at themselves. When they refuse, however, to see what they are, he feels "infinite sadness salted with jokes." He tells us that when the laughing stops, there's "still a big surplus of pain."

Bummy suffers from an odd disorder that he calls "Humanitis": "Suddenly being human is too much for me." He faints, staggers with emotion. He alternately loves and hates the others (and his own reflection in them). He becomes serious: "I don't have the strength to bear my feelings." He leaves the stage; he "dies."

But he soon returns. He sings old songs, and relives old roles: he becomes suitor, slapstick comic, and song-and-dance man. The others join him. Bella is once more the pregnant girl; Max becomes Bummy's vicious father. The various acts become confused. This is conceived strongly: *Bummy wants all the roles to shift violently; he designs "chaos" so that he can start freshly.* He runs through his lines (and compels the others to do the same): "I run and hide, steal, lie, cheat, hate, lust. Thus . . . my pursuit of happiness."

Then he becomes methodical. He slows the action. (He is really in command!) He hands out written parts, not allowing the others to "ad lib." He establishes the need for *reasoned craft.* The stage directions are significant here: "A black cloth has been prepared on the sofa, midstage. There are holes in this cloth for the heads of the chorus." They remind us of the white sheet that once covered Bummy; they imply that drama, death, and birth are joined inextricably.

The "Greek" playlet they perform is *The Upper Depths, or the Birth of Philip Bomovitch.* It is trite and grand—as are all of our lives?—because it mixes language, characters, and events in a deliberately odd pattern. It moves from the chorus saying "Will this be nothing but finite mortal man?" to Bummy claiming "It's great in here. I like it." It has various props: a balloon (the breath of Man); the sofa covered by a cloth; and the darkness of the womb. Its theme is no less than the theme of the entire play—Bummy's birth. (Bummy's various names remind us of Tommy Wilhelm's name changes.)

Bummy seems changed. When the playlet ends, he "seems far removed from them all." He feels "both old and new." He is Lazarus, Christ reborn—no wonder that his performance has "wowed" the supporting players and the audience, including the great impressario, Fiddelman!—but he must still live in *this world*. "Something has happened." He floats.

Bellow could stop here, concluding his play on a *lofty* plane. But he is too serious to rescue his hero entirely. Thus, Bummy may tear up his new contract and toss out the others, but he lacks irony. He is "over the edge" as he hopes to build "The Bummidge Institute of Nonsense." We deserve a modern skyscraper like the United Nations, but the poor, the sad, the bored and tedious of the earth will trust us better for beginning so "humbly." Bummy is "ready for the sublime" as the play ends; we are not sure, however, that he can handle it (or that it is so easily available.)

We are "double-crossed." We are sad because we recognize, even if Bummy doesn't, that there is no "last analysis," no final moment of Truth. The comic work must continue! Bummy has somehow stopped —even though he talks about training programs for the Institute— and he lacks the "mental comedy" needed for higher elevation.

The final effect of *The Last Analysis* is mixed. We are uncertain whether or not to join Bummy as he "saves the world"; we cannot merely laugh or cry. We dangle between different worlds—ours and his, Bellow's and his, Bellow's and ours. Surely, we do know one thing: we have been strangely touched by this powerful, shrewd, and funny play.

Saul Bellow and Mr. Sammler:
Absurd Seekers of High Qualities

by Ben Siegel

Interviewer: "Which of your characters is most like you?"
Saul Bellow: "Henderson—the absurd seeker of high qualities." [1]

Social historians and commentators are now sifting the diverse
cultural forces of the 1960s. That troubled decade, they generally
agree, produced a "new sensibility" of political and cultural radicalism, one varying sharply from the dominant "literary" sensibility of
the later '40s and the '50s. The postwar writings of Lionel Trilling,
Yvor Winters, John Crowe Ransom, Cleanth Brooks, and other key
critics had emphasized "complexity, irony, and paradox," and these
intellectual properties, Daniel Bell observes, fostered a moderate critical attitude that was detached from ideology and excessive social or
emotional involvement.[2]

But by the late '50s, the adherents of the "new sensibility" had rejected the New Critics' sober intellectualism for a new mood and
pantheon. Norman O. Brown, Herbert Marcuse, Jerry Rubin, and
Malcolm X were a few of their heroes, and Marshall McLuhan, Norman Mailer, Leslie Fiedler, and William Phillips were among their
strategists. Before long, the members of this new movement saw themselves as part of an "adversary" or "counter" culture that opposed
their society's materialism, grossness, and decadence. Advocating individual freedom of behavior and expression, they moved quickly
from the championing of "prerational spontaneity" and rejection of
a "technocratic" America to an assault on reason itself. In 1957, Norman Mailer described, in "The White Negro: Superficial Reflections

1 Nina A. Steers, " 'Successor' to Faulkner?" *Show*, 4 (September 1964), 38.
2 Daniel Bell, "Sensibility in the 60's," *Commentary*, 51 (June 1971), 63.

on the Hipster," a few of the behavioral impulses and patterns derived
from years of living with the grim realities of gas ovens and atom
bombs—and what they might mean for the next decade. "If the fate
of twentieth-century man," wrote Mailer, "is to live with death from
adolescence to premature senescence, why then the only life-giving
answer is to accept the terms of death, to live with death as immediate
danger, to divorce oneself from society, to exist without roots, to set
out on that unchartered journey into the rebellious imperatives of
the self." [3]

Mailer's swinging, defiant hipster served not only a youthful Beat
generation but also some of his contemporaries as a personal and literary model for the '60s. Soon, Leslie Fiedler was boldly proclaiming
the demise of the "old novel" and birth of the "new." In "The New
Mutants" he announced a new breed of apocalyptic young American
novelists who were heralding the demise of the humanistic tradition
and its language. Rejecting cultural continuity and progress, as well
as the tired formulas of the "bourgeois novel" (with its Southern,
Jewish, and Hollywood subgenres), writers such as Kurt Vonnegut,
John Barth, Jeremy Larner, and William Burroughs relied on science
fiction's fantasy-and-prophecy powers to portray "the post-humanist,
post-male, post-white, post-heroic . . . post-Jewish world";[4] they did
so to envision more precisely the social and moral nightmare confronting modern man.

More recently, Fiedler has reaffirmed this need for a new novel;
what is required now, he insists, is a novel that reflects the displacing
of literary modernism by postmodernism, one that will "close the gap,
between high culture and low, belles-lettres and pop art. . . . [For]
as certainly as the old God is dead, so the old novel is dead. Certain
writers (Saul Bellow, for instance, or John Updike, Mary McCarthy
or James Baldwin) continue to write old novels and certain readers,
often with a sense of being quite up to date, continue to read them." [5]
But these works represent a world that is no more. His own criticism,
says Fiedler, is clearly "postmodern," for he tries not "to reject those
works of art whose muse is a machine and whose fate seems more
closely linked to the history of Technology than that of the Spirit." [6]

3 Mailer published his essay first in *Dissent*, 4 (Summer 1957), 276–93 and later
in *Advertisements For Myself* (New York: Putnam's, 1959), pp. 337–58; see p. 339.
4 Leslie Fiedler, "The New Mutants," *Partisan Review*, 32 (Fall 1965), 505–25;
see p. 517.
5 Leslie Fiedler, "Cross the Border, Close the Gap," *Playboy*, 16 (December 1969),
252, 230. Literary modernism, as Fiedler sees it, is exemplified by the writings of
James, Proust, and Mann, as well as by those of Pound, Eliot, Valéry, and their
contemporaries.
6 Leslie Fiedler, *Cross the Border—Close the Gap* (New York: Stein and Day,
1972), p. 4.

Advocacy of a machine-and-technology muse is hardly new; neither are disturbed reactions by humanistic critics and authors who feel their beliefs and values threatened. Many such writers were quick to castigate the new movement for its hostility to morality and ideas, for its simplistic faith in innocence and sexual instinct, and for its praise of the angry and violent, the escapist and nihilistic. The new sensibility caters more to the senses than to the mind, argued Susan Sontag in 1965, less to literature—with its "heavy burden" of content and moral judgment—than to the "cooler" arts of music and films, painting and sculpture.[7] Later, Irving Howe doubted whether the new attitude was "compatible with a high order of culture or a complex civilization"; its adherents struck him as frivolous, as interested primarily in avoiding all harsh realities for life's more "relaxed pleasures and surface hedonism."[8] While noting with satisfaction the fading of the new sensibility in the '70s, these critics continue to acknowledge its influence. The harshest condemnation of the new trends was voiced recently by Daniel Bell, to whom the Aquarian youth culture of the '60s still appears to have been "savage, even mindless" in rejecting the temperate rationalism of the '50s. Their social and sexual strivings pointed toward a lost "idealized childhood" as they acted out, "belatedly, their earliest fantasies and sexual demands . . . on a mass scale unprecedented in cultural history."[9]

Most serious American novelists have also eagerly confronted the cultural turbulence of the '60s; they have tried to convey—with pleasure or displeasure—their feeling that insanity has displaced normalcy as the "touchstone of reality."[10] And despite Fiedler's charge that he writes "old novels," Saul Bellow has come closer than any other novelist during the past two decades to transmuting into fiction those forces that isolate the sensitive American from his peers. He has done so in each of his novels, including his latest, *Mr. Sammler's Planet*,[11] in which he probes and dramatizes at length the frenzied rejection by the young and dissident of the computerized social bureaucracy in which they find themselves. He sympathizes with their concerns, but he scorns their behavior and their reluctance even to attempt viable solutions. Negation for its own sake, he makes clear, offers society or the individual few meaningful values.

Some reviewers have professed surprise and dismay at this novel; they find in it a "new Bellow," an aging ideologue exhibiting a new,

---

[7] See Susan Sontag, "One Culture and the New Sensibility," in her *Against Interpretation and Other Essays* (New York: Noonday, 1966), pp. 293–304.

[8] Irving Howe, "The New York Intellectuals: A Chronicle & A Critique," *Commentary*, 46 (October 1968), 47–48.

[9] Bell, "Sensibility in the 60's," 63–64.

[10] Bell, "Sensibility in the 60's," 73.

[11] New York: Viking, 1970. All text references are to this edition.

irrational fear of the young, the radical, and the black. No longer their beloved King Saul—literary innovator, trend-setter, and articulate champion of the rebellious young—Bellow is, in their eyes now, merely one more dated establishment littérateur.[12] As evidence, they point out that Artur Sammler is both European and elderly; both elements, they insist, are firsts for a Bellow hero: never before has Bellow identified with a foreign protagonist, much less one several decades older than himself. Such strictures, admittedly, make good reading, but they are mostly irrelevant and essentially untrue; nor is the surprise and consternation these critics display valid.

For Bellow has managed, in *Mr. Sammler's Planet,* to shift his angle of vision without altering any of the views he has expressed repeatedly in fiction and forum. His primary concern, as always, is at the loss of moral and intellectual authority in America by the rational, the disciplined, the humane. Contributing heavily to the erosion of national thought and art are the pressures and distractions of American city life, the social excesses of history, culture, and news that assault and tire the mind: "All this hugeness," says Augie March, this "abundance, turbulence, Niagara Falls torrent." [13] This cultural surplus is confronted daily by artists and writers—and by every Bellow hero, from the dangling Joseph to the beleaguered Artur Sammler. Each is, like Moses Herzog, a displaced, intellectual victim whose survival depends on his rejecting these exploitative forces. Each tries to wrench from urban disorder a measure of moral coherence. Herzog has only to glance from his window to be reminded that the city, amid dust clouds and clamor, demolishes and rebuilds itself unendingly, while in his head his blood pounds as relentlessly "for order."

Every Bellow wanderer is caught up in this "urban clutter" of noise, dirt, and smell, and each is forced to recognize that all dreams of escape—geographic or spatial—are sentimental nonsense. Spring season or pastoral life, Africa or Mexico, moon or ocean bottom—not one guarantees relief from inner demons or outer pressures. Man must struggle at home for his emotional life, Bellow insists, and in an age that is complex, hostile, and increasingly proud of being revolutionary. But for Bellow, the times are "more dishevelled than revolutionary." [14]

[12] Typical negative readings of the novel are John J. Clayton, "Bellow and the Planet of Our Discontent," *The Valley Review,* 1 (December 1970), 14–15; and Max Schulz, "Mr. Bellow's Perigee, or, The Lowered Horizon of *Mr. Sammler's Planet,*" in *Contemporary American-Jewish Literature,* ed. Irving Malin (Bloomington, Ind.: Indiana University Press, 1973), pp. 117–33.

[13] Saul Bellow, *The Adventures of Augie March* (New York: Viking, 1953), p. 455.

[14] Chirantean Kulshrestha, "A Conversation with Saul Bellow," *Chicago Review,* 23, no. 4, and 24, no. 1 (Spring-Summer, 1972), p. 9.

Several reviewers have defended Bellow by arguing, logically enough, that a novelist does not necessarily share his hero's views. But here, Bellow clearly does: Artur Sammler's reactions to people and events are totally consistent with those expressed by Saul Bellow in fiction and essay, lecture and interview. A decade ago, in "The Writer as Moralist," Bellow noted a "struggle going on . . . between Cleans and Dirties. The Cleans want to celebrate the bourgeois virtues . . . steadiness, restraint, a sense of duty. The Dirties are latter-day Romantics and celebrate impulsiveness, lawless tendencies, the wisdom of the heart." Neither side has a monopoly on virtue, he argued, and each is vulnerable to irrational behavior. "Certain upper-class idiocies are answered by growling from the swamps," so that the differences between them too often are "superficial." [15]

Bellow has often echoed these thoughts, most recently in his essay "Culture Now." There, he lashes out at a number of greedy, self-serving groups: New Left and old right, literary "modernists" and *avant-garde,* "brutal profs and bad-tempered ivy-league sodomites," are among his prime targets. But he is equally harsh with the new intellectual elite—those beguiled "educated readers" of the middle class who romanticize, rather than protest, the abuse and violence heaped on them by radicals and militants. Together, these groups are "bohemianizing" American society while devaluing its history. "All that is not *now,* they say, is obsolete and dead." The grim result is that not merely the nation's literature and media but the total society now belongs to those "demagogues, dunces and businessmen" who form a power caste of "publicity intellectuals." Only the artist, committed as he is to a "commonsense view of things," stands apart, or should.[16]

These few comments alone indicate that Artur Sammler, who repeats most of them, speaks for Bellow—and does so despite his advanced age and foreign birth. Too much, in fact, has been made of Sammler's age, for Bellow's heroes have generally been growing older. Only Joseph, Asa Leventhal, and Augie March were young. Tommy Wilhelm and Moses Herzog were in their forties, Eugene Henderson in his mid fifties, Philip Bummidge and Gooley MacDowell sixty, and Dr. Samuel Braun and Willis Mosby even older. Thus, Sammler, in his mid seventies, continues a careful chronological pattern—and in outlook and temperament he has much in common with several of the older protagonists; he also shares traits with key secondary characters such as Asa Leventhal's crony Marcus Schlossberg, Augie March's Grandma Lausch, and Tommy Wilhelm's father, Dr. Adler. More

[15] Saul Bellow, "The Writer as Moralist," *The Atlantic,* 211 (March 1963), 59.
[16] Saul Bellow, "Culture Now: Some Animadversions, Some Laughs," *Modern Occasions,* 1 (Winter 1971), 162–78.

significantly, perhaps, Bellow presented in his first novels lonely young heroes beset by older opportunists—or "reality instructors"—who sought to dominate or cheat them. These young fellows were themselves overwrought romantics often fearful of their own sanity and excessive natures—whereas their antagonists were "dry, controlled little guys" [17] who could take life and others in stride.

With Artur Sammler, Bellow admittedly varies this pattern. From Joseph to Herzog, his protagonists are loners who, though surviving their varied encounters, end up on tentative terms with society. Sammler too is a loner, but his circumstances are reversed: he defends the social verities and traditions. And whereas earlier the older, secondary figures—as Keith Opdahl, among others, has pointed out—presented those ideas meant to be eccentric, amusing, unreliable, here the elderly hero voices the serious views. [18] The most thoughtful of Bellow's thinking heroes, Sammler has also experienced a great deal, including much violence and death. A Polish Jew by birth, he lost an eye to a German rifle butt, survived a Nazi mass burial in which his wife perished, and roamed Poland with revenging partisans and then alone. His happiest years were as a journalist in London where, snug and smug, he was intimate with the Bloomsbury literary set and with H. G. Wells, about whom he had planned a book.

Now he is an elderly pensioner dependent on his nephew, Elya Gruner, a New York gynecologist with Mafia connections. Seeing himself as a near-posthumous figure, Sammler wants only the calm to live "with a civil heart" and the time to read Meister Eckhardt. Tall, spare, durable, he is a rapid, arrogant walker who sports a large floppy hat and wards off pedestrians and cabs with his furled umbrella. Around him swirl big-city violence, sex, money, variety, imitation. Amid these currents, Sammler (whose name echoes "Uncle Sam," and in Yiddish *zammler* or "collector," and in German "storage battery") stands as a fixed point—a firm observer of the American scene and an exponent of old-style humanism. From that double vantage point he rejects the decade's proliferating lunacies: the immoral politics (of right and left), the hip life styles, and the obsession with originality. "Is our species crazy?" he asks. "Plenty of evidence."

Sammler refers to the friends and relatives, students and strangers who appear before his single eye. Attracted by his sanity and integrity, by his self-control and old-world manners, these urban adventurers force him to act the reluctant or, in Herzog's phrase, "compulsory witness." Almost all are slovenly, promiscuous, eccentric—and young. But if the young people approach moral anarchy and madness, they

[17] Keith Opdahl, "An Honorable Old Man in a World of Obsessed Young Adults," *Commonweal*, 91 (February 13, 1970), 536.
[18] See Opdahl, "An Honorable Old Man," p. 536.

hardly reveal, as some reviewers would have it, "a Bellow in retreat." [19]
What these reviewers ignore is that the *principles* old Sammler admires are those Bellow has advocated since his first novel. *Dangling
Man* ends with the youthful Joseph, exhausted by directionless freedom, proclaiming the joys of "regular hours," "supervision of the
spirit," and "regimentation." [20] In Bellow's next novel, *The Victim,*
Marcus Schlossberg (like Sammler, an elderly Jewish journalist) insists
that man can choose between being "lousy and cheap" or having
"greatness and beauty." Which should he choose? "Choose dignity,"
declares the old man. "Nobody knows enough to turn it down." [21]
Sammler shares both views. Yet he recognizes better than most the
soul's individuality. What he deplores is not each man's need to be
unique, but the current mass obsession with an originality that rejects tested cultural models for the grotesque and bizarre. For if he is
past passion, he is hardly dispassionate as he muses on the connections
between human madness and death. The holocaust and his own escape
from the grave are the experiences by which Sammler measures all
events. These have strengthened his belief in limits, reason, tradition.
Viewing the Upper West Side through a glass darkly, that is, through
his smoked glasses, as well as through bus, apartment, and hospital
windows, he is convinced that New York is the New World's exotic
center; its habitués, protected by "civilized order, property rights, re-
fined technological organization," seek primarily the "free ways of
barbarism." They evoke in him thoughts of culture's collapse, Sodom
and Gomorrah, the world's end. He does not agree with the young
dissidents he encounters that man can survive without rules, dignity,
order, and his sentiments are echoed by Dr. Govinda Lal, the Hindu
biophysicist. "To desire to live without order," says Dr. Lal, "is to
desire to turn from the fundamental biological governing principle"
(*MSP,* 216).

Clearly, intellect and knowledge, Sammler has learned, are not
enough: without a conscience, man is merely an intellectual animal.
Wanting to understand this planet's creatures, he tries to look and
listen without judging. But so doubtful is he of man's future on earth
that he finds tempting the possibility posed by the first lunar shot—
that man "blow this great blue, white, green planet" and move to the
moon. Certainly, time and science have not brought the social progress
predicted by his old friend H. G. Wells,[22] that utopian socialist and
dispenser of romantic fantasies. What they had brought were ideas

[19] See Schulz, "Mr. Bellow's Perigee," p. 120.

[20] Saul Bellow, *Dangling Man* (New York: Vanguard, 1944), p. 191.

[21] Saul Bellow, *The Victim* (New York: Vanguard, 1947), p. 134.

[22] Bellow corresponded with H. G. Wells when the latter wrote to express his
admiration for *Dangling Man.* See Benjamin DeMott, "Saul Bellow and the Dogmas
of Possibility," *Saturday Review,* 53 (February 7, 1970), 25.

sanctioning moral license and indulgence. Now, modern man, having exhausted his planet's resources, looks to the moon for a fresh start. Sammler soon rejects this idea of a lunar haven; the moon venture filling the news media strikes him as a dazzling but wasteful "circus," another reflection of the "lunacy" epitomizing the national mind. Yet, not only all America, he sighs, but all civilized society seeks "the blameless state of madness." He opts instead for this "rotting . . . sinful earth," for whatever its flaws, it remains man's only home. Sammler's sympathies, therefore, are with the limited, the definite, indeed with the bottom of the sea, which embodies, he feels, a descent into dense tangibility, into cool, inward finiteness. These elements symbolize for him man's duties and depth. Yet only a few among the young see that dealing with the near, the commonplace, the responsible is what makes saints and heroes.

Such harsh comments on the young and their culture have stirred anguished cries of "sellout" from former Bellow admirers. His novel, they declare, attacks modernism only to champion tradition and convention to the point of reaction. One reviewer charges Bellow with concocting a "sardonic parody" [23] of his own earlier fiction, and another accuses him of "a smugness . . . common to Jewish mandarin intellectuals." [24] Several are annoyed by his failure to mention the Vietnam War; others find most painful the incident in which Sammler, invited to lecture at Columbia University, is shouted down by his ragtag, longhaired audience. One youth yells that the old journalist can have nothing valid to say because at his age he cannot achieve orgasm. Sammler leaves, pondering the new critical standards. "How extraordinary! Youth? Together with the idea of sexual potency? All this confused sex-excrement-militancy, explosiveness, abusiveness, tooth-showing, Barbary ape howling" (*MSP*, 43). Commenting on this incident, Beverly Gross, in an otherwise perceptive review, summarizes most of these charges: "This outburst, meant to characterize the student movement and the consciousness of the New Left, characterizes more than anything else what has gone wrong with *his* novel. When an artist who is no blunderer—and Bellow is a supreme artist—furnishes so false a moment, it is something of a revolution. Bellow has failed to give credibility to the opposition." The student here, she goes on, "is recognizable only as a nasty caricature. He is part of a whole corpus of signs and tendencies that this novel is proclaiming against. He is being used." [25] But Gross, like the others, has missed

23 James Neil Harris, "One Critical Approach to *Mr. Sammler's Planet*," *Twentieth Century Literature*, 18 (October 1972), 235–70.

24 D. P. M. Salter, "Optimism and Reaction in Saul Bellow's Recent Work," *Critical Quarterly*, 14 (Spring 1972), 64.

25 Beverly Gross, "Dark Side of the Moon," *The Nation*, 160 (February 8, 1970), 154.

—or chosen to miss—Bellow's point. Rather than "put down the new cultural dissidents," Bellow, as Robert Alter rightly insists, "views them with a compassionate sadness." [26]

Nor does Bellow attack modernism and radicalism, but only their misuse: the abuse or distortion, in any form, of human knowledge, language, and experience is what angers him. Bellow has often made this clear—as in a 1965 interview: "What does the radicalism of radical writers nowadays amount to?" he asked.

> Most of it is hand-me-down bohemianism, sentimental populism, D. H. Lawrence-and-water, or imitation Sartre. For American writers radicalism is a question of honor. They must be radicals for the sake of their dignity. . . . Their radicalism, however, is contentless. A genuine radicalism, which truly challenges authority, we need desperately. But a radicalism of posture is easy and banal. Radical criticism requires knowledge, not posture, not slogans, not rant. . . . True radicalism requires homework—thought.[27]

Even more distasteful to Bellow than rhetorical posturing is the waste of human potential, the squandering of natural gifts and material advantages, such as that exhibited by young Wallace Gruner and his sister Angela. Wallace, dismissed by his father as a "high I.Q. moron," is a caricature of educational and technological futility (two prime targets, ironically, of the radical young). Compared by some readers to Tommy Wilhelm, that other inept son of a successful Jewish doctor, he does reveal several similar character and behavior traits. But Bellow has again reversed the circumstances: Tommy is rejected by his father and cheated by an older worldling, Dr. Tamkin; Wallace and the oversexed Angela live off their father, Elya Gruner, the novel's most sympathetic figure. Indeed, the older males (Sammler, Gruner, Dr. Lal, and even the dead Ussher Arkin), despite human flaws, conduct themselves with a style and dignity lacking in the next generation; together, they reaffirm a deeply felt sense of responsibility or community. Wishing to explain himself to his quizzical Uncle Sammler, Wallace declares pathetically: "I'm a different generation. I never have had any dignity to start with" (*MSP*, 241). Wallace, Angela, Sammler's own neurotic daughter Shula, and the other young people convince the old man that their collective "liberation into individuality" has brought them much more "misery and despair" than success or joy. Sammler is appalled. "Hearts that get no real wage, souls that find no nourishment," he sighs. "Falsehoods, unlimited. Desire, unlimited. Possibility, unlimited. Impossible demands upon complex realities, unlimited" (*MSP*, 229).

26 Robert Alter, "A Fever of Ethnicity," *Commentary*, 53 (June 1972), 68.
27 Gordon Lloyd Harper, "Saul Bellow," in *Writers at Work: The Paris Review Interviews, Third Series*, ed. George Plimpton (New York: Viking, 1968), pp. 189–90. [Included in this collection, p. 5.]

Sammler underscores his disenchantment with the young by rejecting his own early beliefs, especially those derived from Marx and
Freud. Now he is more impressed by Max Weber, especially by
Weber's castigating of those "specialists without spirit, sensualists
without heart" who imagine they have "attained a level of civilization
never before achieved" (*MSP*, 54). He is keenly aware, however, that
the older generation hardly lacks the spiritless and sensual; the
affluent and powerful in particular have failed to provide America
with the moral leadership and authority that would have prevented
so many disorders and disruptions. The trouble is that the rich are
themselves "winners in struggles of criminality, of permissible criminality" (*MSP*, 75). Whether he clamors for originality or for power,
modern man has overburdened his moral and emotional capacities.

These current values and life styles are embodied for Sammler in
the brazen black pickpocket who, in camel's-hair coat and Dior shades,
operates on the Fifth Avenue bus. Sammler reports him to the police,
who are not interested. The thief corners Sammler in his apartment
house lobby, contemptuously unzips his own fly, and forces the old
man—no sound uttered—to look at his bared genitals, then leaves.
What are Sammler and the reader to make of this? The choices are
many: black man confronting Jew; noble savage versus effete moralist;
or perhaps, as Sammler himself thinks, raw, lawless energy (sexual
ego) dismissing reason, decency, discipline. Has not Angela Gruner
been acting similarly? Indeed, thinks Sammler, "a sexual madness" is
overwhelming the Western world; even an American president, according to rumor, has exposed himself similarly to the press. Sammler
recalls the terrifying denuding by the Nazis of their victims and his
own nakedness in the Zamosht Forest. The world's terrors are un-
ceasing. In any event, the half-blind old humanist feels that he and
all he represents have been reduced to impotent absurdity.

Making this sad point several times, Bellow hardly champions, as
some have claimed, either humanism unqualified or thought without
action. He had challenged years ago, with his "poor-man's Socrates,"
Gooley MacDowell, the person of mere thought or ideas. A lifelong
rationalist, Gooley seeks at sixty a "pay-off" for his years of "devoted
studies," for he finds that in today's trying world, only to breathe or
only to have thoughts renders life barren. "Look at us," he complains,
"the more plentiful our ideas the worse our headaches." In fact, an
individual today "needs heroism," Gooley adds, "even to be decent,"
and to win just average contentment he must harbor strong "feelings
of being that go beyond thought." [28]

The strangest misreading of Bellow has been by those who see the

---

28 Saul Bellow, "Address by Gooley MacDowell to the Hasbeens Club of Chicago," *Hudson Review*, 4 (Summer 1951), 222–27.

pickpocket not merely as an expression of "Jewish outrage at the state of the nation" [29] but of the novelist's "hostility" to black skin.[30] This "racist" view requires the reader not only to ignore the impressive black figures in *Henderson the Rain King* but also to scan *Mr. Sammler's Planet* with one eye closed. For Sammler, the graceful, catlike thief resembles a masterful African princeling, and his fall makes clear that neither Sammler nor Bellow approaches the law's moral complexities as a rigid constructionist. Indeed, when Sammler sees the pickpocket choking—almost deservedly—his young friend Lionel Feffer (near the Lincoln Center, no less), he feels responsible: he had told Feffer of the thief and that shrewd opportunist had been taking pictures of the black. Sammler, made painfully aware once more of his old-man's helplessness, calls upon his son-in-law, Eisen, who is standing by indifferently, to act. Eisen, newly emigrated from Israel, is a foundry worker turned artist, who paints living people as corpses. Spurred to action by Sammler, he smiles, shrugs, then bloodies the pickpocket with a bagful of his artwork—metallic sculptures commemorating Israel's existence. These events clearly suggest, as Irvin Stock points out, that in Eisen, "the traditional allegiances of both Jew and artist—to life, to man—have been reversed." [31] Bellow also implies that Jews hardened by death camp and war can bring even black potency to earth; certainly, the two earlier confrontations between blacks and Jews in the novel have also been reversed. Ironically, Sammler, who in the Zamosht Forest killed a German soldier with deliberate pleasure, is now appalled by Eisen's ferocity. "This is much worse," he tells himself. "This is the worst thing yet" (*MSP*, 290). Near murder is for the old humanist too high a price even for law and order.

Bellow cannot resist a laconic comment on Sammler's moral confusion: he has Eisen (also a death-camp survivor) reject the older man's hairsplitting. "You can't hit a man like this just once," Eisen stutters. "When you hit him you must really hit him. Otherwise he'll kill you. You know. We both fought in the war. . . . If in—in. No? If out— out. Yes? No? So answer" (*MSP*, 291–92). Sammler lacks an adequate response. He can only recall that he had himself committed murder, and the action had taught him "that reality was a terrible thing, and the final truth about mankind overwhelming and crushing." Trying

---

[29] Schulz, "Mr. Bellow's Perigee," p. 122.

[30] An interesting but rigid view of Bellow's black pickpocket is that of Morris Dickstein. Bellow presents this character, writes Dickstein, "without irony or qualification, as elemental amoral force that threatens 'civilization,' an embodiment of the spirit of a barbarous age." Indeed, Bellow's novel is for Dickstein "a paranoid manipulation of stereotypes and racial fantasies." See Morris Dickstein, "Malamud's Best Book in Years About a Black and a Jew: The Tenants," *New York Times Book Review* (October 3, 1971), 16.

[31] Irvin Stock, "Man in Culture," *Commentary*, 49 (May 1970), 90.

to reject so "vulgar and cowardly" a conclusion, he has been reminded repeatedly that extreme moments are met only by moral extremes—with philosophic niceties proving absurdly inadequate. One recent description of the humanist-as-hero seems apt here. "Standing next to the existential man," Harold Simonson writes, "the traditional humanist as a fictional character can only be described with ridicule and hollow laughter. His cultivated taste and learning show him sadly inadequate to confront his real condition." [32]

Bellow clearly agrees and underscores this point in the final events of the novel. The two figures with most claim to style and grace, Elya Gruner and the pickpocket, are brought low: Elya dies before his time, the princely thief lies beaten and arrested. When the world bears down heavily, Bellow's heroes are not reluctant to turn to God. Herzog, for instance, extricated from jail by a devoted brother (also named Elya), gratefully addresses a letter to God, in which he declares that he has always desired to do God's "unknowable will," taking this will, and God, "without symbols." [33] Sammler, too, sends a message upward; as the younger kin seek ways to profit from Gruner's death, he stands alone with the corpse. Not for him are Tommy Wilhelm's self-pitying tears before the dead; he improvises a *Kaddish*, a mourner's prayer, for this nephew who, by his compassion and concern, has reminded him that "There is still such a thing as a man—or there was. There are still human qualities." Despite flaws and vanities, Elya Gruner had reached out to others and, without shirking or quibbling, had always done "what was required of him." Elya "was aware," Sammler informs God, "that he must meet, and he did meet—through all the confusion and degraded clowning of this life through which we are speeding—he did meet the terms of his contract. The terms which, in his inmost heart, each man knows. As I know mine. As all know. For that is the truth of it—that we all know, God, that we know, that we know, we know, we know" (*MSP*, 313). Elya Gruner is to be included, Sammler thus insists, among those who have kept man's covenant with God. Not great in number, they are enough to prove that this "crazy species fought its criminality," and that if man can not escape his animality, he is at least "an animal of genius" (*MSP*, 305). Let no one claim ignorance of this contract, says Bellow, because man knows intuitively, without discussion, "the difference . . . between good and evil." [34]

---

[32] Harold Simonson, *Strategies in Criticism* (New York: Holt, Rinehart & Winston, 1971), p. 112. Simonson refers to Sartre's Self-Taught Man (*Nausea*) and Virginia Woolf's Mr. Ramsay (*To the Lighthouse*). He might well have added Artur Sammler.

[33] Saul Bellow, *Herzog* (New York: Viking, 1964), p. 333.

[34] Sanford Pinsker, "Saul Bellow in the Classroom," *College English*, 34 (April 1973), 977.

As he does in each of his novels, Bellow here shows his readers man at his worst and best, reminds them again that, regardless of circumstances, the individual can do more than lament his fate; if nothing else, he can give thought to his conscience and responsibility to others. He can also reject the cries of doom and disaster sounded repeatedly in fiction and media. "Things are grim enough," Moses Herzog decides, "without these shivery games"—to which Bellow himself offers amen. The crux of all his writing, he insists, is believing in human beings, and this caring or believing or love alone matters." [35] What else does Bellow now suggest man do? What he has suggested many times before. In the magazine version of the novel, he has Sammler provide a direct answer: act reasonably, moderately. "Without limits you have monstrosity, always. Within limits? Well, within limits monsters also appear. But not inevitably." [36] Bellow omits this "advice" from the book version. Yet the thought may be worth recalling in the years ahead.

[35] Saul Bellow, "Distractions of a Fiction Writer," in *The Living Novel: A Symposium,* ed. Granville Hicks (New York: Macmillan, 1957), p. 20.

[36] Saul Bellow, "Mr. Sammler's Planet, Part II," *The Atlantic,* 224 (December 1969), 140.

A Discipline of Nobility:
Saul Bellow's Fiction

by Marcus Klein

In the 1950s the sensible hero journeyed from a position of alienation to one of accommodation. Accommodation to the happy middling community of those years, to the suburbs, to the new wealth and the corporate conscience, to the fat gods. But the accommodation was aware of itself and, for the spirit's ease, it saved a tic of nonconformity. That was the substance of David Riesman's lessons in autonomy, and no social prescription of the decade was so well-liked as his. The journey was the *reisemotif*, so to speak, of serious American fiction in the decade, and of less serious American fiction, too. When the retrieved awareness was small, as often happened, when Marjorie Morningstar accepted Mamaroneck and Sloan Wilson his tailor, when, that is, the progress toward accommodation was most successful, accommodation looked most like retreat.

Saul Bellow's novels, altogether the most exciting fiction of those years, worked too—quite beyond any question of Bellow's intentions —within the motion from alienation to accommodation. Indeed, from a certain distance Bellow's novels find their definition as a systematic exploration of the concerns of all the Wilsons and the Wouks. Only —and of course it makes all the difference—they were more aware, more imaginative, and more severe. Bellow's characters, despite the variousness of mood and style of his work, remain much the same: a youth and a fat man, with a quirky philosopher loitering nearby. And they face problems which are reducible to a single problem: to meet with a strong sense of self the sacrifice of self demanded by social circumstance. Alienation, the sense of separate and unconciliating identity, must travel to accommodation. Bellow's inspiration is finally in other, deeper sources, but as the novels have worked themselves out they have dealt in the terms presented by the history in which they have found themselves. The dialogue between alienation and accommodation is what first of all they are about.

Dangling Man, published in the mid-1940s, took its terms from the '40s and pushed a dour hero over the arc from the impossibility of alienation to the death in accommodation. Joseph in his idiopathic freedom is functionless and unbearably isolated, but when, by hurrying his draft call, he seeks accommodation, he sacrifices the freedom of the self. The problem, whose formal construction Bellow perhaps borrowed from debates in *Partisan Review,* is insoluble, and in Bellow's next book, *The Victim,* it yields to a more tangible problem in responsibility. Asa Leventhal must balance what he owes a man who is at once his persecutor, his victim, and also his companion in this universe against what he owes himself. He discovers that he has a moral obligation in each direction—and that the issue is not only a moral one. Life is a battle in which each engagement suggests the necessity of disengagement, and *vice-versa.*

It may be a comic battle. This is a proposition which all of the dozens of high adventures of Augie March will want, serially, to prove, and which Augie finally will want to preserve intact. Except that it can't be preserved. There is too much running and brawling in the proposition, and no possibility of real freedom or community or love. For that reason *Augie March* never really ends.

In *Seize the Day* Bellow suddenly made the problem and his fiction severe by bringing to the last extremity a hero who can run and brawl no longer, who must find a principle of life in this world that has beaten him—or die. Tommy Wilhelm (together with Bellow) manages it, though he just manages it, in his last, desperate, resonating adventure. He finds himself weeping at the bier of a stranger, and in the same motion discovers that he is moving "toward the consummation of his heart's ultimate need." That need, the whole of the novel comes to reveal, is the need not to die. At the moment of death, his motion is toward existence, the vitality that defines and unites everyone, and his weeping is an acceptance of it and therefore an act of love toward life.

What has been caught, but just caught, is a progress of the soul through its freedom, from isolation to affirmation of ordinary life in the world. The affirmation is made again in the first movement of *Henderson the Rain King.* "Grun-tu-molani," man-want-to-live, an ancient African queen whispers to Henderson, and his heart fills with joy. But Henderson is ridden by high energies and lofty ambitions, and equipped therefore for the discovery that the principle of reconciliation is not enough. He needs further adventures, as the principle needs extension. Man wants to live, but in what shape and form? The communal principle fails Henderson as soon as he learns it when, in an impetuous gesture of good will, attempting to rid a cistern of frogs, he blows up his host's water supply. The idea of community imposes the idea of service, and Henderson possesses that idea fiercely. He would make men better, and free them from the law of decay. But his passion for service must be chastened and trained, and his further adventures under the tutelage of Dahfu, an African king who is part Wilhelm Reich, part Zarathustra, and part King David, provide him with just that spiritual exercise. He is put to lessons in self-transcendence. He must learn to contain humiliations. He must overcome fear. Like Zarathustra, he must empty himself in order to become a man again. Having done so, he can return to his home in Connecticut, to his wife, and he can make plans to enter medical school.

It is to these Nietzschean terms that the dialogue of *Dangling Man,* between alienation and accommodation, has come. The terms now, well over a decade later, are in no close sense the same terms at all. Bellow has got beyond them. But they are clearly consonant with their originals. They refer to the same problem, and the five novels show a strict struggle with it. What is remarkable is that Bellow has played it all by ear. The orderliness of his progress, and the intellectual unity, have after all been the wonderful accident of his commitment. The novels, with perhaps the exception of *The Victim,* are not even well-made. They spill over on themselves; they work themselves out according to the demands of character and frequently, one feels, out of the demands of gimmicks. They exhibit novelistic failures: *Dangling Man* is enclosed and short of action; Augie's exuberance runs down in the middle and becomes repetitive; Henderson suffers turgidity among his other sufferings. But they are shaped, and that is the excitement one feels in them, by an energy of total commitment, by an imagination that will confront human needs and greeds as they spill all over themselves and yield to clarity only after heavy labor.

A large and suffering appreciation of maelstrom, of personality filled with its own chaos and set down in the chaotic circumstances and the obscure obligations of the ordinary world, has shaped the novels and made them into a coherent vision. Bellow's alienated hero before he is alienated is a terribly oppressed individual, and it is with the feeling of his oppression that the fiction no doubt begins. Human beings crowd upon Bellow's hero and attempt to subjugate him. Human beings become burdensome to him. And it is not only those others who directly assault him who threaten his freedom. He begins in a condition of individuality imperiled, and his career is a series of adventures through a metropolis of perils. Bellow's hero lives among clutter, boredom, distraction, things. "Things done by man overshadow us," says Augie. "And this is true also of meat on the table, heat in the pipes, print on the paper, sounds in the air, so that all matters are alike, of the same weight, of the same rank, the caldron of God's wrath on page one and Wieboldt's sale on page two." Augie's complaint is diagnosed as *moha,* opposition of the finite, a curious complaint which is the start in fact of all the Bellovian protagonists.

It is the sheer weight of chaotic existence that first of all defines them. "The novelist is distracted," Bellow says in one of his discursive pieces. ". . . there are more things that solicit the attention of the mind than there ever were before." The novelist is menaced with "death by distraction," and not only the novelist: everyone on every level is exposed to the danger. We are menaced by the sheer distraction of sheer wealth. "The world is too much with us, and there has never been so much world," Bellow has said elsewhere. There is so much money now and there are so many possessions. "Love, duty, principle, thought, significance, everything is being sucked into a fatty and nerveless state of 'well-being.' " The fat gods of the new materialism are all about us demanding our energies.

We are menaced, distracted, and overborne by the sheer clutter of things. And of course it is to the point that Bellow, unlike the past masters, Hemingway and Faulkner, is entirely a city writer. (*Henderson* takes place mostly in Africa, to be sure, but not in the green hills of Africa. It is an Africa teeming with people and political intrigue, and with furniture; an Africa urbanized.) In the city there is much more to contend with. Things and others both are close and thick in Bellow's novels, and though Bellow is not without affection for nature, there is no escape into rural simplicities. In urban circumstances the rites of love are enormously difficult. Bellow's cities—Chicago and New York—are dense with neighbors and noise, with streetcars, subways, families, friends, soot, and filth. Joseph, living in a six-sided box within a Chicago rooming house, is victimized by the old man next door who coughs all night, leaves the door to the toilet open, steals socks, and throws empty whiskey bottles into the alley. *The Victim* begins: "On some nights New York is as hot as Bangkok," and all the gagging heaviness of a New York summer, the light of the sun like "the yellow revealed in the slit of the eye of a wild animal," the subways, the sweat, the listless crowds in the parks, the invincible dirt, the struggle for air, is brought upon Asa Levanthal's moral burden. Augie's Chicago, while it spawns heroic vitalists, is what he calls it in his first sentence, a "somber city." Those vitalists are all Machiavellians, omnipresent, dangerous, reaching out with too many clever hands. The somber city provides neither a recollection of Edenic childhood nor expectation of heaven. Augie is set down into "deep city vexation" and "forced early into deep city aims," and "what," he wants to know, "can that lead to of the highest?" His initiation into love is of the kind the city affords, love paid for and second hand. "That's what city life is.

And so it *didn't* have the luster it should have had, and there *wasn't* any epithalamium of gentle lovers . . ." The character and the fate which are Augie's study are located first in his response to the enormousness and complexity of Chicago. "Crusoe," he says, "alone with nature, under heaven, had a busy, complicated time of it with the unhuman itself, and I am in a crowd that yields results with much more difficulty and reluctance and am part of it myself."

The clutter of the city weighs upon the shapes Tommy Wilhelm and Eugene Henderson, too. His existence lies upon Tommy Wilhelm like a hump, he is "assigned to be the carrier of a load which was his own self," but it makes a difference that he must carry it along upper Broadway on a summer's day. On a day after a sleepless, noisy New York night. Through the dust of the street and the fumes of the buses, through "pushcarts, accordion and fiddle, shoeshine, begging, the dust going round like a woman on stilts," talking to himself because there is no one else to talk to among the millions of a city like New York. "The traffic seemed to come down Broadway out of the sky, where the hot spokes of the sun rolled from the south. Hot, stony odors rose from the subway grating in the street." And when Dr. Tamkin, the tutelary confidence man of the novel, a deity of this inferno, tells Tommy that the world is full of murderers, Tommy answers helplessly that "there are also kind, ordinary, helpful people. They're—out in the country."

Henderson goes out in the country, first as gentleman pig farmer, then as an African explorer, but the spirit, the heat, the humanity, and the junk of the city are always at his back. His farm, become a pig kingdom, swarms with grunting animals. The city's steaming pavement becomes the strange, obscurely threatening "calcareous" rocks of King Dahfu's country. The heat of the city becomes the boiling African sun, felt as the jungle fever which oppresses Henderson throughout his spiritual adventuring. Tamkin is recreated in King Dahfu, Henderson's guiding spirit, king of the warlike Wariri, another prince of darkness. The clotted Broadway crowd becomes the frenzied savages who batter Henderson to his knees in the ceremony in which he is made the Rain King.

Henderson abandons things and people to make the trip to Africa. It is the notion of junk that is the immediate motive of his going. Climbing through the rooms of an old lady just dead, he is overwhelmed by her collected rubbish: "Bottles, lamps, old butter dishes, and chandeliers were on the floor, shopping bags filled with string and rags, and pronged openers that the dairies used to give away to lift the paper tops from milk bottles; and bushel baskets full of buttons and china door knobs." And he thinks, "Henderson, put forth effort. You, too, will die of this pestilence. Death will annihilate you and nothing will remain, and there will be nothing left but junk." He puts forth effort to escape, but the city stays with him nonetheless. In Africa he talks city talk: "Now listen, Your Highness, don't sell me down the river. You know what I mean? I thought you liked me." He thinks, in Africa, in city metaphors and of city events; the city maintains its pressure, and alive within his other speculations is the city idea of people, nameless, faceless, with whom no communication is possible. Tommy Wilhelm was condemned to talk to himself in a city where every other man spoke a language entirely his own, and Henderson is brought to the vision of Babel raised to include the universe: "This planet has billions of passengers on it, and those were preceded by infinite billions and there are vaster billions to come, and none of these, no, not one, can I hope ever to understand. Never!" He goes on to reflect that this matter of quantity, come upon in another view, need not bury you alive, that it is marvelous and not depressing— but the reflection comes of his struggle and not of his primary condition.

Under the mass of such quantity and confronted by such chaos in the external world, Bellow's hero in his first motion moves toward unburdening and sloughing off. Civil society is too much, and indeed in extreme moments even the cultural accumulations, the very history and wisdom of civilization, are too much and are rejected. Most emphatically by the aging wise man, another Zarathustrian prophet, of Bellow's monologue called "Address by Gooley MacDowell to the Hasbeens Club of Chicago":

> Around our heads we have a dome of thought as thick as atmosphere to breathe. And what's about? One thought leads to another as breath leads to breath. By pulling [it] into universal consciousness, can [we] explain everything from Democritus to Bikini? But a person can no longer keep up, and plenty are dying of good ideas. We have them in the millions, in compilations, from the *Zend Avesta* to now, all on file with the best advice for [one] and all human occasions. . . . Look at us, deafened, hampered, obstructed, impeded, impaired and bowel-glutted with wise counsel and good precept, and the more plentiful our ideas the worse our headaches. So we ask, will some good creature pull out the plug and ease our disgusted hearts a little?

It is a prayer Augie, too, records: "Anyway, there's too much of everything of this kind, *that's* come home to me, too much history and culture to keep track of, too many details, too much news, too much example, too much influence, too many guys who tell you to be as they are, and all this hugeness, abundance, turbulence, Niagara Falls torrent. Which who is supposed to interpret? Me?" And Tommy Wilhelm is overcome by the sheer information in Tamkin's discourses, and Henderson, an overwhelmed millionaire, under the spur of a similar impulse fills beautiful pieces of architecture with pigs and then, seeking Eden, makes a safari to the precivilized past, "the real past," he says, "no history or junk like that." And if all history and culture are rejected in a style that borrows widely from the world's accumulation of literature, that fact is more than irony. Bellow's style, which beginning with *Augie March* has become a racy vehicle bearing great freights of knowledge, is a thing that simultaneously admits and dismisses clutter. All its process of literary echoing goes to lend the rejection authority.

The matter has become more and more apparent, but since the beginning all Bellow's heroes have started in a gesture of escape from burdens, an extreme romantic gesture. It is a gesture which in its extremity brings Bellow into touch with one of the defining impulses of American character, into touch with at least all the classic Redskins of American letters, from Leatherstocking to Whitman to Mark Twain to Hemingway, all those who light out for the woods, the open road, the Territory, and into touch perhaps with the Palefaces, too. (The extreme need to escape burdens, to be free of all the clutter, is certainly as well a distinction of Hawthorne and Henry James.) Bellow's hero is tempted frequently to epiphanies of love for mankind in general, though never for things, and his motion is brought to various thematic significances, but he is in the first instance activated by the need to rid himself of the weight of the chaos.

He can escape from under that weight into harmony with natural laws vaguely realized as beneficent, or he can escape into himself, locate all value and reality in his person, or he can in various ways attempt to reconcile himself with external existence in all its chaos. And it is out of those three possibilities, the first two stretching toward the last, that the action and the total thematic construct of Bellow's novels have come.

Neither as a metaphysical conception nor in the pleasantness of its phenomena is Nature ever dominant as a motif, though it has become more emphatic as the novels have succeeded each other. Bellow's city imagination is not comfortable with the Natural Laws. He has little nature to bring to them. But his hero entertains a yearning for them and a provisional trust that they are good, because the circumscription of the possibility of escape demands it. Joseph dismisses "nature" when it is presented to him by a friend who complains of the treelessness and too-human deadness of New York, dismisses it as nostalgic sentimentality. Nevertheless his whole struggle toward what he calls the "facts of simple existence" is involved in a turn of the seasons toward fruitful harmony. The chaotic winter submits to spring. Joseph begins his journal in the dark Chicago December and surrenders himself, relieves himself of his freedom, in April. Bellow accents the matter by having Joseph look forward throughout his winter to walking in the park in his spring coat on the 21st of March, and he shifts the mood of the novel toward resolution with the coming spring.

Asa Leventhal, locked in New York's inhuman heat, has moments of freshness and deep breathing at sea on the Staten Island ferry, and the plot of the novel moves him toward the relief that will come with Labor Day. The attempted suicide of his antagonist, Allbee, on the eve of that day makes possible Leventhal's birth into a possible world, and the day itself brings cooling breezes. Nature as transcendent reality brushes Leventhal lightly once—for a brief moment of half-sleep he feels the whole world present to him and about to offer him a mysterious, it would seem redeeming, discovery. But the discovery blows by him and at the end of his action, having abandoned ultimate questioning and now re-entering a darkened theatre with his wife, he is no closer to a notion of reality.

But Augie comes, if not conclusively, at least wholeheartedly to the natural laws, his "axial lines" called "Truth, love, peace, bounty, usefulness, harmony!" which, he says, quiver right through him when striving stops. They excite him in the moment after his perception of them to pastoral ambitions. He wants to own and settle on a Midwestern farm, to marry, and to teach orphans. His adventures carry him, however, into complexities which won't permit cessation of striving. The axial lines, he says, are "not imaginary stuff . . . because I bring my entire life to the test." There is no doubting his sincerity, but this is one of the moments when Augie's hopefulness becomes shrill. His whole life does not validate the perception. The novel does not earn that leap into faith. In fact the novel is honest beyond Augie's knowing and it does not permit him so easy an escape. Nor is it an escape that Tommy Wilhelm, so strictly confined by authentic troubles, can practically afford to take. Not, anyway, in its romantic simplicity. Tamkin does offer him nature. "Creative is nature," he says. "Rapid. Lavish. Inspirational. It shapes leaves. . . . You don't know what you've got within you." But it is no solace to a middle-aged slob rapidly and lavishly dying in the middle of New York City. Tommy is simply confused by the offer.

It is Henderson who most clearly moves toward harmony with the natural laws. He goes among noble savages and to live with the beasts in the field—and if his Africa has the feel of Chicago and the smell of New York, that is apparently despite Bellow's first intention. Moreover it is Henderson who most clearly demonstrates the naïveté of the escape into nature. He makes a journey into the heart of darkness to discover the horror of it. He goes to Africa to discover Reality. A voice within him says constantly, "I want," and that is what it ultimately wants. "Truth" and "Reality" are ambitions always at his lips. His soul's progress is marked by a succession of emblematic beasts. First a porcine pig farmer in a sty of piggish phenomena, he comes in the first stage of his journey upon a motley tribe of pious cow-worshipers and then he tries to do what none of them will do, to deal at first hand with a plague of frogs. He fails, but in failing he has pursued nature to a certain depth. His next, and most important, stop, with a tribe of lion-worshipers, brings him face to face with the thing itself. Under the tutelage of Dahfu—himself a refugee from civilization come home to meet Reality—Henderson is put to the task (following disciplines derived from the somatic psychology of Wilhelm Reich) of assuming and absorbing Dahfu's pet lioness. She is all lion, Dahfu observes. "Does not take issue with the inherent. Is one hundred per cent within the given." She is the way to Being, the end of Becoming, the unchanging truth prior to the cycle of desire and fear. She will force Henderson to the present moment. "She will make consciousness to shine. She will burnish you." She *is* Being—or, as it turns out, penultimate Being—itself. (Being, of course, not seen as daffodils. Bellow is never so lacking in severity as that.) And Henderson has some small success in overcoming his fear of the lioness and then in absorbing lion-ness. He meets the inhuman thing. In the same way, it happens, and within the same image as previous Bellow heroes have met it— Asa saw the yellow of the sun like that in the slit of the eye of a wild animal, "say a lion, something inhuman that didn't care about anything human and yet was implanted in every human being, too," and Augie had adventures with the lion's American equivalent, an eagle with a "pressed-down head, the killing eye, the deep life of its feathers." But Henderson goes further. The lion is pure fire, he says, forcing him to close his eyes. So are the stars pure fire, he realizes, and not small gold objects. He develops his consciousness of the matter beyond ways that are permitted Asa and Augie. He discovers that the inhuman fire is at the center of his humanity, too.

With that discovery he should achieve harmony. Here is the very principle of Augie's axial lines. But Henderson is hurried to a further pitch of Reality. Dahfu's lion is a pet lioness after all. Henderson is now made to confront the authentic lion, male and wild:

> Then, at the very door of consciousness, there was a snarl and I looked down from this straw perch . . . into the big, angry, hair-framed face of the lion. It was all wrinkled, contracted; within those wrinkles was the darkness of murder. The lips were drawn away from the gums, and the breath of the animal came over me, hot as oblivion, raw as blood. I started to speak aloud. I said, "Oh, my God, whatever You think of me, let me not fall under this butcher shop. . . ." And to this, as a rider, the thought added itself that this was all mankind needed, to be conditioned into the image of a ferocious animal like the one below.

That lion castrates and kills King Dahfu. The voice of the lion is the voice of death itself. And this Real, far from being the escape from chaos, is chaos and old night itself. To submit to the harmony it offers, on the principle that the lion outside is inside, too, would be to accept the inhumanity of the inhuman Real. Henderson had in one of his discourses with Dahfu parried Eliot by saying that human-kind could not stand too much *un*reality, but Eliot wins the point. Henderson now reflects on the great inescapable rhythms of life, Augie's axial lines once again, but he reflects that he can't afford to worry about them. The old queen's advice, "Grun-tu-molani," man-want-to-live, comes to mean going about the business of living despite the death-dealing, chaotic Real.

That is very much, if not explicitly, the ground upon which Augie finally mounts his optimism. If Augie is only incidentally concerned with the nature of the real Real, he is completely engaged with the natural laws as they impinge on his larky and boisterous freedom, and the *animal ridens* rises in him *despite* their influences. His adventures are escapes from all determinisms, human and suprahuman. And that is the ground upon which Tommy Wilhelm, finally made to confront death as ultimate reality, can choose to live. The escape from under the weight of external chaos into the natural laws does not work. It is no escape at all. At the center of the universe are violence and death. The vague yearning for the natural laws lucent in the earlier novels is quite extinguished when the fiction works it out to the test.

There is an alternative dodge for Bellow's oppressed hero in the assertion of his own character as the locus of reality and value. In the face of cluttering chaos and with a swagger, he can assert personality broadly. "A man's character is his fate, says Heraclitus," says Augie with relishing approval, and if at the end he learns that a man's fate is his character, why, that is a fate good enough for him. Tamkin advises Tommy:

> Seek ye then that which art not there
> In thine own glory let thyself rest.
> Witness. Thy power is not bare.
> Thou art King. Thou art at thy best.

It is advice under which Tommy staggers. The hero of one of Bellow's short stories, "The Trip to Galena," a young man engaged in a war against the overburdening boredom of things and people, proposes that "a man is bound to do everything in his lifetime." He will conduct war by the simple exertion of personality. And Henderson, whose person is explicitly reflected in his body, is great and joyous in his body. His very suffering delights him because it is an exercise of personality. At the center of the universe, then, in this action, is the individual self. The self constantly threatened, however, and presenting an obligation. The Bellovian hero will protect his personality from the outside or, because he can't live in a nutshell, insinuate it in and out of chaotic experience; but he will maintain it, attempt to maintain it, always unbroken.

At the end the assertion is merely a dodge, and the escape is blocked precisely because the inhuman outside *is* within—that, finally, is why "alienation" is impossible. Nor can personality remain untouched. The attempt at self-preservation raises severe moral problems. And at the end the person must indeed be broken in order to achieve life. But the motion of the escape meanwhile irradiates Bellow's writing. It is the inspiration of his comedy. Because the need is desperate, the assertion of the person is extreme—with *Augie March* and thereafter, though there are hints of the mood before, the assertion is raised in various characters to burlesque. Bellow's personalist hero yelps, quite the gamecock of a new, urban wilderness, quite like his backwoodsman prototype impelled to brashness by dispossession and inadequacy and the feeling of threatening powers everywhere. He sings himself with quite the same nervy insolence with which Walt Whitman met the world, and like that witty comedian he makes a great gesture of including the whole world in himself, but then he adopts shifts and evasions and contrarieties to keep free of it. And like Whitman, he celebrates himself by the exercise of a free-wheeling, inclusive, cataloguing rhetoric, gripping great bunches of facts in sentences that just manage to balance, racing through various levels of diction, saying with every turn, "Look at me, going everywhere!" It is a gaudy fireworks of a style, in itself a brilliant affirmation of the self. At the same time it performs the ironic function, by its calculated indiscriminateness (in Bellow and in Walt Whitman, too), of discarding everything it picks up. It is therefore the perfect expression of the dynamic, disengaging, mock hero.

Dahfu accuses Henderson of being a great avoider, and the same accusation may be made against all of Bellow's personalists. Augie is the clearest instance. His famous "availability" is the flamboyant self-asserting part of him, but it is perfectly and in every engagement countered by his "opposition." At the end he still has all his availability; his great appetite for life and engagement is intact precisely because he has spent it in no experience. He is presented taking what amounts to still another oath of unsusceptibility to all the "big personalities, destiny molders, and heavy-water brains, Machiavellis and wizard evildoers, big-wheels and imposers-upon, absolutists." The oath is redundant, for his unsusceptibility is continuous. Indeed it is a moral failing, and one which Augie is made to realize. The one advice by his many advisers which cuts deep is that he can't be hurt enough by the fate of other people. That is a failing in love, and the most strenuous part of Augie's action is in the problem it poses. It is a failing he never rectifies, for to do so would stop him cold.

Augie is a kind of Huck Finn, with his something adoptional about him, his participation in a linear series of adventures, his resilience, his mounting good humor. The comparison has been noted. But he is like Huck, too, in his reluctance to be civilized. He eludes. He is not to be caught by the shaping influences. He won't be determined. Moreover, he is Huck confined to a city populated by endless duplications of the King, the Duke, and Colonel Sellers. No matter that his adventures take him over two continents, he is always in Chicago, without a Territory to light out for—and so he is put to more muscular shifts of duplicity. What the Mississippi and the Territory could do for Huck, Augie must do for himself. His only territory is his personality, which he must keep free. Life is dramatic for Augie, it is process, and the process is that kind of evasion that keeps all events and the person from settling.

A new discipline and another notion of the possibilities of freedom will be needed by the personalist hero who is to avoid evasion and be hurt enough by the fate of other people. Bellow comes to it, but after *Augie* as before the strong assertion of independent personality secures all of his lyricism, and without restriction to the personalist protagonists. Radical self-assertion, assertion of the real, untypical self, is an act of courage in Bellow's squeezing world. There is glamor in it which just for itself for the moment transvalues all moral obligations. It commands Bellow's love even for the very Machiavellians he loathes —sometimes, it should be added, with the disastrous result of turning them quaint.

Almost in the very beginning, in 1942 with his second published story, "The Mexican General," there appeared the first in Bellow's line of resolutely vital knaves. The General is a provincial opportunist who has secured his opportunity with the assassination of Trotsky. He is an arrogant ghoul, well-mistressed, a vile entrepreneur at the funeral of the Revolution, and he is made to bear a moral of political corruption. But he is also equipped with Lawrentian innuendoes of personality—he has Indian vigor, he is alive, he has personal force, he is an *Übermensch* just not yet attained to moral transcendence, and the pale moral sophisticate of the story is reduced by him to a fascinated helplessness. There is no doubt that the Mexican General is intended as a villain, but, perhaps despite his intentions, Bellow celebrates him. There will be many like him, with variations in virtue: Kirby Allbee and (also in *The Victim*) incidental chieftains, the patriarch Schlossberg; the matriarch Mrs. Harkavy; then Augie's

Grandma Lausch and his "first superior man," William Einhorn—and indeed every one of the thirty-odd Machiavellians in his adventures; then Dr. Tamkin; then King Dahfu with his "strong gift of life" and his extra shadow-casting intensity, and Henderson himself. All of them are, if not reincarnations of the General, at least apparently related to him. The descendants inhabit Bellow's shorter pieces as well: plays, stories, monologues, and a curious and festive interview (published in *The Reporter*) with Joe "Yellow Kid" Weil, an aged oligarch among the Chicago confidence men and among the Chicago intellectuals of Bughouse Square, "an elegant and old-fashioned gentleman" of "round phrases and leisurely speech," a reader of Nietzsche and Herbert Spencer, a masterful man who has refused to be society's obedient slave.

The virtue in the exercise of personality for its own sake is clearly a virtue derived from necessity. It is derived as well, seemingly, from the lessons in necessity inherent in one tradition of Yiddish literature, the tradition of what has been called *dos kleine menschele*, the little man of the Eastern European ghetto, the *stetl*, who is forced by the presence of perils everywhere to ingenious ways of personal survival. One of those ways is in mock-heroism. Yiddish conversation itself, a vessel of the spirit that produced *dos kleine menschele*, is, Bellow himself has said,

> full of the grandest historical, mythological, and religious allusions. The Creation, the Fall, the Flood, Egypt, Alexander, Titus, Napoleon, the Rothschilds, the sages, and the Laws may get into the discussion of an egg, a clothesline, or a pair of pants.

The conversation of Augie and his major successors is full of the same, sprouting comparative references to heroes from Jacob to Caesar to John Dillinger to Sir Wilfred Grenfell, to epical events from the Diaspora to the campaigning events of World War II. This manner of living on terms of familiarity with greatness, Bellow goes on to say, contributed to the ghetto's sense of the ridiculous. It also performed a more delicate feat of irony, and one to which Bellow is sensitive. On the one hand, the mock-heroics of the little man render all conventional heroism absurd. Mock-heroism in Bellow's fiction serves that function. But the mock-heroics of Bellow's protagonists and antagonists (both) are far from those of tradition—the tradition of Chaucer and Rabelais and Swift. They are not practiced with such broad and easy security. On the other hand, the acts themselves constitute real heroism, a mode of strong self-assertion in a community that disallows the self. Given the prison of restrictive circumstances of the *stetl*, and then those of Bellow's city, it is the only mode by which personal identity can be emphasized. Augie's mythical mouth-

fuls provide rough fun; they burlesque his own bravado and dilute
all pretension. At the same time they call Julius Caesar and John
Dillinger to witness. There is courage in the insolence of it. The
bravado is a thin mask for the bravery, rather than vice versa. Augie's
frisky speech is the power he puts forth to win from all oppressive
circumstances a right to exist.

The exercise of personality is everywhere in Bellow's world an act
of courage. The salvation of the self, whether by defiance or evasion,
is an honored behavior. The self is where felt reality is, and where
meaning may be. But the rocks upon which simple exulting personality would founder were discovered at the beginning. Joseph, whose
whole struggle was for the means by which the self might be preserved
in a time of death, comes upon the disappointing fact of his own
baseness and then on the necessity of goodness in community. Alone
and allowed to test his dreadful freedom, he becomes irritable, self-
indulgent, oversensitive, quarrelsome. Perhaps he has not achieved
the highest freedom. Freedom should be the condition of dignity. But,
meanwhile, he does not know what to do with the freedom he has.
His free self becomes burdensome to him, and he has a continuous
lesson in the end of ordinary free self-hood in Vanaker, the lonely,
disgusting old man next door, grunting, hacking, thieving, and smell-
ing away his existence. It is when Joseph sees a rat scurrying through
some garbage that he resolves to give up his freedom and his self.
The self he has held so dear is an "imprisoning self," and the end
of his speculation about "ideal constructions" is that the highest of
them is that which *unlocks* the imprisoning self. Alienation is not to
be made into a doctrine. The other side of freedom is isolation. Alienation is, moreover, morally reprehensible. "What we really want,"
Joseph discovers, "is to stop living so exclusively and vainly for our
own sake, impure and unknowing, turning inward and self-fastened."
Joseph's talent is "for being a citizen, or what is today called, most
apologetically, a good man," and "goodness," he is forced to know,
"is achieved not in a vacuum, but in the company of other men, attended by love."

The notions of inherent baseness, of human nature sharing the
bestiality of nature itself, and of love as an imperative lurk everywhere
for the personalist hero. At some point in his adventuring each of
Bellow's heroes finds the beast within. Asa Leventhal must wrestle
with his own inhumanity. Augie, rich in spirit and rowdy as he is, is
unable to stay with his purest feelings. He is confronted by the last
of his many advisers with a vision of the human soul as composed of
secrets, lies, and diseases. Tommy Wilhelm is confronted by Tamkin's
notion of a corrupting "pretender soul" turning all human beings into
murderers. ("Yes, I think so too," says Tommy. "But personally . . .

don't feel like a murderer. I always try to lay off. It's the others who et me.") Henderson sees himself as a bargain basement of deformities, is whole existence proposed in metaphors of beasts. And in one short rical instance, in an Easter sermon by one of Bellow's quacky truth-elling rejuvenators, cannibalism is imploded as the law of life. "The ermon of Dr. Pep" begins in a protest against hamburger for the bad onscience in its disguise of the slain beast and ends in a protest gainst the suicide by which a gentle humanity disguises its murders. Ien must eat, and murder is the cost of civilization.

But that statement is merely ecstatic. Bellow's major heroes, com-elled to live beyond the lyrical moment, confront the beast within nd the human propensity to murder, and they cannot rest in their erception. They must—each of them—as well confront the moral onditions of civilization, the cost of which would seem to be precisely he self.

Each of the major protagonists is forced, like Augie, to suffer con-usion between love and an independent fate. Not only that, he must train to reconcile those impossible opposites. That is what the struggle or accommodation comes to. Joseph strains and fails—or he ends not uite in failure but in a desperate attempt to reacquaint himself with rdinary communal reality. Asa Leventhal, a self-enclosed, self-ighteous victim, is assaulted by the imperative of brotherhood, which t the end he cannot accept. But he does reach a large idea of what t is to be exactly human. An old man in the lavatory of a movie heatre tells him that Boris Karloff is a law unto himself. One wouldn't e Boris Karloff. To be neither more nor less than human, Asa dis-overs, is to be "accountable in spite of many weaknesses," and with hat discovery he achieves a tentative goodness. Augie, not hurt enough y the fate of other people, particularly fails the severe test of ro-nantic love. The test, his affair with Thea, is most particularly rich in onfusion—not only for Augie; Bellow too has groped his way through t. Thea's love is murderous. But it is real love, a way of discovering ther people. If it is strange to Augie, then, Augie himself comes to dmit, that is his own fault. The struggle for Augie is to make it less trange. And Tommy Wilhelm and Henderson, too, struggle to admit ove to their freedom, to be themselves and at the same time to have a lace in the human community.

Tommy Wilhelm at the last extremity of his need seizes the day and noves toward the consummation of his heart's ultimate need. But it s with *Henderson* that the consummation is first achieved and ren-lered, achieved by a Nietzschean notion of heroic self-transcendence ased on freedom, a notion that has been hinted at in all the previous novels.

Despite all circumstances of oppression, despite the violence of nature and the violence of men, despite the cocky, assertive "I," despite all determinisms and despite finitude and death, the individual *is* free and free to choose. He can become better. Joseph felt that by some transcendent means human beings could distinguish themselves from brute things and he considered that the universal quest was for pure freedom, but the practical means to transcendence were not at hand. In *The Victim* the patriarch Schlossberg suggests as equal possibilities that man is "lousy and cheap" and that he has "greatness and beauty." But if those are equal possibilities, then one *can* choose. The means of transcendence are at hand. And what would one choose? "Have dignity, you understand me?" he says. "Choose dignity." But for As there are practical difficulties. Augie's Einhorn preaches a similar doctrine of self-transformation, as does Augie himself, in passing. And Tamkin strenuously offers Tommy Wilhelm the possibility of choice Tommy *can* seize the day and thereby choose life. But not yet nobility, a word much favored by Bellow and meaning the coalescence of self-lessness and selfhood. The individual who would exert his freedom toward such transcendence will need great spiritual capabilities to begin with, and then hard discipline.

Henderson is the man, and, in terms of a succession of metamorphoses, he gets such discipline.

By Bellow's own inspiration or by astonishing coincidence, Henderson's career follows with great closeness, with only one initial deviation, that of the spirit in the first parable of *Thus Spake Zarathustra* Says Zarathustra:

> Of three metamorphoses of the spirit I tell you: how the spirit becomes a camel; and the camel, a lion; and the lion, finally, a child.
>
> There is much that is difficult for the spirit, the strong reverent spirit that would bear much: but the difficult and the most difficult are what its strength demands.
>
> What is difficult? asks the spirit that would bear much, and kneels down like a camel wanting to be well loaded. What is most difficult, O heroes, asks the spirit that would bear much, that I may take it upon myself and exult in my strength? Is it not humbling oneself to wound one's haughtiness? Letting one's folly shine to mock one's wisdom?
>
> Or is it this: feeding on the acorns and grass of knowledge and, for the sake of the truth, suffering hunger in one's soul?
>
> Or is it this: stepping into filthy waters when they are the waters of truth, and not repulsing cold frogs and hot toads?
>
> Or is it this: loving those who despise us and offering a hand to the ghost that would frighten us?
>
> [*Walter Kaufmann translation*]

1 All excerpts from *Thus Spake Zarathustra* are quoted with permission from *The Portable Nietzsche*, trans. by Walter Kaufmann. Copyright 1954 by The Viking Press, Inc.

Henderson is not a camel—he is a Connecticut millionaire, not a Bedouin, and so without that opportunity—but he is a strenuous spirit who would bear much and who demands the extremest test of his strength. He engages the Zarathustrian burdens of humility and folly. If he does not feed on acorns and grass, he raises and identifies with pigs that do, and he suffers hunger in his soul. He does precisely, among the first of his African tribes, meet the test of frogs in the filthy waters, but without humility, and it is to his sorrow that he repulses them. And he strains to love those who despise and reject him.

Says Zarathustra:

> All these most difficult things the spirit that would bear much takes upon itself: like the camel that, burdened, speeds into the desert, thus the spirit speeds into its desert.
>
> In the loneliest desert, however, the second metamorphosis occurs: here the spirit becomes a lion who would conquer his freedom and be master in his own desert. Here he seeks out his last master: he wants to fight him and his last god; for ultimate victory he wants to fight with the great dragon.
>
> Who is the great dragon whom the spirit will no longer call lord and god? "Thou shalt" is the name of the great dragon. But the spirit of the lion says, "I will." "Thou shalt" lies in his way, sparkling like gold, an animal covered with scales; and on every scale shines a golden "thou shalt."
>
> My brothers, why is there a need in the spirit for the lion? Why is not the beast of burden, which renounces and is reverent, enough?
>
> To create new values—that even the lion cannot do; but the creation of freedom for oneself for new creation—that is within the power of the lion. The creation of freedom for oneself and a sacred "No" even to duty—for that, my brothers, the lion is needed. To assume the right to new values—that is the most terrifying assumption for a reverent spirit that would bear much. Verily, to him it is preying, and a matter for a beast of prey. He once loved "thou shalt" as most sacred: now he must find illusion and caprice even in the most sacred, that freedom from his love may become his prey: the lion is needed for such prey.

Henderson speeds from the meek, reverent, cow-worshiping Arnewi into the desert. There he destroys himself, body and soul, in order to become a lion, and in the very process he learns something about the possibilities of self-transformation. He learns, moreover, what it is to contain one's freedom. The lion, Dahfu tells him, is pure Being. It is entirely itself, it is all unobliging will, and, heavy with the clutter of existence, on all sides oppressed, Henderson secures from it a way of confronting the oppressing, death-dealing universe. The lion is for Henderson, and Dahfu, the intensity of the self beyond all reverence, the avatar of freedom, and Henderson, as lion, looks forward to new creation.

Says Zarathustra:

> But say, my brothers, what can the child do that even the lion could not do? Why must the preying lion still become a child? The child is innocence and forgetting, a new beginning, a game, a self-propelled wheel, a first movement, a sacred "Yes." For the game of creation, my brothers, a sacred "Yes" is needed: the spirit now wills his own will, and he who had been lost to the world now conquers his own world.
>
> Of three metamorphoses of the spirit I have told you: how the spirit became a camel; and the camel, a lion; and the lion, finally, a child.

The last of Henderson's tutelary spirits is the child he adopts on his plane back to America. The airplane makes a fueling stop and he runs with the child in his arms around the airport in Newfoundland. What, specifically, Henderson has newly found is his way back, after he had been lost to the world, to his ordinary life, but he comes back now in a new movement with a new will to creation: "I guess I felt it was my turn now to move, and so went running—leaping, leaping, pounding, and tingling over the pure white lining of the gray Arctic silence." A self-propelled wheel. And he is provided with a sacred "Yes." He has always had a "service ideal." It had been crushed, but now it has been newly invented, he will enter medical school, and his suicidal violence has been transformed to love.

Thus spake Zarathustra, and it is perhaps of note that Zarathustra at that time sojourned in the town that is called The Motley Cow.

That is not to suggest anything programmatic about *Henderson*. The novel is not a manual for living. If the Nietzschean parable is at the center of it, the parable is elaborated, indeed sportively elaborated. It is a funny book and it goes off all sorts of ways. Nor is it to suggest that *Henderson* is the summit of a mountain of thought up which Bellow has been scrabbling the years thus far of his novelist's career. Bellow, too, has been disorderly and boisterous, full of strong assertions and apothegms which have the finality only of the fullest fiction, which crack on the next turn of events and mood.

And there will be more events.

But the novels have, all this while, been going somewhere—not, of course, toward any summit at all, nor toward any solution to anything. Bellow's domain for investigation is nothing less than the bases of all moral behavior, wherein one expects no solutions except by fiat or by sermon. Fiction is only the jittery act of reaching. When the goal is sufficient, as in Bellow's fiction it is, and when in spite of jitters the reach is serious and long and one can see that it is reaching, fiction becomes crucial. As in Bellow's case it has.

Postscript *1973*

When I wrote this essay, more than ten years ago, I of course realized that it would soon be out of date. I was attempting a usual kind of academic enterprise, a complete-works analysis—of a work which not only was not complete but which had been defining itself to that point by its particular urge to outstrip its own calculations, by the sheerly contingent nature of its resolutions. The attempt seemed to me to be plausible nevertheless, and even useful, because the problems adumbrated by the work were, as I thought, so clearly the givens of contemporary American civilization. I had for my subject both the fiction of Saul Bellow and also "issues" certifiably of basic public concern. My argument was that the fiction of Saul Bellow was *exemplary*. The material of Bellow's fiction was the response of sensibility and imagination and intelligence and personality—the privacy of everybody, but in its highest instances—to the moment in history. The significant, symptomatic canting term of the moment in history seemed to me to be "alienation." Everybody, after any preliminary motion of thought, was alienated. The term had come to be honorific and pretentious; Bellow had made it mean something, something hurtful, and by so doing had rescued all of us from feelings of privileged malaise. Where there had been symptom, he had created severity, dilemma, and challenge.

If my essay was quickly out of date, I think now that it did discover some true patterns in Bellow's fiction and that it had a validity even as prediction. Those characterizing shiftings between "alienation" and "accommodation" which I thought were to be discovered in the earlier novels are repeated at least in *Herzog* and in the play *The Last Analysis*.

Herzog and Bummidge are, again, men who begin in concentrated, claustral self-examination, and who from obsession with the self break forth into world views, universal theories, metaphysical speculation, history—in short, into the public environment. The problem for both of these protagonists, still, is that the one shift is as impossible as the other. The privacy of the individual is a literal impossibility, and as a principle it is immoral—by definition. On the other hand, the public truth is crushing and, finally, too abstract to be real. Meanwhile, their adventuring consists of desperate attempts to make conjunctions, to find a principle of concurrence between private reality and formulations of universal truth. Bummidge performs psychoanalysis upon himself in order to cure his "Humanitis," an "emotional disorder," as he defines it, "of our relation to the human condition." *"Je sens mon coeur et je connais les hommes,"* says Herzog—twice, at first with conviction but then, the second time, dubiously.

They are aspirants to goodness, once again, meaning precisely the establishment of knowledge of kinship with the collective will of all of the millions of others beyond the self. "But let's stick to what matters," says Herzog. "I really believe that brotherhood is what makes a man human. . . . The real and essential question is one of our employment by other human beings and their employment by us." Meanwhile, as was the case with Bellow's earlier heroes, the authority for their aspiration is entirely a function of their failures of kinship. Failure in this sense is the revelation of Bummidge's—or anyone else's —psychoanalysis. Moses Herzog, forty-seven years old, twice divorced and with two children behind him, undone by lovers and a failure as a lover, a bad father having been an ungrateful child and an indifferent citizen, is a man who has risen, as he says, from humble origins to complete disaster. What the two of them really know about brotherhood is that it is constantly betrayed from both without and within. All potential brothers tend to be exploiters. The individual soul, doting on its own uniqueness, pitying itself, distorts and sickens all connections. So Bummidge asks himself, "What's the matter, Bummidge? Don't you like other human beings?" And he answers:

> "Like them! I adore them! Only I can't bear them. I love 'em like a dog. So ardent, so smoochy. Wagging my tail. This sick, corrupt emotion leaks out of me."

The universal theories and world views do not meet the test of their individual failures. The failures remain authoritative. But in both instances—as was the case with Bellow's earlier heroes—the adventurers end in an assertion that despite everything, a true principle of concurrence can be found. The definition of the principle is still entirely provisional; but it is to be known that it is something less than any formal intellectual construct, and that it is a given of the human condition. For the comedian Bummidge, salvation will be discovered in purgative laughter. Like Augie before him, he knows that man is (fortuitously, blessedly) the laughing animal. Laughter can transform the butcher shop which the human situation has become. Having passed, as he says, by means of his own device through the stages of brutality and mediocrity, he is ready at the end to establish his Institute of Nonsense, designed to rid the soul of the debris of its peculiarities and perversities. Herzog, the certified intellectual and specialist in Romantic Thought, has all the while been trying to write a great book which might overturn "the last of the Romantic errors about the uniqueness of the Self" and which would end "with a new angle on the modern condition, showing how life could be lived by renewing universal connections." The kind of connection which he finally discovers in his own life is Romantic in the Wordsworthian sense: he acknowledges the Nature within his nature. His convalescence from his private disasters has taken place in June. His little daughter is named June. His girl friend Ramona, who takes sex as her religion, is by calling a florist. He moves into his decrepit old farmhouse in the Berkshires, and when Ramona comes to bring him her comfort, he reacts by bringing her wild flowers, and at this point the knowledge comes to him that he is done with the fury of addressing letters to the world.

The assertion is made desperately, but buoyantly. Much has been sloughed off, most notably a debris of grand theories about the nature of the human condition. As Bellow himself has said (in his *Paris Review* interview in 1966), *Herzog* concludes with a first step, "The first *real* step." And the same is true of *The Last Analysis*. This first step is not itself subjected to any testing. The good hope with which it is broached does not rest on any reason, any assessment of probabilities. The end in both instances is another beginning, which is not pressed to an end.

These terminal affirmations, in all of Bellow's fiction and up through these instances, have nevertheless not been arbitrary. They have been the inventions of characters who have been able to perceive that their various kinds of isolation, of "alienation," have been at least partially self-inflicted, or in any event potentially resolvable by reference to the self. It is all a matter of perspective, of course. These characters discover that despite heavy private woes and despite terrific propaganda to the contrary—"the commonplaces of the Wasteland outlook," in Herzog's words, "the cheap mental stimulants of Alienation, the cant and rant of pipsqueaks about Inauthenticity and Forlornness"—despite so much, adjustments can be made, and just what they will consist of is not yet so very important.

Mr. Sammler's Planet is a different matter. The perspective prior to this, even in such relatively somber novels as *Dangling Man* and *The Victim,* has been comic. The various selves have in their inceptions been presented with the energy sufficient for sheer provisionality. They rebound from all terminations.

Like the other characters, Sammler does affirm the human connection in spite of many provocations to the contrary. It is the object of the action of the novel to make him do so. In his long life he has already once witnessed the end of rational good will, that which was particularly symbolized by his Bloomsbury days and by H. G. Wells. He has suffered human madness egregiously: a Polish Jew in the time of the Holocaust, he has in fact once been murdered, and, having managed to crawl back from the grave from beneath other corpses,

he has been a murderer. Now in New York, with his one good eye—
the other was smashed in with a rifle butt by a German soldier—he
witnesses what seems to promise to be the second collapse of the world.
All evidences indicate the triumph of "dark romanticism," that triumph ironically made possible by liberal enlightenment—

> "the struggles of three revolutionary centuries being won while the
> feudal bonds of Church and Family weakened and the privileges of
> aristocracy (without any duties) spread wide, democratized, especially
> the libidinous privileges, the right to be uninhibited, spontaneous,
> urinating, defecating, belching, coupling in all positions, tripling, quad-
> rupling, polymorphous, noble in being natural, primitive, combining
> the leisure and luxurious inventiveness of Versailles with the hibiscus-
> covered erotic ease of Samoa."

Evidence suggests that sexuality and feces have become the measure
of all things, and theft, exploitation, and aggression have become the
ordinary events of life.

And yet he does at the end affirm. The occasion for affirmation is
not now his own need, as has been the case with the previous heroes,
but one unheroic—indeed, slightly foolish—example of human goodness. There has been his nephew and benefactor Elya, who as he was
husband, father, provider, doctor, and at the cost of private desires,
lived a useful life—who asserted obligation where in literal fact none
was; he had taken Sammler as his uncle in order to benefit him, in
order to extend his family obligation. When he dies—and in the last
words of the novel—Sammler will pray for him and derive the indi-
cated lesson:

> Remember, God, the soul of Elya Gruner, who, as willingly as possible
> and as well as he was able, and even to an intolerable point, and even
> in suffocation and even as death was coming was eager, even childishly
> perhaps (may I be forgiven for this), even with a certain servility, to do
> what was required of him. At his best this man was much kinder than
> at my very best I have ever been or could ever be. He was aware that
> he must meet, and he did meet—through all the confusion and de-
> graded clowning of this life through which we are speeding—he did
> meet the terms of his contract. The terms which, in his inmost heart,
> each man knows. As I know mine. As all know. For that is the truth
> of it—that we all know, God, that we know, that we know, we know,
> we know.

These sentiments have been uttered before. Indeed, on occasion in
the same words. Herzog in one of his imaginary colloquies objects to
Professor Hocking that we do not have to be taught the need for overcoming subjectivity, correcting it by useful duty, for "we know this,"

says Herzog, "We know, we know, know it!" The strenuous passivity in the sentiment is to be found also in Augie March's "axial lines." And the direction within the sentiment to useful duty is to be found in Henderson's ultimate decision for movement.

Meanings have shifted, however. Sammler's insistence is not validated by any energy for comic rebounding, but quite the opposite. Though he specifically rejects the perspective from apocalypse, he has nonetheless been presented at his inception with the strong sense of an ending. The character we have in the present moment of the novel has been shaped by it. This is true as a matter of the gross eventualities of the character. Sammler is an old man. He is an accidental survivor. He has once been returned from the dead, and he is dying again. And it is true as a matter of the tonality of the relationships he still has. Even his daughter is something of an imposition upon him. He speculates, assesses, and compassionates. He takes perspective altogether from "the luxury of nonintimidation by doom."

The character whom we have in the present has already arrived at critical adjustments of the self, such precisely as might enable him to insist on human goodness without an accompanying urgency, virtually without emotion. Having once been witness to and to some extent participant in the end of the world, he has seen through the ways of the world; that which he witnesses in New York—the kingly black pickpocket of the phallic assertiveness, that Columbia student who measures wisdom in terms of sex and feces, raunchy Angela, scheming Wallace, and all of the others—confirms his knowledge. What he knows in particular is that the modern world has licensed a terrific willfulness which is serviced even (or perhaps primarily) by its liberal rationalism. The Nazis had offered one kind of proof. The life and work of H. G. Wells, about which Sammler is a presumed expert, constitute another true emblem and prophecy for the contemporary condition. On the one hand, Wells was a compulsive explainer, and by that much, an enemy to the soul's own natural knowledge. As rampant scientist, he obscured and trivialized ideas; as social activist, he was—so Sammler's sense seems to be—destructively glib. On the other hand, Wells in his life was a man who had admitted no restraint. And so the new Age:

> The children were setting fire to libraries. And putting on Persian trousers, letting their sideburns grow. This was their symbolic wholeness. An oligarchy of technicians, engineers, the men who ran the grand machines . . . would come to govern vast slums filled with bohemian adolescents, narcotized, beflowered, and "whole."

Or not necessarily narcotized. In just a slightly different vision the mark of the new Age is:

Child, black, redskin—the unspoiled Seminole against the horrible
Whiteman . . . Millions of civilized people wanted oceanic, boundless,
primitive, neckfree nobility, experienced a strange release of galloping
impulses, and acquired the peculiar aim of sexual niggerhood for everyone. Humankind . . . demanded accelerated exaltation, accepted no
instant without pregnant meanings as in epic, tragedy, comedy, or
films.

Confirmations of this vision are to be found everywhere, and Sammler made his adjustment to it long ago. He is challenged to new
speculations, however, by the separate willfulnesses of those who are
near to him, and then, formally, by Dr. Lal, the Hindu author of
The Future of the Moon. But both sets of challenges are somewhat
less than they might be. Those who are near to him are not remark-
ably dear to him. And the vision of Dr. Lal can be both tentatively
honored and then dismissed by Sammler because it proves to be not
really dissimilar to his own, only not so fully realized. Dr. Lal, too,
assumes that a terrific willfulness is basic reality, and he would assert
that it is to be found not only in persons but in atoms and cells. The
argument between Lal and Sammler is restricted to the consequences
of this assumption, with Lal taking the melioristic view. This willfulness is capable of producing beautiful kinds of order, if only it can
be allowed adequate room. The moon is the new frontier. There are
technical problems associated with the colonization of the moon, but
the project must be broached. He is on the side of accommodating
lunacy.

Lal's argument is undermined, first by the implications of the scene
in which it is most fully presented. His immediate auditors, as he sits
discussing with Sammler, are, besides Sammler, Sammler's daughter
Shula and his niece Margotte. They are after all specimens—rather
mild ones—of Lal's clientele. Both are tremendously attentive to Dr.
Lal, quite as a consequence of their frustrated willfulness. They are
not in search of creative order. The root of the will of these odd,
aging, rather crazed creatures is their genitalia. They have designs
on Lal. The place of the discussion is Elya's house, and meanwhile
Elya's son Wallace is up in the attic searching through the plumbing
for money which his father has supposedly hidden away. Wallace
wants to buy an airplane with the money. He wants to fly. Wallace is
also a dilettante technician, in many fields. He figures odds, knows
formulas, likes taxonomy, invents schemes. He is a great dreamer, a
sounder of the Attic Pipes and certainly a potential astronaut. He
brings the discussion between Lal and Sammler to an abrupt end by
breaking a pipe and flooding their living room. The trouble with
Wallace is that with all of his calculations, his will is absolutely random, and therefore destructive.

And Lal's argument is undermined secondly, and emphatically, by the character of Sammler himself. Early in the novel, Sammler compares the contemporary surfeit of "explanations" to an invading sea, such as will be released from the pipe in the attic, and he sees himself as being engaged in a kind of exercise in good plumbing:

> A Dutch drudgery, it occurred to Sammler, pumping and pumping to keep a few acres of dry ground. The invading sea being a metaphor for the multiplication of facts and sensations. The earth being an earth of ideas.

He seems to be registering an important distinction. But what or which ideas? He in fact spends most of his waking hours reading the work of Meister Eckhart, from which he presumably draws an "idea" of the mystical reality of God, God as idea, and the nothingness of creatures. Neither he nor Bellow really tries to assert that idea, however. It is true because it is appealing, and it is appealing because— though neither Sammler nor Bellow says just so much—it seems to provide an adequate challenge to human willfulness. It is not for nothing that Artur Sammler was named by his mother for the great Artur Schopenhauer, whose system contains the information, as Sammler recalls it, "that only Ideas are not overpowered by the Will." Not that Sammler necessarily entertains a Schopenhauerian idea of Idea, but he chooses the kind of idea that will not be victimized by its opposite.

Indeed, the novel alludes to the system of the great Schopenhauer with some frequency, though not systematically. Schopenhauer had declared that his system had the result of making the ancient Hindu philosophy newly available, though his system went further, and Sammler finds himself interpreting and correcting the philosophy of a latter-day Hindu. In the complicated interchange between Will and Representation in the system, Will produces Representation—and Sammler acknowledges that one must "make peace . . . with intermediacy and representation." Schopenhauer's location of the seat of the human Will, as Sammler recalls, is the organs of sex, and Sammler is surrounded by persons whose entire authority for acting is in the primacy they give to sex. And so even unto smaller matters: Sammler insists on brevity in written intellectual discourse, and on the importance of a knowledge of Latin, thereby following the specific advice of Schopenhauer.

But it is primarily a mode of character that is derived from the system, or that—more accurately, certainly—is discovered incidentally to be confirmed by the system. Will is terrible, and the goal of the philosopher is liberation from Will. That liberation is difficult because man, too, is an objectification of Will; freedom is nevertheless possible for human beings when Will turns upon itself and denies itself. Men can accomplish that denial through knowledge of Will. And the result will be detachment from earthly existence, quiescence, the end of the ceaseless striving of the Will, and compassion for those who still strive.

Such character suggests a moral principle, which is not different from that which was asserted by Bellow's previous heroes. Elya is Sammler's exemplary hero because Elya had opposed his own private desires and by doing his duty made himself greater than his own willfulness. "The pain of duty makes the creature upright," Sammler says, "and this uprightness is no negligible thing." But the conception —the invitation to participate in ordinary life—is now very chilly. And ironically so, after all. Bellow's previous heroes have come to their various expressions of community and participation by the process of rebounding from prideful isolation. They have refused to be alienated, sometimes seeming to force-feed themselves with a sense of the richness of human life. Sammler is never alienated. He is remote and austere, quite beyond any alienation, and he discovers in the richness of human life cause for revulsion. There is too much of human community, too much of brotherhood, too much of employment and being employed.

The assertion of brotherhood has become an affirmation of contract. The breaking of the error of the uniqueness of the self has become self-denial. And if there is a sense of universal connections, that sense contains no joy. There can be no doubt, of course, that Bellow is working with authentic materials of contemporary history, and what now is implied by the total of Bellow's work so far is minimalization of faith in the human connection.

Saul Bellow and Norman Mailer:
The Secret Sharers

by Earl Rovit

Sometimes in the history of literature, and especially during periods of uncertain stress and unsettled attitudes, two opposing figures may jut above the artistic jostling of the times, there to contend for the favor and loyalty of their contemporary audience. One thinks, for example, of Stendhal and Balzac, of Tolstoy and Dostoevsky, of Hemingway and Faulkner. We tend to forget that even though such rivalries are eventually reconciled in the long-term perspectives of literary taste, still, during the period of struggle itself, the opposition of art-styles, temperaments, and the flamboyancies of topicality may engender extreme militance in the readership of the rival authors. With no intention of exalting the importance of their status by the implied comparisons, I think it is fair to say that American prose of the 1950s and '60s has been heavily dominated by the collision of claims and counterclaims invested in the radically differing modes of thought and style inherent in and associated with the works of Saul Bellow and Norman Mailer.

Further, I suspect that we may underestimate somewhat the degree to which their writings have been interpreted and evaluated in Academe as well as in the marketplace, in terms of the real and fancied antagonisms between them. I can easily remember when a strong expression of approval for *Herzog* or *Mr. Sammler's Planet* was automatically—and with some justice—considered a negative judgment on *An American Dream* or *Why Are We In Vietnam?*, and vice versa. In fact, there has even been a small movement among some literary fashion designers to label Bellow a "Modern" and Mailer a "Postmodern," and to imply that preference for one or the other be coupled with the dogmatic profession of a faith in a past that never was or a future that never will be. History, of course, has a habit of arranging its own pasts and futures; in the passage of time it assigns its own values and shakes jagged irreconcilabilities into relative harmonies, and I dare say we will gradually recognize that in spite of their apparent incompatibility, Bellow and Mailer, like all serious artists, have really been working on parallel lines all along. Art is, ultimately, an issue of incredibly complex dialectics: the relentless struggle within the writer's personality; his efforts to shape his own artistic voice within the conventions of his form; the argument that he hurls at his most trenchant critics; the subtle or violent pressure that his work exerts against the inertia of his potential audience. At their most creative, these transactions are necessarily inconclusive; when neither side achieves a sweeping victory, the works of art that survive may gain a partial validation through the very ordeals of trial and opposition. In any case, we are still some years away from all but the most tentative evaluations; however, because Bellow and Mailer have been so dramatically at odds, and because their conflict has so strongly patterned the literary landscape of American fiction in the years following World War II, it is useful to look more closely at the ambiguous nuances of their interrelationship.

Rather than seizing immediately on some of the more blatant differences between the two, we might first note the surprisingly wide areas of confluence that both writers share. Though Bellow—a Gemini to Mailer's more celebrated Aquarius—is almost eight years older, both men are first-generation urban Jews of middle-class background and socialist sympathies, both have been richly nurtured in the best education that America could offer them, both have been accorded early success and generous rewards as writers by the Establishment, and both have accepted with total seriousness the dictum that the democratic artist must take an active role in the critical interpretation of his culture. Both writers have been unashamed "intellectuals," albeit of very different varieties. Bellow has consistently delighted in the traditional play of ideas, whereas Mailer has had an equally consistent passion for ideologies and theories, tirelessly manipulating them into dazzling patterns, even as he has, in turn, been sometimes tiresomely manipulated by them. Or, to focus on this area from a slightly different angle, Bellow has characteristically channeled his intelligence toward questions concerning the moral possibilities of contemporary life; he has staunchly identified himself as a writer who very consciously wrestles with the desperate ambiguities of morality in a world where religious sanctions no longer operate, save as a sentimental judgment and an unappeasable nostalgia. Mailer, on the other hand —and this is well below the often eccentric bravado and fustian of his rhetoric—appears to be at his deepest root a soul in a fiery religious search, an experimenter in an erratic pursuit of the Absolute, a writer with a powerful moralistic sensibility, intolerant of any compromise and insidiously attracted to categories of experience such as Sex and Time, God and the Devil.

The problematic theme to which Bellow has been irresistibly drawn from *Dangling Man* to *Mr. Sammler's Planet* is that of trying to reconcile *virtue* with the fact of self-consciousness: can modern man attain "dignity," can he live a "good" life when he must assume the traditional function of God, when he himself must judge his own frailties, cowardices, and ignoble motives? Mailer's search, in contrast, has aimed inexorably at discovering or creating some *holiness,* or "wholeness," in a world perversely governed by entropy. His novels and journalistic ventures have tended to become dramatized exercises in testing or groping for that stance of moral muscularity that may release an essence of purity in a plastic world—that may create some bastion of permanence that will withstand the cancerous corrosions of change. Thus, whereas Bellow's struggles to arrive at a workable moral identity have led him inevitably into the ambiguous modes of comic and grotesque irony—that style that is the last-ditch defense against despair—Mailer, like a compulsive ascetic, has been impervious to humor and tolerance and ambiguity, adopting the sometimes visionary and the sometimes tedious role of the artist as seer, pundit, egotistical crank, and Establishment scourge.

Neither writer is what one might call a natural storyteller—not, at least, in the sense that Faulkner or I. B. Singer or John Barth so abundantly is. For Bellow, a story-line seems more than anything else a weblike scenario that he weaves more and more tightly around his captured protagonist; it is primarily a method of presenting the stifling power of the human predicament in order to measure his hero's ability to endure the harrowing weight of his own life. In effect, the typical Bellow plot is rarely more than a device to bring his protagonist and his reader into a heightened emotional awareness of the thin sliver of freedom that life permits to consciousness. In fact, one can readily imagine Bellow under different circumstances being perfectly comfortable as an eighteenth-century essayist—formidably intelligent, comprehensively "liberal" in a crisply satirical way, and slightly contemptuous of such errant frivolities as fiction. In Mailer's work, the story-line appears to be almost arbitrary and incidental to the sporadic pronouncements of "truth" that the continuity of events (usually encounters of violence and/or sex) provides for; Mailer is as likely to proclaim these "truths" in his own *ex cathedra* or *ex cloaca* voices as he is in dialogue, interior reflection, or gestures of symbolic action. If we can imagine Bellow as an essayist of the Enlightenment, we can as readily see Mailer as a self-anointed lay preacher of any age—a

Moog-synthesizer-throated amalgam of Captain Ahab and Peck's Bad Boy usurping Father Mapple's pulpit to justify his more-than-human ways to his own White Whale.

Nor, except in *The Naked and the Dead* and *The Victim,* is there much indication that either writer is especially concerned with employing fictional structures as strategies of conveying meaning. That the two dominant novelists of our time choose the novel form almost in spite of themselves, and that they exploit that form while virtually ignoring its most central resource is a strange commentary on the temper of our age and the desires of our reading audience. It suggests, in part, the extent to which serious writers have surrendered the craft of storytelling to the pulps, the cinema, television, and even the various agencies of the news media. It suggests also the severe distrust with which our age judges fictional structures as methods of projecting clear and reliable images to dispel the murk of our confusions. At any rate, though Mailer can always be counted on for flights of verbal excitement (*Why Are We In Vietnam?* is his one sustained solo), and though Bellow conveys a brilliant stylistic exuberance in *The Adventures of Augie March* and in the first section of *Henderson the Rain King,* I think it fair to say that neither man has made any radical experimentation or exploration of the novel form itself. Perhaps both have been so vividly engrossed in *substance*—in the urgencies of the ideas that move them—that they have been tolerably satisfied to leave the conventional solutions of style and structure pretty much in the places where they found them. And this makes all the more interesting the fact that their artistic beginnings were in the same literary region; a kind of "hard" realism. Behind Bellow stands that earlier Chicago giant, Theodore Dreiser, as well as the French and Russian realists and the spoken and written Yiddish tradition. Behind Mailer we also find Dreiser, except that here, *An American Tragedy* is filtered through James T. Farrell, Dos Passos, and, of course, Hemingway.

Clearly, these literary influences are much more pervasive than the mere conventions of tone and subject matter. They imply spontaneous preferences that may emanate from a profound temperamental need shared by both men. Ultimately, and most concretely, the naturalistic tradition may help Bellow and Mailer to express their deepest sense of reality—to locate it, to strive to understand it, and to drive their total energies in an effort to articulate it. Here, I think, we may begin to discern the very different focuses of their work—here in their differing responses to a Dreiserian sense of reality. Both Bellow's and Mailer's earliest works (*Dangling Man, The Victim, The Naked and the Dead*) take for granted an objective reality that is essentially indifferent—if not actively hostile—to man; an utterly claustrophobic environment that can be adequately defined only in terms of interlocking power-relationships, within which Bellow's early heroes dangle as pathetic victims, and which Mailer's officers and infantrymen express in barely more than animal responses and as animated embodiments. From the beginning, Mailer's has been the harsher and more uncompromising point of view. The bleak world-structure of *The Naked and the Dead* allowed no flexibility to human behavior; there was no space between history and personality, no area of supple resilience between the impersonal forces that shape and the human sentience that coexists. But Bellow (who has singled out *Jennie Gerhardt* as the novel that best illustrates Dreiser's power) never fully succumbed to the stark naturalistic view. Joseph, Leventhal, and Tommy Wilhelm are clearly victims, but they are victims who are intensely aware of themselves as victims. And it is precisely Bellow's commitment to the fact of their developed self-awareness that has led him to exploit the introspective space between history and personality —the precious human space in which morality, humor, grace, and creativity may conceivably exist. In fact, the steady current of development from Bellow's earliest work to his latest can be appreciated partially in terms of his painstakingly honest efforts to widen that space between—to present victim-man with valid opportunities to enlarge his human capacities. Augie, Henderson, Herzog, and Sammler are continually victimized, but they are not victims; for want of a better descriptive term, we could call them "survivors."

Mailer's direction has been dramatically different. Although he has never repeated the wholesale naturalistic doctrine that informed *The Naked and the Dead,* and although he has hurtled out of the somewhat doctrinaire Marxist Darwinism of his first novel into a thrilling steeplechase over the barriers of Reichian revisionism, and in and out of the thickets of Existentialism and New-Left Apocalypticism, he has remained more or less true to his first view of the universe. It strikes me as significant, for example, that after the Gothic failures of *Barbary Shore* and *The Deer Park*—failures in part dependent on the curious inability of either book to locate itself in reference to reality—Mailer turned to journalism. And what he has done in his brilliantly original reportorial adventuring is to reembrace covertly that solid objective reality that structured his first novel. In other words, by placing himself aggressively in front of the historically real and actual—a heavyweight prize fight, a national nominating convention, a march on the Pentagon, a moon launching, or the poignant career of a Hollywood sex symbol—Mailer is able to cope with a world he himself never made. Because he has not created and is not responsible for that world, he can attempt to transform it (along with his own self) interpretatively into his own special fictions. In this sense, his earlier abortive attempts to project a persuasive illusion of reality in *Barbary Shore* and *The Deer Park* may be seen as symptomatic of a double refusal on his part: on the one hand, Mailer may be stubbornly refusing to recant the dogmas of naturalistic determinism that he had first proclaimed in *The Naked and the Dead*; on the other hand, he may also be refusing to accept the bleak condition of creative impotence that these very dogmas impose upon him. There is no MOS for a creative artist in the Table of Organization that sustains the cosmos of Anopopei, and Mailer is clearly frustrated by the necessary passivity that realism requires of his surrogate narrator-heroes, Mikey Lovett (*Barbary Shore*) and Sergius O'Shaughnessy (*The Deer Park*). Artists *manqués,* they are burdened with the obligations of creating the worlds of their respective novels and acting in those worlds at the same time; they manage neither task particularly well.

Mailer's attempts to resolve this dilemma delineate the volatile shifts in direction that his career has taken since the 1955 publication of *The Deer Park*. His emergence as a journalist can thus be understood as an action entirely consistent with his well-publicized disgust with "victim-literature," and with his theatrical struggles—personal, political, and novelistic—to invent or incarnate a "hipster-hero" who will prove immune to the paralysis of living in a universe of cause-and-effect determinism. In *An American Dream* and *Why Are We In Vietnam?*, novels that become increasingly extreme in their departures from realistic reference, Mailer appears to be trying to avoid the strictures of naturalism without confronting them head-on. Such a procedure strikes me as highly exciting and even more highly dangerous for a committed realist to undertake. For if *The Armies of the Night* or *Of A Fire on the Moon* succeed in communicating the personality of a creative passion and intelligence (Mailer's), they do so through the agency of the world that we all share undeniably with Mailer. In his last two novels, however, that world is radically distanced, and the projected worlds of Rojack and D. J. may simply be outside our capacities of recognition.

Mailer's metaphysics—or as much of it as I can understand—seems to be founded on an inexorable either-or basis: Hip or Square, cancer or schizophrenia, victim or rebel, God or the Devil, nothingness or wholeness. Intellectually absolutistic and prone to solipsism, Mailer will either have his cake and eat it too, or insist that everyone must do without cake. And though this attitude can be amazingly useful in forcing a reader to attend to a brand-new pattern in a familiar landscape (even in *The Prisoner of Sex* and *Marilyn*, Mailer captures at moments the entire attention of his reader), it has severe disadvantages as the basis of structuring a novel. Bestowing a totalitarian authority on the consciousnesses of Rojack and D. J., Mailer eludes the responsibilities of realism without endorsing an alternate position. Rojack's world is as vivid and puerile as a crude animated cartoon, and despite the occasionally brilliant verbal texture of *Why Are We In Vietnam?*, D. J.'s world evokes no dimension beneath or beyond its own volubility. When fiction casts off the supports of realism, it must strive to sustain itself as parable, parody, urgently rooted fantasy, or as an aesthetic structure self-defined by its own created metaphor. To my mind, Bellow's one nonrealistic novel, *Henderson the Rain King*, manages this transition with great effectiveness, but Mailer's last two novels float narcissistically free from the grip of human experience. Rojack and D. J. are narrator-minds deliberately swollen into states of mindlessness in order that they may posture as successful rebels. Mailer is still unwilling or unable to deny the formative pressure of history, but in *An American Dream* and *Why Are We In Vietnam?* he pretends to ignore it. Engorged by the sweet taste of their own egos, his free-swinging (but far from "dangling") rebel-heroes comport themselves in a never-never land located between the past and the future—a mythical pseudomystical *now* of supersensuous immersion and courageous instinctual response. Mouse-drab and timid in comparison, Bellow's survivors pick their way gingerly through the detritus of their experience, straining to maintain a precarious balance between the irrevocabilities of the past and the dwindling possibilities of the future.

Thus, both writers found their early work on very similar legacies. Both inherit a defining naturalistic concept of world order, and both wage valiant battle against the paralyzing burden of that concept— Bellow cautiously exploring and exploiting the introspective space within, Mailer leaping out of the frame completely. Bellow's work has developed along relatively traditional lines. Composed in a period of some thirty years, his individual fictions have a strong family resemblance to one another, and his thematic concern with the ambiguities of morality and personality has grown suppler and more tensile with his increasing craftsmanship. Along with this mastery, his later novels seem to breathe an air of richer repose; Bellow gives the impression of moving with larger ease and freedom through the bleak foreground of his own world as he gains confidence in the reality and value of the creative self-consciousness. One consequence of this, apparent in *Mr. Sammler's Planet*, is a greater receptivity to the possibilities of religious experience; however, a less happy by-product is the tone of acerbic self-righteousness that tinges that novel. Nevertheless, the steady publication of serious, well-wrought novels over a long period of time augurs well for their survival and suggests that Bellow's art will continue to grow and unfold with slow richness and quiet surprise.

Mailer's work, on the other hand, is much more difficult to view as a whole. In a sense, each of his books is a brand-new beginning; and any one of his novels could be mistaken for the dazzling debut of a highly promising young first novelist. All his books share an uneven virtuosity in style, an interest in focusing on men facing extreme crisis-situations, an unflagging concern for the proper measure of courage, and a razzle-dazzle breathlessness in their presentation—a histrionic sense of the hero-magician yanking the absolutely newest and most relevant rabbit of all out of his tall, black, inexhaustible hat. How or if Mailer will find a way of resolving the knotted dilemma that seems to me to lie at the very core of his work—his unnegotiable demand that man be creative in a deterministic universe—I do not know. Perhaps the compromise accepted by his naturalistic predecessors such as Steinbeck, Dreiser, and Norris—the reluctant or enthusiastic embrace of some unorthodox variety of mysticism—may still be an open option for Mailer. (Apparently, a temperament that is beguiled by the theoretical comprehensibility of a completely ordered and completely meaningless natural universe is equally beguiled by the potential revelation of a completely ordered and completely meaningful supernatural universe. It would seem that it is not the problem of *meaning,* but that of *mystery,* that challenges such a temperament.) At any rate, all readers of Mailer are well aware of his frequent references to states of expanded consciousness, telepathic communication, electromagnetic forces, the more-than-human power of the will, and the knowledge that the glandular and olfactory organs can impart to man if he has the creative courage to expose himself to their uses. There is some indication that Mailer is willing to weigh these matters at more than metaphorical seriousness, and he may yet move assertively into a full-fledged membership in Godhead. It is also posssible, however, that his dalliance with the occult is just an aspect of the rhetorical fireworks that are his stock in trade. It would be foolhardy to predict Mailer's next moves or jumps, but I think that until he makes a significant attack on his central unresolved "problem," his novels *as wholes* will lack that sharp realistic edge that is always present in the best passages of his writing.

Finally, most remarkable in the comparison between Bellow and Mailer are, I believe, the large areas of tacit agreement between them —in my judgment, agreement that is more nearly congruent than that between either man and any other significant writer of their generation, with the possible exception of Robert Lowell. Putting aside as irrelevant their distinctive temperamental differences, one might expect to find a close mutuality of vision and technique, or, at the very least, a genial complementarity. But this, of course, is precisely what we fail to find. Instead, I suggest somewhat fancifully that each has almost consciously chosen the other as his "other"—his double, an-

tagonist, alter ego, favorite enemy, living embodiment of those facets
of his creative personality that he must resolutely oppose and, indeed,
ruthlessly suppress. Baldly stated in this manner, the formula is too
pat and too easy, but it may be worth a certain credence. Both writers
begin their careers in virtual agreement as to what constitutes "reality," and in their efforts to arrive at an honorable position that will
allow them an escape from the round robin of "the victim-bit," each
finds in the other a formidable rival whose way he has consciously
chosen *not* to follow. When Mailer insists that the one role he will
avoid at all costs is that of "the nice Jewish boy from Brooklyn," and
when one can discern throughout Bellow's work the constant attrac-
tion, fascination, and aggressive disapproval of life lived on the apocalyptic edge of abandonment, the critic may be excused for supposing
that this intense dialectic may be the projections of a conflict within
the creative depths of both writers. (Kirby Allbee and Charles Eitel,
for example, are interesting possibilities of reverse identifications.)
Mailer, a man whose stormy private life has been as public as his
expert manipulation of the mass media could make it, has maintained
a supreme silence over the materials of his childhood and adolescence,
almost as though he were officially born on the day *The Naked and
the Dead* was published. And Bellow, "that nice Jewish boy from
Chicago," has compulsively exploited the autobiographical indeli-
bilities of his growing-up years in his novels, while keeping a precious
decorum over his private personality.

Thus, it seems to me that in a particularly concrete way each writer
clarifies the other, much in the fashion of identical but reversed mirror
images. In a moment of candid self-recognition, Mailer defined himself
as "a radical conservative"; with equal force Bellow could be categorized as a conservative radical. In the same manner, their contrasting
attitudes toward their own Jewishness, toward women, and toward
politics, and their notions of such concepts as Time, History, Evil, and
the value and function of Art, are likely to bear the same closely opposed relationship. I suppose that it is for this reason that the antago-
nism between their work is so much more striking than any possible
contrast between the work of either of them and that of, for example,
Updike, Barth, Hawkes, Salinger, Malamud, or Styron. A fratricidal
struggle, especially a symbolic one, sucks all the oxygen from the air
and gives the impression of a total engagement that mobilizes the
whole environment into opposing alignments. I cannot pretend to
know what their relationship has ultimately meant to the literary
landscape in America; in fact, it is entirely possible that in the long
run, it may be merely a casual and insignificant spasm on the peripheries of what may prove to have been the truly central issues of
our time. But viewing it in the perspective of several decades, their

relationship may enable us to appreciate the achievements and failures of each writer in an especially meaningful way. And because it is their achievements that are partly responsible for the literary standards of their entire generation and the one that has followed, a keener appraisal of the opposition between Bellow and Mailer ought to tell us a good deal more about ourselves as a reading audience than we might otherwise be able to deduce.

Chronology of Important Dates

1915   Bellow born in Lachine, Quebec, July 10.

1924   Moves with family to Chicago.

1933   Enters the University of Chicago.

1935   Transfers to Northwestern University.

1937   Graduates from Northwestern with honors in anthropology and sociology. Enrolls in the University of Wisconsin, but leaves school upon marrying Anita Goshkin; a son, Gregory, was born of this marriage.

1941   Publishes first short story, "Two Morning Monologues," in *Partisan Review*.

1944   Publishes first novel, *Dangling Man*. Serves briefly in the Maritime Service during World War II.

1947   Publishes *The Victim*.

1948–52   Awarded a Guggenheim Fellowship. Travels in Europe, and teaches at the University of Minnesota, New York University, and Princeton University.

1953   Publishes *The Adventures of Augie March,* which wins the National Book Award for Fiction.

1956   Publishes *Seize the Day*. Marries Alexandra Tschacbasov; a son, Adam, was born of this marriage.

1959   Publishes *Henderson the Rain King*.

1960–62   Edits the magazine, *The Noble Savage*. Marries Susan Glassman in 1961; a son, Daniel, was born of this marriage.

1964   Publishes *Herzog*, which wins his second National Book Award. *The Last Analysis* premieres on Broadway, and closes after twenty-eight performances.

1968   Publishes *Mosby's Memoirs*. Becomes a Professor on the Committee on Social Thought at the University of Chicago.

1970   Publishes *Mr. Sammler's Planet*, which wins his third National Book Award.

Notes on the Editor and Contributors

EARL ROVIT, Professor of English at the City College of New York, is the author of *Herald to Chaos, Ernest Hemingway,* and *Saul Bellow;* he has also published three novels.

JOHN CLAYTON, the author of *Saul Bellow: In Defense of Man,* teaches modern fiction and creative writing at the University of Massachusetts.

DENIS DONOGHUE, Professor of Modern English and American Literature at University College, Dublin, is the author of *The Third Voice, Connoisseurs of Chaos, The Ordinary Universe, Jonathan Swift, W. B. Yeats,* and *Thieves of Fire.*

MARCUS KLEIN, Professor of English at the State University of New York at Buffalo, is the author of *After Alienation: American Novels in Mid-Century* and *The American Novel Since World War II.*

IRVING MALIN is Professor of English at the City College of New York; his publications include *New American Gothic, Jews and Americans, Saul Bellow's Fictions, Isaac Bashevis Singer,* and *Nathanael West's Novels.*

RICHARD PEARCE is Professor of English at Wheaton College. He is the author of *Stages of the Clown: Perspectives on Modern Fiction from Dostoevsky to Beckett* and *William Styron.*

RICHARD POIRIER is Director of Graduate Studies in English at Rutger's University and the author of *The Comic Sense of Henry James, A World Elsewhere, The Performing Self,* and *Norman Mailer.*

M. GILBERT PORTER teaches contemporary literature and literary criticism at the University of Missouri at Columbia; his study of Saul Bellow's fiction will appear in 1974.

BEN SIEGEL is Professor of English at California State Polytechnic University, Pomona; his books include *The Puritan Heritage: America's Roots in the Bible, Biography Past and Present,* and *Isaac Bashevis Singer.*

VICTORIA SULLIVAN, co-editor of *Plays By and About Women,* teaches in the English Department of the City College of New York.

RUTH R. WISSE, Associate Professor of Yiddish Literature in the Department of Jewish Studies at McGill University, is the author of *The Schlemiel as Modern Hero* and the editor of *A Shtetl and Other Yiddish Novellas.*

Selected Bibliography

Works by Saul Bellow

"Address by Gooley MacDowell to the Hasbeens Club of Chicago." *Hudson Review*, 4 (Summer 1951), 222–27.

The Adventures of Augie March. New York: Viking, 1953.

"Culture Now." *Modern Occasions*, 1 (Winter, 1971), 162–78.

Dangling Man. New York: Vanguard, 1944.

"Deep Readers of the World, Beware!" *New York Times Book Review* (February 15, 1959), 1, 34.

"Distractions of a Fiction Writer." In *The Living Novel: A Symposium*, ed. Granville Hicks, pp. 1–20. New York: Macmillan, 1957.

Henderson the Rain King. New York: Viking, 1959.

Herzog. New York: Viking, 1964.

The Last Analysis. New York: Viking, 1965.

Mr. Sammler's Planet. New York: Viking, 1970.

Mosby's Memoirs. New York: Viking, 1968.

Seize the Day. New York: Viking, 1956.

"A Sermon by Dr. Pep." *Partisan Review*, 16 (May–June 1949), 455–62.

"Some Notes on Recent American Fiction." *Encounter*, 21 (November 1963), 22–29.

"Two Morning Monologues." *Partisan Review*, 8 (May–June 1941), 230–36.

The Victim. New York: Vanguard, 1947.

"Where Do We Go From Here: The Future of Fiction." *Michigan Quarterly Review*, 1 (Winter 1962), 27–33.

Works about Saul Bellow

Alter, Robert. *After the Tradition*. New York: Dutton, 1969.

Axthelm, Peter M. *The Modern Confessional Novel*. New Haven: Yale University Press, 1967.

Baumbach, Jonathan. *The Landscape of Nightmare.* New York: New York University Press, 1965.

Bezanker, Abraham. "The Odyssey of Saul Bellow." *Yale Review,* 58 (1969), 359–71.

Clayton, John J. *Saul Bellow: In Defense of Man.* Bloomington, Ind.: Indiana University Press, 1968.

Crozier, Robert D. "Theme in *Augie March.*" *Critique,* 7 (1965), 18–32.

Detweiler, Robert. *Saul Bellow.* Grand Rapids, Mich.: Eerdmans, 1967.

Donoghue, Denis. *The Ordinary Universe.* New York: Macmillan, 1968.

Dutton, Robert R. *Saul Bellow.* New York: Twayne, 1971.

Enck, John. "Saul Bellow: An Interview." *Contemporary Literature,* 6 (1965), 156–60.

Galloway, David. *The Absurd Hero in American Fiction.* Austin, Texas: University of Texas Press, 1966.

Geismar, Maxwell. *American Moderns.* New York: Hill & Wang, 1958.

Gindin, James. *Harvest of a Quiet Eye.* Bloomington, Ind.: Indiana University Press, 1968.

Goldberg, Gerald J. "Life's Customer, Augie March." *Critique,* 3 (1960), 15–27.

Guttmann, Allen. *The Jewish Writer in America.* New York: Oxford University Press, 1971.

Hall, James. *The Lunatic Giant in the Drawing Room.* Bloomington Ind.: Indiana University Press, 1968.

Handy, William J. *Modern Fiction.* Carbondale, Ill.: Southern Illinois University Press, 1971.

Harper, Gordon L. "The Art of Fiction XXXVII: Saul Bellow." *Paris Review,* 9 (1966), 48–73.

Harper, Howard M., Jr. *Desperate Faith.* Chapel Hill, N.C.: North Carolina University Press, 1967.

Hassan, Ihab. *Radical Innocence.* Princeton, N.J.: Princeton University Press, 1961.

Josipovici, Gabriel. *The World and the Book.* Stanford, Calif.: Stanford University Press, 1971.

Klein, Marcus. *After Alienation.* New York: World Publishing, 1964.

Malin, Irving, ed. *Saul Bellow and the Critics.* New York: New York University Press, 1967.

Malin, Irving. *Saul Bellow's Fiction.* Carbondale, Ill.: Southern Illinois University Press, 1969.

Opdahl, Keith M. *The Novels of Saul Bellow.* University Park, Pa.: The Pennsylvania State University Press, 1967.

Pearce, Richard. *Stages of the Clown.* Carbondale, Ill.: Southern Illinois University Press, 1970.

Rovit, Earl. *Saul Bellow*. Minneapolis: University of Minnesota Press, 1967.

Rupp, Richard H. *Celebration in Postwar American Fiction*. Coral Gables, Fla.: University of Florida Press, 1970.

Scheer-Schäzler, Brigitte. *Saul Bellow*. New York: Ungar, 1972.

Schulz, Max F. *Radical Sophistication*. Athens, Ohio: Ohio University Press, 1969.

Shulman, Robert. "The Style of Bellow's Comedy." *Publications of the Modern Language Association*, 83 (1968), 109–17.

Sokoloff, B. A. *Saul Bellow: A Comprehensive Bibliography*. Folcroft, 1972.

Tanner, Tony. *City of Words*. New York: Harper & Row, 1971.

———. *Saul Bellow*. Edinburgh: Oliver and Boyd, 1965.

Weber, Ronald. "Bellow's Thinkers." *Western Humanities Review*, 22 (1968), 305–13.

Weinberg, Helen. *The New Novel in America*. Ithaca, N.Y.: Cornell University Press, 1970.

Wisse, Ruth R. *The Schlemiel as Modern Hero*. Chicago: The University of Chicago Press, 1971.

TWENTIETH CENTURY VIEWS

American Authors

(continued on next page)

(continued from previous page)

TWENTIETH CENTURY VIEWS

British Authors

(continued on next page)

(continued from previous page)

TWENTIETH CENTURY VIEWS

European Authors

AESCHYLUS, edited by Marsh H. McCall, Jr. (S-TC-99)
BAUDELAIRE, edited by Henri Peyre (S-TC-18)
SAMUEL BECKETT, edited by Martin Esslin (S-TC-51)
BRECHT, edited by Peter Demetz (S-TC-11)
CAMUS, edited by Germaine Brée (S-TC-1)
CERVANTES, edited by Lowry Nelson, Jr. (S-TC-89)
CHEKHOV, edited by Robert Louis Jackson (S-TC-71)
DANTE, edited by John Freccero (S-TC-46)
DOSTOEVSKY, edited by René Wellek (S-TC-16)
EURIPIDES, edited by Erich Segal (S-TC-76)
FLAUBERT, edited by Raymond Giraud (S-TC-42)
GIDE, edited by David Littlejohn (S-TC-88)
GOETHE, edited by Victor Lange (S-TC-73)
HESSE, edited by Theodore Ziolkowski (S-TC-110)
HOMER, edited by George Steiner and Robert Fagles (S-TC-15)
IBSEN, edited by Rolf Fjelde (S-TC-52)
IONESCO, edited by Rosette C. Lamont (S-TC-108)
KAFKA, edited by Ronald Gray (S-TC-17)
LORCA, edited by Manual Duran (S-TC-14)
MALRAUX, edited by R. W. B. Lewis (S-TC-37)
THOMAS MANN, edited by Henry Hatfield (S-TC-36)
MOLIÈRE, edited by Jacques Guicharnaud (S-TC-41)
PIRANDELLO, edited by Glauco Cambon (S-TC-67)
PROUST, edited by René Girard (S-TC-4)
SARTRE, edited by Edith Kern (S-TC-21)
SOPHOCLES, edited by Thomas Woodard (S-TC-54)
STENDHAL, edited by Victor Brombert (S-TC-7)
STRINDBERG, edited by Otto Reinert (S-TC-95)
TOLSTOY, edited by Ralph E. Matlaw (S-TC-68)
VIRGIL, edited by Steele Commager (S-TC-62)
VOLTAIRE, edited by William F. Bottiglia (S-TC-78)